Encouraging Participative Consumerism Through Evolutionary Digital Marketing:

Emerging Research and Opportunities

Hans Ruediger Kaufmann
University of Nicosia, Cyprus

Agapi Manarioti
The Brand Love, Cyprus

A volume in the Advances in
Marketing, Customer Relationship
Management, and E-Services
(AMCRMES) Book Series

www.igi-global.com

Published in the United States of America by
    IGI Global
    Business Science Reference (an imprint of IGI Global)
    701 E. Chocolate Avenue
    Hershey PA, USA 17033
    Tel: 717-533-8845
    Fax: 717-533-8661
    E-mail: cust@igi-global.com
    Web site: http://www.igi-global.com

Library of Congress Cataloging-in-Publication Data

Names: Kaufmann, Hans Ruediger, 1958- author. | Manarioti, Agapi, 1979-
  author.
Title: Encouraging Participative Consumerism Through Evolutionary Digital
  Marketing : Emerging Research and Opportunities / by Hans Ruediger Kaufmann
  and Agapi Manarioti.
Description: Hershey, PA : Business Science Reference, [2017] | Includes
  bibliographical references.
Identifiers: LCCN 2016057708| ISBN 9781683180128 (h/c) | ISBN 9781683180173
  (eISBN)
Subjects: LCSH: Internet marketing. | Consumer behavior.
Classification: LCC HF5415.1265 .K384 2017 | DDC 658.8/72--dc23 LC record available at
https://lccn.loc.gov/2016057708

This book is published in the IGI Global book series Advances in Marketing, Customer Relationship Management, and E-Services (AMCRMES) (ISSN: 2327-5502; eISSN: 2327-5529)

British Cataloguing in Publication Data
A Cataloguing in Publication record for this book is available from the British Library.

All work contributed to this book is new, previously-unpublished material.
The views expressed in this book are those of the authors, but not necessarily of the publisher.

For electronic access to this publication, please contact: eresources@igi-global.com.

Advances in Marketing, Customer Relationship Management, and E–Services (AMCRMES) Book Series

ISSN:2327-5502
EISSN:2327-5529

Editor-in-Chief: Eldon Y. Li, National Chengchi University, Taiwan & California Polytechnic State University, USA

MISSION

Business processes, services, and communications are important factors in the management of good customer relationship, which is the foundation of any well organized business. Technology continues to play a vital role in the organization and automation of business processes for marketing, sales, and customer service. These features aid in the attraction of new clients and maintaining existing relationships.

The Advances in Marketing, Customer Relationship Management, and E-Services (AMCRMES) Book Series addresses success factors for customer relationship management, marketing, and electronic services and its performance outcomes. This collection of reference source covers aspects of consumer behavior and marketing business strategies aiming towards researchers, scholars, and practitioners in the fields of marketing management.

COVERAGE

- Web Mining and Marketing
- Telemarketing
- Ethical Considerations in E-Marketing
- Cases on Electronic Services
- Social Networking and Marketing
- Database marketing
- Cases on CRM Implementation
- Relationship marketing
- CRM and customer trust
- CRM strategies

IGI Global is currently accepting manuscripts for publication within this series. To submit a proposal for a volume in this series, please contact our Acquisition Editors at Acquisitions@igi-global.com or visit: http://www.igi-global.com/publish/.

Titles in this Series

For a list of additional titles in this series, please visit:
http://www.igi-global.com/book-series/advances-marketing-customer-relationship-management/37150

Strategic Marketing Management and Tactics in the Service Industry
Tulika Sood (JECRC University, India)
Business Science Reference • ©2017 • 393pp • H/C (ISBN: 9781522524755) • US $210.00

Narrative Advertising Models and Conceptualization in the Digital Age
Recep Yılmaz (Ondokuz Mayis University, Turkey)
Business Science Reference • ©2017 • 360pp • H/C (ISBN: 9781522523734) • US $205.00

Socio-Economic Perspectives on Consumer Engagement and Buying Behavior
Hans Ruediger Kaufmann (University of Applied Management Studies Mannheim, Germany
& University of Nicosia, Cyprus) and Mohammad Fateh Ali Khan Panni (City University,
Bangladesh)
Business Science Reference • ©2017 • 420pp • H/C (ISBN: 9781522521396) • US $205.00

Green Marketing and Environmental Responsibility in Modern Corporations
Thangasamy Esakki (Nagaland University, India)
Business Science Reference • ©2017 • 294pp • H/C (ISBN: 9781522523314) • US $180.00

Promotional Strategies and New Service Opportunities in Emerging Economies
Vipin Nadda (University of Sunderland, UK) Sumesh Dadwal (Northumbria University,
UK) and Roya Rahimi (University of Wolverhampton, UK)
Business Science Reference • ©2017 • 417pp • H/C (ISBN: 9781522522065) • US $185.00

Strategic Uses of Social Media for Improved Customer Retention
Wafaa Al-Rabayah (Independent Researcher, Jordan) Rawan Khasawneh (Jordan University
of Science and Technology, Jordan) Rasha Abu-shamaa (Yarmouk University, Jordan) and
Izzat Alsmadi (Boise State University, USA)
Business Science Reference • ©2017 • 311pp • H/C (ISBN: 9781522516866) • US $180.00

For an enitre list of titles in this series, please visit:
http://www.igi-global.com/book-series/advances-marketing-customer-relationship-management/37150

DISSEMINATOR OF KNOWLEDGE

www.igi-global.com

701 East Chocolate Avenue, Hershey, PA 17033, USA
Tel: 717-533-8845 x100 • Fax: 717-533-8661
E-Mail: cust@igi-global.com • www.igi-global.com

Table of Contents

Preface

MARKETING TODAY: SURFING ON THE WAVES OF DIGITAL CHANGE OR DROWNING?

During the last nine decades marketing experienced an evolutionary process from product, sales, branding, and relationship marketing eras to the current identity era. Whilst these eras were mainly based on a one-way communication between marketers and consumers aiming to attract the respectively desired consumer behaviors to the brand, today, the current digitalization era represents the, so far, highest level of identity expression by the consumer. Now, brand-consumer relationships are not only based on a two-way communication but are even initiated by the consumers. Latter express their social identity via the brand by influential brand communities and by becoming co-creators of the brand by becoming increasingly involved in idea generation and product development and promotional campaigns. This reflects the shift of mindsets required from marketers. Marketing messages are less 'encoded' by the marketer and 'decoded' by the consumer, but rather emerge through a continuous communication and interaction on the 'same eye level' requiring different communication characteristics such as trust and relevance. The chances of the digitalization era for the marketers consist of developing consumers from simple minglers to committed brand lovers spreading their love across their networks. Besides an ever stronger emotional attachment to the brand by a more intensive two-way communication and an implicit stronger involvement of consumers as co-creators, digitalization contributes to this love by providing ever more customized products and services which should be highly relevant and timely to the respective real life situations of the consumes by analyzing a so far hugely untapped source of digital or 'big' data. On the other hand, these chances might turn into severe threats of alienating consumers if marketers do not succeed in accepting a more emancipated consumer role, enhancing their communication skills targeted towards sustainable and ethical relationships or acquiring the conditional technical and analytical skills. Importantly, a counterproductive effort when implementing digital marketing is to overlook the key feature that made the social media a revolutionary innovation: sharing. This book addresses these contentious questions and aims to prepare the marketer of today for the new era by a continuous reflective discussion to synthesize the dichotomies of offline and digital marketing mindsets and to provide her/him with a fundamental skill set in an interesting and pragmatic manner:

In Chapter 1, we set the stage by contrasting the traditional and newly required digital marketing mindset, develop a definition and discuss the main terminology. An emphasis is put in this chapter to illuminate the newly required diverse skill set of a marketer of today spanning management, strategic, operational and communicative marketing as well as research skills. Well intended key rules for success in transcending the traditional and digital marketing paradigm are provided. Chapter 2 familiarizes the reader with the technological background knowledge for an effective consumer centered design of an enthusiastic, sophisticated, genuine or pleasant website personality to attract customers, keep them loyal and increase the share of their wallets. The logic behind the Search Engine Optimization is explained as well as the creation of effective customer service experiences. Chapter 3 provides specific factors to explain the development of an engaged and committed consumer and her/his online shopping behavior as well as to generate e-customer profiles. Furthermore, based on the Lego and Sears case studies, it puts online communities and its media behavior in the context of value creation. Representing the latest stages of consumer brand relationships, frameworks for co-creation and brand love are provided. Chapter 4 dedicates to engage consumers via social media. Surveys on the global use of social media, networks and platforms are provided. In a world of me-formation, importantly, the psychological factors favoring social media use, such as 'like', 'share' or 'comment' lead to a categorization or segmentation of media users. The role of social media for humanizing a brand follows. Finally, the case study 'do it like a girl', regarded as a milestone in social media, points to the ability of social media to change consumer behavior. Besides website and communities, Chapter 5 complements the elements of an e-product focusing on content. Its structure is suggested to be designed according to the 70:20:10, 80:20 or the thirds rule. Many suggestions to build an audience relating, for example, to various types of content, photos, blogs, videos, mobile apps, hash tags or micro sites, to mention but a few, are given. The online related marketing strategic and mix factors for a pay per click campaign are discussed followed by an expert interview with Persado's Product Director on the creation of a cognitive content platform. Chapter 6 concludes with a thematic potpourri both, contrasting and integrating online and offline marketing. Based on the previous chapters hypothesized frameworks for integrating online and offline marketing and its channels as wells as 'food for thought' for the development of digital business models and suggestions for a performance measurement metrics system are provided. Facing an ever increasing power of the consumer, essential ethical questions are briefly discussed.

THE VALUE OF THE BOOK AND IMPACT

Against the background of the rather scattered knowledge body of digital marketing, this book differentiates by its intention to holistically zoom in the most relevant and updated aspects of digital marketing in a compact way for marketing practitioners/consultants, academics and students alike. It is suggested to serve as an introductory pragmatic standard source of knowledge rather than a detailed and comprehensive reference guide and might best be used for training purposes. This is reflected in chapter questions and a number of best cases as well as a practitioner interview. Consequently, the book was written with a dedication to engage and interact with the reader. In doing so, it critically engages the reader with an applied and interdisciplinary applied science approach favoring a managerial/practitioners' perspective. The reader is familiarized with selected psychological, sociological and marketing/consumer behavior knowledge to better understand the emergence of the phenomenon and the mindset of its heavy users. This is regarded a precondition for the implementation of consumer centered digital marketing strategies and tactics rather than just mechanically developing the skills to just apply the new tools. Perceiving a gap as to strategic digital marketing aspects, i.e. the integration of online and digital marketing strategies or digital business models, the book takes both, a strategic and operational perspective. Whilst focusing on a pragmatic applied orientated view, the book discusses and summarizes the current cutting edge theories in the field. Furthermore, it aims to provide the readers with current empirical research to familiarize them with updated findings on relevant topics and to sensitize them for areas for further research.

Acknowledgment

We want to thank the editors and reviewers for their support and insightful comments - without their input this book could not have been accomplished. Special thanks goes to the practitioners that granted us their expertise, Mr. Petros Ziogas, Mr. Alexios Ballas and Mrs. Areti Provata and to our colleagues who provided their manifold contributions and reviews, especially Fateh Ali Khan Panni. We are also grateful to the International Business School at the University of Vilnius who granted the right to use the material developed initially for a research project and to be further developed. Finally, we want to thank our families and friends for standing by us through this still exploratory journey into the world of digital marketing.

Hans Ruediger Kaufmann
University of Nicosia, Cyprus

Agapi Manarioti
The Brand Love, Cyprus

Chapter 1
E–Marketing in a Digitalized World

ABSTRACT

In this first chapter, we introduce and discuss the fundamental terminology while exploring the distance between digital and traditional marketing. Although we strongly believe that there are no constants in today's dynamic business environment, we propose a set of propositions that might be helpful to the transition of marketing to its digital offspring. Building on experience, best practice, literature and research, we highlight the multifaceted role of the digital marketer by explaining the 7 sets of skills that they need in order to succeed. In a nutshell, this chapter grounds on the idea of a much needed mindset shift that will distinguish the competent digital marketers.

Questions

1. "Why bother with online marketing when you are that good with the traditional one"?
2. What are the main commonalities and differences between online and traditional marketing?
3. What are the rules of digital marketing?
4. Do I have the skills to be a competent digital marketer?

DOI: 10.4018/978-1-68318-012-8.ch001

"WHY BOTHER"?

Probably many of our readers have heard the voice in their heads asking this question. "Why bother with online marketing, when you are that good at traditional? After all, this is the real thing, digital is a hype that will pass". The truth is we have asked ourselves the same question, long before start writing this book. But, in the meanwhile, we also found the answer (as you have obviously done, too, since you are reading a book on digital marketing): Because digital marketing is not an add-on, it's an imperative, as the American Marketing Association admits (www.ama.org). Because it's a paradigm shift, not a hype. It's a new modus operandi that shapes consumer behaviour while responding to these changed attitudes, at the same time, a whole new world of marketing opportunities, far outside our comfort zone. Perhaps, some years ago, including a digital aspect on our marketing efforts was a differentiating factor; today, it is a prerequisite, a sine qua non dimension. How good we are on the strategy and implementation and how satisfied the users are by their experience, this is the differentiator, for now, and the majority of companies are just doing their baby steps on the field. Naturally, some years later, resourceful strategy design and execution will also be a common place and a new element will separate the winners from the laggards and so on. Because this is a constant in life and in digital marketing as well: everything changes.

If we asked you to propose a definition of digital marketing, what would it be? Can you think of some words that you would definitely include in your short description? Below, there are 3 different approaches to digital marketing:

The use of digital technologies to create an integrated, targeted and measurable communication which helps to acquire and retain customers while building deeper relationships with them – Digital Marketing Institute (DMI). (Royle & Laing, 2014)

Digital Marketing is a sub branch of traditional Marketing and uses modern digital channels for the placement of products e.g. downloadable music, and primarily for communicating with stakeholders e.g. customers and investors about brand, products, and business progress. (Royle & Laing, 2014)

Achieving marketing objectives through applying digital technologies and media. (Chaffey & Ellis-Chadwick, 2012)

The commonplace among all three definitions is the aspect of technology, as digital marketing is defined by the use of the new, digital channels and media. Apart from this, each definition underpins a different side of the digital marketing, an understanding that highlights its multifaceted nature: The DMI definition adopts a strategic point of view, focusing on relationship building with a targeted audience in as measurable manner. The Simply Digital Marketing proposal is more tactical, focusing on product placement and promotion, while the main argument of the last one is integration- how we achieve marketing objectives (not merely online marketing objectives) with the support of the technological advancements.

Reading between the lines, there are two major discussions coming of these definitions: First of all, digital marketing is about building relationships not just selling products or attracting clicks. The new capabilities of the digital technologies that provide us with ample, click-by-click data on the consumer behaviour, along with the community building angle of the social media, take digital marketing strategies to a deep psychological level of personal goals satisfaction, far more meaningful than the "trying to make them buy" approach. Website metrics are precious when they focus on the big picture, otherwise, they become self-referential and, eventually, useless in the strategic brand building scope of digital marketing- remember the "paralysis by analysis" situation?

Secondly, it's the call for integration. Digital marketing is a part of the overall marketing strategy, it is not a separated strategy but a piece of the puzzle. One might think that we are stating the facts now, but there is compelling evidence, as discussed later in our book, that companies fail to embody digital to marketing function, leaving the digital marketers isolated and the digital strategies unbound to any strategic objective.

Having said that, let us propose a definition of digital marketing that, we believe, balances all the aforementioned points:

Using digital technologies and media to build relationships with targeted audiences, as a part of an integrated and measurable marketing strategy.

Differences and Commonalities Between Online and Traditional Marketing

When we discuss digital marketing, it is important to consider both words equally: yes, it is digital, not traditional, therefore new terms are coined, new rules apply, new behaviours occur. But, it is still marketing, the activity, set of institutions, and processes for creating, communicating, delivering, and exchanging offerings that have value for customers, clients, partners, and society at large (American Marketing Association, 2013). As marketing as whole monitors and responds to consumer needs, digital marketing is an advancement to adapt to the overwhelming penetration of the internet in our lives. And, despite the complex skills that a competent digital marketer has to have, they first need to know marketing. It is our strong belief that in order to become a digital marketer, a solid marketing background- at least in terms of formal education as a starting point- is needed. And this is how we take sides on the hot debate that Mark Ritson's article on Marketing Week (Marketing Week, 2016) has fueled, about whether marketers need to have some formal education on marketing or not. Building relationships through online communities and create self-expressive content that will engage the users to the brands, beyond the context of the online world, demands a deep understanding of the customer behaviour, motives, and goals and the ways brand building can respond to them. If you go out there, armed with creative thinking and inspiration and knowing all the tips and tricks of digital marketing but have very limited knowledge of how consumers think, feel and make decisions, it is possible to find it very difficult to gasp the strategic potential of online marketing- and of your career.

On the other hand, having studied marketing doesn't make you a digital marketer. The new environment mandates a shift in the mindset and a new set of analytical and technical skills that will allow you to understand and exploit the new possibilities. As you will read this book, you will probably notice how strongly we insist on this "mindset shift" concept. Looking at the fundamental differences between online and traditional marketing will make clear why:

- When you practice traditional marketing, you are not expecting a two way communication: the brand talks to the customers, period. However, in the online environment, the power has been transmitted to the users, who can now respond, review, comment, promote or challenge our marketing statements. Marketing departments structure strategies and plans, but at the end of the day, if the users decide to start a conversation, they will (and the marketers' reflexes are of great value here). It might seem that the brand is exposed to public discussion- and it kind of is- but, on the bright side, don't underestimate how significantly the effect of responsible and meaningful marketing is multiplied, through the power of the word of web.

- On the same token, executives have been violently taken away their privilege to decide behind closed doors. Today, transparency is an imperative and those who fail to comply are punished and humiliated. News travels faster than ever and, it seems really hard to hide malpractices and doubtful decisions as the next PR disaster are just a tweet away. Marketers need to be alerted and ready to control any suchlike situation while deploying strategies to allow perceived access to the consumers inside the decision making sanctum.

- In traditional marketing, despite our persistent efforts for customization, we mostly talk to masses. In the digital environment, it is the exact opposite: technology has provided us with so many tools for segmentation and targeting that we are able, like never before, to talk separately to each of our customers. As we explain later, target groups have been replaced by personas and although we have never been more distant, we can claim that we know our customers better than ever.

- The content of the marketing messages has always been very important, but, in the traditional context, is was about the brand, its feature, and the value proposition. Digital marketing challenges this premise: users go online to talk about themselves- there are huge streams of "me-formation" published each minute (Kaufmann & Manarioti, 2016). They are not willing to sit and listen the brand promoting itself, whatever not relevant to them is dismissed. Therefore, digital marketing is about creating content that is meaningful and relevant to the user while subtly promoting the brand identity or a specific offering.

- Taking this a step further, content that is too stiff, too polished, and too professional is not easy to engage to. The internet, and the social media in particular, are a more informal, direct, person to person medium and what is, in reality, called for is a transition towards a "brand-as-a-person" situation (Chen et al., 2015).

- Brands that have achieved to motivate their users to co-create are the winners of the digital marketing battle. Having access to brand related, user generated content is a great success for the brand, a pursuit that it is significantly facilitated by the abilities of the new technologies. For example, a form of co-creation refers to brand content created and shared by the uses, spontaneously or as a response to a brand prompt. Introducing a hashtag contest (e.g. like the #MoveYourLee contest by VF Corporation or the #ShareaCoke by Coca Cola) that invites users to share their experience with the brand can be a very personalized tactic that strengthens the feeling of sharing and belonging between community members while creating positive word of mouth for the brand. How could you do so in the traditional marketing setting?

- Last, but not least, comes the subject of metrics. When we measure the effectiveness of a TV commercial or a print ad, we mostly focus on reach and frequency, as a means to calculate how many people potentially received our message. In digital marketing, there are some major differences: we have the ways to know exactly how many people received our message, where did they find it, how long have they been exposed to it and what they did next. But, at the end of the day, performance metrics are not enough- conversion is what actually matters: how many sales did we generate from Banner A, how many newsletter subscriptions from pop up B, how many website visits from our PPC (pay-per-click) campaign. On the social media arena, specifically, there is a very important mediator, engagement. Reaching many users is of importance only because it raises the chances of likes, shares, and comments- otherwise, if users don't respond, reach doesn't mean much (we will come back to it, later). And, for the skeptics that hear again the "Why bother" question in their heads, research has found that the more users engage with a brand online, the higher the chances to choose the brand, both online and offline (Google, 2014).

THE RULES OF ONLINE MARKETING

In general, in contexts that are as dynamic and ever changing as the digital environment making a list of rules seems like a desperate effort to put the chaos in an order, to control somehow an uncertain future. But, on the other hand, they are handy and they do make complexity simpler- so here they are, ten rules of online marketing. As rule Number 1 implies, they are valid today but might be completely irrelevant tomorrow, so stay alerted!

- **Rule No 1- One Thing is Constant: Everything Changes**: If you don't believe us, read a book or an article on the digital related subject, published five (or fewer years ago). You will easily understand that great advancements of the day are outdated features today, new concepts have emerged and even newer will come up soon. What you know today will be common sense tomorrow, so don't stop searching and learning.

Figure 1. Rules of digital marketing

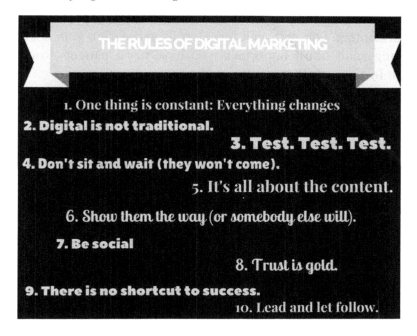

- **Rule No 2- Digital is Not Traditional**: It's what we discussed earlier; the goal of marketing is always the same but applying traditional practices or mindsets to digital marketing is a lost cause. Challenge your beliefs, keep an open mind and be ready to re-learn what you knew about marketing, this is the gateway to the digital world.
- **Rule No 3- Test. Test. Test:** Test your content, test your headlines, test your images, test your buttons, and test your campaigns. Why? Because you can. It's cheap, it's easy and it's precious. Get the habit to create multiple versions of your online material and to monitor your audience's reactions before you select the final version. Usually, in the traditional environment, running A/B testing is costly and time consuming, so we keep it for the very important decisions, but read Rule No 2 and test.
- **Rule No 4- Don't Sit and Wait (They Won't Come):** You might build an amazing website and yet never manage to beat the simple and plain wordpress blog of your competitor. Launching a website and then sit and wait for the visitors to come is not the way the internet works. Yes, it might be effective in the case of a new store at a popular mall, or of a new product prominently placed on a supermarket shelf, but it

will not be on the internet. You have to meticulously work on the way the search engines will find you and how they will positively evaluate your content, you will seek for referrals and design your social media strategy and- most important- you have to be patient- Rome wasn't built in a day, neither is your success.

- **Rule No 5- It's All About the Content:** Some believe that "Content is King" and we actually agree: content is the king, today (remember Rule No 1?). Brands that understand the meaning of content management- as a strategy to build a relationship with the users on the basis of sharing opinions and expertise about a subject of common interest- are the ones that excel in digital marketing, at the time being. Creating good content, apart from spending a lot of time and effort, means breaking the narrow boundaries of the brand category and be bold enough to start a broader conversation- e.g. if you sell butter, invest on a website about pastry recipes, if you sell athletic apparel, launch a fitness mobile app like Nike did etc.

- **Rule No 6- Show Them the Way (Otherwise Someone Else Will):** Never do anything online that is not clearly bounded to a conversion goal. As simple as that. If you publish a Facebook post in order to generate website traffic, always include a link to the landing page. If you run a campaign to promote a sales offer, make a clear Call-To-Action prompt. Don't expect the users to find their way to your website (chances are that they won't bother). Clearly, show them the way you want them to follow.

- **Rule No 7- Be Social:** If you are still skeptical about the impact of social media, don't feel bad about it- most marketers report that they feel the same (Stelzner, 2016) - but the sooner you get over it, the better. Social media marketing is founded on the profound psychological need of reward seeking and belonging ((Zhu & Chen, 2015) and marketers have countless opportunities to fulfill these need in ways that benefit both the brand and the users.

- **Rule No 8- Trust is Gold:** Consumers are cautious towards marketing and advertising and this is yesterday's news. Therefore, they are constantly looking for evidence that a brand, a website, a social media profile etc. worth their trust. Even the ranking on the search engine is a proof of trustworthiness, along with reviews, social media engagement, lack of bad reputation etc. Think your brand as a person that builds an identity through posts, tweets, replies, hashtags and content in general. Does that person seem to behave in a coherent manner, does it make sense? If your brand was a person, would you trust him/ her? Make sure your brand looks, feels and acts in a reliable manner and you will be rewarded.

- **Rule No 9- There is No Shortcut to Success**: Depending on the way you approach life, this is either very good or very bad news: you have to work hard in order to enjoy long lasting, sustainable outcomes of your digital marketing strategies. Which means that if you have a competitor that seems to gain ground just by investing in hypes, but actually fails to steadily produce high quality, relatable content while you do, you will probably win, in the end; but it also means that you need to invest lot of time and effort to design and implement your strategy, post by post, tweet by tweet, keyword by keyword.

- **Rule No 10- Lead and Let Follow:** Do you have a Snapchat account (this is a question that makes sense in 2016, perhaps it will sound ridiculous a year later). If you want to lead, as a marketer and as a brand representative, you should work on your ability to monitor new trends, to understand what will shape tomorrow and how your audience will respond to a new social platform, an update on the Google algorithm, a change in Twitter's hashtag format. You, as a digital marketer, you have to be digitally active, to be an early adopter and to always keep you mind open- this is the best way for you to lead. All the rest, the risk averse, the technophobics, the "I know Facebook and that's enough" marketers can just follow. Choose your side wisely.

The Digital Marketer

A research published in 2014, emphatically identified a gap in the skills of the digital marketers, highlighting the many different levels of literacy that the addition of "digital" has brought about (Royle and Laing, 2014). Later, in 2016, the Social Media Marketing Industry Report also found that marketers are not yet able to understand exactly the way their digital marketing (social media marketing in particular) efforts work and to clearly explain how to measure ROI (Stelzner, 2016). Most of us, working in the marketing field, have experienced this gap in the real world, as we are or have been challenged to monitor new trends and to the extent our plans to new territories, ruled by conversion and engagement metrics. This conversation brings us to admit that being a good digital marketer is a complex profession that demands a unique combination of knowledge and skills from different areas. Taking the

Figure 2. The digital marketer
(Adapted from Royle & Laing, 2014)

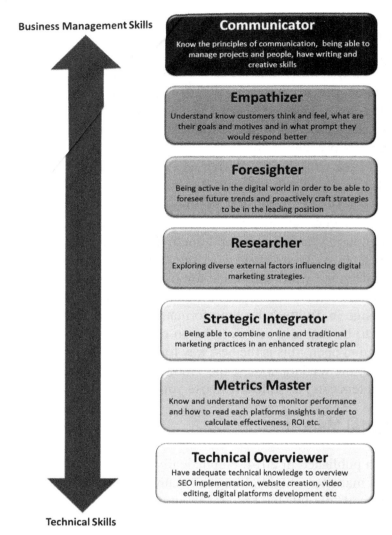

lead from the Digital Marketer Model proposed by Royle and Laing in their publication (Royle and Laing, 2014), here are the building blocks of digital marketing competency:

In a continuum from business management skills to core technical skills, the middle is the place where differentiation occurs, at least for now: being a strategic integrator means that the digital marketer is able to balance traditional and digital marketing and to combine them in synergistic strategies. We emphasize this skill a lot, because here is where the "mindset shift" is mostly needed: adding a digital ankle in our strategies without being able to bind it with our core marketing objectives and our traditional marketing practices, literally says nothing. The meaning here is about succeeding in integrating mobile apps with in store experiences, TV campaigns with social media content, sales scenarios with website features in an omni channel marketing where different tactics produce a cumulative outcome. Take the example of beacon systems in malls, where push notifications with limited time offers or other brand messages are sent to consumers when they approach a store. Sales offers are a (very) traditional marketing practice but when combined with the geo-location abilities of mobile technology they can produce a very impactful campaign, with a notion of exclusiveness and community belonging.

Digital marketers are very closely involved with technical personnel, from web designers to mobile apps developers, 3D animators, SEO analysts etc. Obviously, it is unrealistic to expect one person to know all the above- and much more than these, after all, multitasking is good, but specialization is better. However, marketers must definitely be able to overview, guide, create briefs using the correct terminology, understand key concepts and ultimately communicate with technical professionals, if they are to maintain control over their strategies. This is a challenge, given that technological advancements are very rapid and usually difficult to understand by those who are not trained to. Being active online, following influential blogs and keep eyes, ears, and mind open is a good plan for becoming an effective "technical overviewer".

On the same side of the continuum, becoming a metrics master means that you know how to exploit the wealth of insights provided by tools like Google Analytics and, most important, how to make sense out of them. As mentioned earlier, marketers struggle to measure the impact of their initiatives and, although this is also the result of falling short in the Strategic Integrator performance, it reflects their perplexity on the metrics matter. Digital platforms, including social media, have inherited tools to provide marketers with insights since this is a major advantage of digital versus traditional marketing: we are in the privileged position to monitor every single click and have access inside the mind of our users. If we fail to make use of this privilege, we practically void the value proposition of digital marketing itself. Naturally, becoming a metrics master is not easy, it takes effort and time, as it calls for analytical and numerical skills and the ability to translate ratios and metrics in human behaviour. The good news is that, for starters, there are loads of handy webinars and eBooks that will provide you, at least, with what you fundamentally need to know and understand.

As we move up in the skills continuum, we approach the core areas of marketing competency in the most traditional use of the term. Being a *researcher* means having the skills and knowledge to find and collect information from our environment, including social, political, economic, environmental etc. factors and synthesize them to make conclusions that will allow us to better understand our consumers' behaviour. Needless to say, that an isolated marketer, immobilized behind an office, without constant firsthand experience with the field is a marketer in vitro. Being a researcher, means being out there visiting points of sales (in the cases of brick and mortar) or visit eshops in the case of online traders, being active on the social media and get involved in conversations with the consumers, read trend reports and stay updated and, most of all being able to combine all the input above in favor of better decision making.

William Ford Gibson, the noir prophet of the cyberspace, once said "The future is already here- it's not just very evenly distributed" and his quote pretty much describes the equilibrium in digital marketing. The next mega trend of the near future has already been discovered and it is probably making its first steps into the digital world. It could be Snapchat or Augmented Reality, it could be a universal use of hashtags or the wearables or something entirely new that is already known to few. The foresighter keeps these new trends on his/her radar and has the experience and the skills not only to foresee what the next big trend will be but to take action as well and futureproof their brands. A very trustworthy source of information that will help marketers foresee the future are the customers themselves, their shifted goals, motives and needs and how imperative they are becoming. If you understand how people think and make decisions, in the fundamental psychological level where goals, needs, and motives reside, then it will be easier to predict their forecoming preferences and their reactions to new value propositions. Of course diving into people's minds and psyches demands for a solid understanding of psychological and sociological issues but, equally important, it asks for *real time* empathy and emotional connection. Being an empathizer is a hard-to-find skill, describing people that manage to get over their personal thoughts and perceptions and get in their audiences' shoes. If we see our brands or our marketing tactics solely from our marketing perceptive, we might end up being self-referential and myopic- we do what is right by the book but neglect how people will receive it. During our careers, we have come across many cases of marketing fails, that were well designed and theoretically backed up but not appropriate for the time and place they were launched. Despite the good intentions and the literacy of the marketers in charge, their lack of empathy condemned their efforts. On the other hand, being able to receive our own messages, from the position of the audience/ consumer/ user will allow us to understand if we are really relevant if we are relatable and to whom, if what we say is really meaningful or just empty marketing language. Being an empathizer is a skill that, when backed up with the right metrics it can become a source of strong, sustainable advantage. Finally, a good marketer is also an effective manager and leader, a proficient worker of words and a competent business person. When initiating change and bearing change being a communicator is a trait that might determine success or failure. Specifically, in the subject of integration, between traditional and digital marketing practices- and executives, it is the leadership skills of the marketer that will unite the different approaches into a seamless strategy. As you will read later, there is compelling evidence that today one of the main reasons why companies fail to integrate the different aspects of marketing is the "walls" among the marketing teams. The solution to this is a matter of leadership and it's this new type of marketer that will be charged to resolve it.

Along with or even beyond everything else, marketers should maintain high morality standards and set the bar for themselves. The large volumes of information, this digital stalking of consumers raises vivid debates about privacy and a question on how protected can consumers be against malicious marketing practices. Truth is that perhaps the greatest power consumers own today is this of commenting and sharing; a doubtful practice can become an avalanche of bad reputation and, literally, one post is enough to set the fire. But, apart from this, it's real to say that marketers have access to more information- therefore more power- than ever. It is our personal obligation, as professionals and as parts of the society, to resist to the temptations of short term glory in favor of long term sustainable advantages.

THE BOOK STRUCTURE

As you might have already noticed, the commonalities and differences between online and traditional marketing have, at large, inspired the rules of marketing, that dictate the characteristics of the digital marketer. The structure of this book is the last link of this chain, as at the end, you will have the tools and theoretical back up to develop each one of the aforementioned skills:

Chapter Number 2 is focused on the design of the website, introducing some technical aspects but from a marketing point of view. It is not our purpose as marketers to develop code and design websites, but we have to know how the user experience reflects on our branding perception and how brand values are translated in websites. After all, the website is becoming a part of the brand image and it has to be perceived as such. Also, search engine optimization is covered in chapter 2, as it is bound to the website structure but also to strategic aspects, like targeting and positioning. As we have already said multiple times, technology and SEO principles (from a technical perspective) change quickly, but it is the main idea that will remain: our decisions while designing and writing content for a website are led by our audiences and what they like, what they look for, what they need, not the other way round. The sooner we realize this and we make an 180o turn our mindset, the sooner we will get dynamically in the digital marketing arena.

Chapter 3 is all about the consumer behaviour and how it has changed due to the internet and the digital tools, introducing the ideas and meanings that are necessary to develop the researching and empathizing skills. Today, online shopping has taken over many industries, mobiles are emerging as main purchase channels, while consumers are empowered and therefore they have become more demanding as they seek simultaneously for extrinsic and intrinsic rewards. On the other hand, the social media and the structure of the internet, in general, facilitates the development of brand communities, relieved from geographical boundaries, and built upon the shared values among customers and brands. As communities are highlighted as a major marketing opportunity, the concept of co-creation emerges as the active participation in creating value for the brand. All these new concepts are heavily based in theory, but in this new context, they are actualized via the new technological tools.

Chapter 4 is dedicated to the social media, as social media marketing is a discipline of digital marketing that is in full bloom today. Despite the common perception that the social media are a trend, a hype imposed to us by peer pressure, truth is that they actually respond to our persisting need of belonging, sharing and get rewarded for this. Facebook, Twitter, Instagram, Snapchat etc. are built on our fundamental need to express ourselves and connect with likeminded others and here lies the opportunity for brands to communicate their personality and invite people to identify with it. But, on the dark side, now brands are exposed to public discussion as any disappointed customer can share their experience and initiate an avalanche of the bad reputation that even evolves to a crisis. Or a satisfied customer can write a positive review that will start a chain of positive Word of Mouth, leading to visible positive impact to sales and brand value. This new context needs to be understood and monitored by the digital marketer, and when so, it can become a source of sustainable competitive advantage.

In Chapter 5, we introduce the term "Content as product", showing how important content management is for any given brand. This is an entirely new concept that it might not be easily compared with any equivalent from the traditional marketing literature, but it is in the heart of any successful strategic integrator. Creating relatable content that will satisfy the needs of the audiences and will motivate them to engage with the brand sometimes calls for a transgression, beyond the traditional boundaries of the product category. Marketers are asked to find the golden section where consumers' interest intersect with brand messages and build a whole content strategy right there. As a result, a new online marketing mix emerges, one that evolves all the familiar meanings and concepts into new ideas that cannot be overseen.

Finally, the last chapter integrates major issues of digital marketing (like ethical considerations, big data and business models) reviewing the wealth of related literature that has been published throughout the years. Interestingly, you will find out that classic marketing models remain valid and valuable, even if channels have changed. Vice versa, new debates have been initiated and new reactions have been monitored, as results of this changing era. Finally, this chapter attempts a sneak preview in the future, where reality will probably get new meanings and new opportunities will present themselves to the braves of the marketing field.

Answers

1. Borrowing from the American Marketing Association, digital marketing is not an add-on, it is an imperative. Defined as the use of digital technologies and media to build relationships with targeted audiences, as a part of an integrated and measurable marketing strategy, it is the response to the dramatic change of the consumer behaviour as a result of the internet penetration in our lives. Brands that pursue long lasting, meaningful relationships with their targeted consumers, cannot afford to refrain from what is described as the digital revolution.

2. Regardless if it's digital or traditional, it is always marketing. Which means it is a consumer focused, analytical and synthetic strategic process to create and propose meaningful offerings. But, in the digital environment,

users are empowered and willing to respond, to discuss, to co-create or co-destroy brands and marketers need to tailor their strategies to the new context. Among the very few things that one can be certain about in marketing is that going digital with a traditional mentality will not take you anywhere.

3. When everything changes as rapidly as in the digital marketing area, the first rule is that there are no rules. Things cannot be written in stone, yet, it is good to remember that digital revolution calls for a mindset shift, because digital marketing is not traditional. It has new rules and new potentials that allow us to test different alternatives and closely monitor our audiences' reactions but also mandate that will go out and find our customers rather than sit and wait for them to come. The digital environment provides us with new ways to engage with our customers and build communities, based on self-expressive content, shared ideas and trust and makes the marketer a content creation, on top of everything else. This is our ammunition: high quality, relatable content, hard work and an open, forward thinking mind.

4. Being a digital marketer is demanding, as it calls for a complex set of skills, but, at the time being, there are so many resources to acquire these skills that make knowledge very accessible and success very possible. As digital marketers, we need to be strategic integrators and successfully combine traditional with digital marketing actions, while having a strong understanding of technical aspects that will fall under our supervision. Strong numerical skills are also called for, in order to translate conversions, traffic, bounce and other metrics into human behaviour- and while constantly monitoring the external environment and advancements, to come in a place where the marketer will be a foresighter, too. Exactly as in traditional marketing, being a researcher that collects information from different angles to build consumer personas and exercising empathy with them is also a key talent and a combination of knowledge and soft skills. Finally, being a pioneer that initiates change and introduces novel concepts to traditional environments, demands for communication and leadership skills that will motivate people to give a chance to the future, even when it seems overwhelming.

REFERENCES

American Marketing Association. (2013). *Definition of marketing*. Retrieved from https://www.ama.org/AboutAMA/Pages/Definition-of-Marketing.aspx

American Marketing Association. (2016). *Digital*. Retrieved from https://www.ama.org/topics/digital/ Pages/default.aspx?k=contentsource:%22Main%22%20 AND%20AMATopicTags:%22Digital%22%20AND%20 (%20ContentType:%22AMATextPage%22%20OR%20 ContentType:%22AMAToolPage%22)&tab=9#SearchResults

Chaffey, D., & Ellis-Chadwick, F. (2012). *Internet marketing: strategy, implementation and practice*. Pearson Education.

Chen, K., Lin, J., Choi, J. H., & Hahm, J. M. (2015). Would You Be My Friend? An Examination of Global Marketers Brand Personification Strategies in Social Media. *Journal of Interactive Advertising*, *15*(2), 97–110. doi:10. 1080/15252019.2015.1079508

Googleapis.com. (2014). *Brand Engagement in the participation age*. Retrieved from https://think.storage.googleapis.com/docs/brand-engagement-in-participation-age_research-studies.pdf

Kaufmann, H. R., & Manarioti, A. (2016). The Content Challenge: Engaging Consumers in a World of Me-Formation. In The Impact of the digital world on management and marketing (pp. 271–285). Academic Press.

Ritson, M. (2016). *Maybe it's just me, but shouldn't an 'expert' in marketing be trained in marketing?* Retrieved from https://www.marketingweek. com/2016/07/12/mark-ritson-maybe-its-just-me-but-shouldnt-an-expert-in-marketing-be-trained-in-marketing/

Royle, J., & Laing, A. (2014). The digital marketing skills gap: Developing a Digital Marketer Model for the communication industries. *International Journal of Information Management*, *34*(2), 65–73. doi:10.1016/j. ijinfomgt.2013.11.008

Stelzner, M. (2016). Social Media Marketing Industry Report. *Socialmediaexaminer*. Retrieved from http://www.socialmediaexaminer. com/report/

Tiago, M. T. P. M. B., & Veríssimo, J. M. C. (2014). Digital marketing and social media: Why bother? *Business Horizons, 57*(6), 703–708. doi:10.1016/j. bushor.2014.07.002

Zhu, Y., & Chen, H. (2015). Social media and human need satisfaction: Implications for social media marketing. *Business Horizons, 58*(3), 335–345. doi:10.1016/j.bushor.2015.01.006

Chapter 2

Technological Background Knowledge to Use the Internet as a Marketing Tool

ABSTRACT

Websites are the cornerstone of digital marketing, the online premises of brands and companies, therefore, this chapter focuses on them. Making web design decisions stretches far beyond personal aesthetics, and there is compelling evidence that customers respond and evaluate the overall online experience differently even when a slight detail is changed. This chapter reviews the school of thoughts and models that apply to strategic website design, from the marketer's point of view. Later, we present the main concepts on Search Engine Optimization, since it is significant to website success and tightly bonded to the website architecture. The chapter concludes with a glance at fundamental metrics, as an effort to explain and decode how website related decisions are quantified, measured, evaluated and related to marketing objectives.

Questions

- Why are over-confident marketers threatening website success?
- Which are the 7 dimensions of a website?
- There is always a catch: what is it?

DOI: 10.4018/978-1-68318-012-8.ch002

- Why is the website personality crucial for our internet marketing decisions, and why is this so important for the brand experience?
- How many layers do websites have?
- How can we know what constitutes a positive web experience for our user?
- How do the search engines measure relevance and importance?
- What is the golden rule of Search Engine Optimization (SEO)?

CONSUMER CENTERED EFFECTIVE WEBPAGE DESIGN AS A MEANS TO INCREASE WEBSITE REACH AND LOYALTY

In the physical brick and mortar world, the website can be regarded as the equivalent of the store window; but in this new era, with so many dot.com businesses, on plenty occasions the website is the whole store itself. Designing and updating a complete and useful website is not a matter of choice any more (like brand presence can be sustained without any digital presence), but a decision that determines the present and future success of brands, since consumers are migrating online and mobile in their overwhelming majority. According to livestats.com (2016), more than 3 billion people around the world have access to the internet today- a figure approaching 50% of the world population, while, back in 2006, internet penetration was as high as 17.6%. In the United States, 88.5% of the population have access to the internet compared to 79.3% in Europe. Figure 1 presents the countries with the highest internet penetration in 2016 with islands, small countries and Scandinavia to be leading the table:

In fact, probably everyone we know has access to the internet. This understanding clearly calls the marketers to quickly adopt - if not done yet- an online marketing strategy, starting from building a website that meets their stakeholders' needs. In this process, a strong synthesis between technical and marketing know-how is required; no part can produce a sufficient and competent outcome without the other. This is due to the website being a multifunctional tool as it serves, amongst others, diverse functional/ informational, sales and marketing and social/ relational purposes. Its success is the sum of integrated technological, design, business and marketing excellence. As proposed by Smith and Chaffey (2005, p. 172) a website may have 3 levels of objectives:

Table 1. The 20 countries with the highest internet penetration in 2016

Country	Penetration (%of Pop)
Iceland	100.0%
Faeroe Islands	98.5%
Norway	98.0%
Bermuda	97.4%
Andorra	96.5%
Denmark	96.3%
Liechtenstein	95.8%
Luxembourg	95.2%
Netherlands	93.7%
Sweden	93.1%
Monaco	93.0%
U.K.	92.6%
Finland	92.5%
Qatar	92.0%
United Arab Emirates	91.9%
Bahrain	91.5%
Estonia	91.4%
Japan	91.1%
New Zealand	89.4%
U.S.	88.5%

Source:www.livestats.com

- **Customer Acquisition:** Converting visitors into customers.
- **Customer Loyalty**: Repeated visits.
- **Higher Share of Customer's Wallet**: Selling additional relevant products to the same customer.

As in any strategic process, the first question marketing practitioners should ask themselves before preparing the brief for the website is: What is my brand's/company's objective? What purposes this website will serve? Applying the saying, 'well begun is half done' and, in this case, the initial step is crucial, as designing a website is an idiosyncratic and not a "one size fits all" process. Hence, before approaching a web developer, you should have decided the major objective of the website for the time being; for example, at the current life cycle stage of our internet presence, are we targeting high reach or high loyalty? Then involve the technical team to guide you through the technological and designing features that will take you to your goal. As we have come across multiple occasions where the marketer insisted on a specific layout and features, based on subjective and ill-informed opinions, we strongly suggest to ask and value the web developers'/ web designers' input to transform a website to a useful means to the end. In case you are looking for statistical findings to back up our suggestions, there is extensive research on the subject abound which concludes that website features designed for one purpose (for example higher reach) are not equally helpful when the target is different (for example increased loyalty) and vice versa (i.e. Tarafdar & Zhang, 2008).

In order to bring about the desired objectives and consumer behaviors, let us outline the 7 dimensions of website features (Ting et al., 2013) that will be used to some extent to ultimately engage the targeted user:

- **Interactivity:** The level to which the website allows two-way communication between information providers and information users to establish partnerships. These relationships can be transactional, i.e. exchange of information, support etc., or social, as the website becomes the spine of a community for their members to interact amongst each other and with the brand and to enjoy participatory and social benefits.
- **Navigation:** Measuring how easy it is for the users to acquire the information they want on the website, including standard menu structure, home page links, SEO, standard page design and the indication of user position in the menu. The ease of navigation has been found to be significant for both, targeting reach and loyalty, revealing that internet users prefer simple rather than fancy structures (Tarafdar & Zhang, 2008). Note that in times where mobile penetration is growing rapidly, all the above parameters of navigation should be responsive to different devices to preserve- rather than spoil- the user experience.
- **Functionality/ Usability:** Competency to use the internet to its fullest potential and keep up with new technology, i.e. incorporating social and personalization tools. From a branding point of view, an outdated design sends unfavorable messages when it comes to the brand's reflex on evolution and innovation.
- **Marketing:** Promotional messages and tools designed to communicate products/ services, the company, the brand and its identity. Again, for a website to be effective subject to a measurable goal, every marketing action on the website must be linked to a Call-To-Action, a conversion target that can be explicitly measured and compared, in order to

capture the progress and success of our marketing efforts; the Internet provides with the tools and the opportunities and if we decide to spare this wealth of analytics, this opportunity that can result to competitive advantage is wasted.

- **Service:** Competency to provide value-added activities, related to the business field, but not as a part of the business transaction. Services and information that are useful for the visitor are considered as "good content" and are much appreciated by users and the search engines, for example, currency convertors in a finance related website, weather information on a hotel website etc.
- **Innovativeness:** Creative ideas designed for products, services or the brand that are both novel and valuable differentiate the website from its competitors. Given that complicated processes discourage the visitors, innovation should be focused on the essence of the services provided and its usefulness for the audience. Therefore, innovativeness has a significant technical angle but is mostly a matter of strategic and marketing decisions.
- **Online Processing:** Competency to conduct secure online transactions and provide order status. Although, at first sight, it might not seem applicable to all businesses, the trend is towards online processing and no brand can afford to forego it.

An additional and quite familiar perspective to marketers in terms of designing a web page is provided by Eisenberg (in Smith & Chaffey, 2005), a prolific writer and columnist that proposed an adaptation of the popular AIDA model, otherwise used as an advertising strategy, to web design:

- **"Attention:** The site must grab attention when the visitor first hears about it or even when the visitor actually arrives. We achieve attention through graphics, animation, interaction and easy access to relevant information.
- **Interest:** Once we have the customers' attention, it's our chance to provide more detailed information and incentives to engage them.
- **Desire:** There are many marketing tactics to trigger desire, from investing on Fear of Missing Out (limited offer, only one seat left), to giveaways and free stuff such as free information, free screensaver, free services to unlimited more.
- **Action:** The prompt to act - Call to Action (CTA)-, e.g. to ring up, subscribe or order that should be clear and easy to use (p.176)."

Albeit very useful, internet related frameworks always have a drawback: they can easily become irrelevant as trends become standards very quickly, and today's innovations are tomorrow's prerequisites. Recent internet history has proven that devices change, search engine algorithms are updated and new online specific marketing concepts emerge. The only permanent factor in this change is the fact that the marketers must be in close connection with their audiences and strive for an ever better understanding of their goals, needs, and motives. Caveat: Internet marketing principals are not put in stone, and a brand that wants to enjoy leadership must learn and apply the new rules, daily.

THE WEBSITE PERSONALITY

If your website was a human, how would you describe her/him?

The answer to this question is the essence of the website personality, a concept very affine to brand personality, coined by Aaker (1997, p.347) as "the set of human characteristics associated with the brand". On the same token, researchers later developed the concept of store personality (D'Astous & Levesque, 2003) that ultimately evolved to website personality construct (Poddar et al., 2009) in an effort to explore the traits of online commercial stores. Although related, the initial concepts of brand and store personality have some fundamental differences, mainly on the dimensions of each personality type. Given that there are more similarities between a Web store and an offline store than between a webstore and a brand, the website personality construct is based on the store personality. Note that the research was limited to commercial websites (e-shops) but the conclusions can be generalized to all websites, given that website satisfaction impacts purchase and revisit intentions.

Website personality refers to the mental representation of an online store on dimensions that are similar to and reflect the dimensions of human personality (Poddar et al., 2009), that have been proposed to be the following:

- Enthusiasm
- Sophistication
- Genuineness
- Solidity and
- Unpleasantness.

For a website to be "enthusiastic" means that visitors perceive their experience with it as fun and joy, thanks to the color schemes, the design and an overall feeling of friendliness and welcoming. Sophistication refers to websites that are elegant, classy and upscale to their design, their content and quality of service as well. Genuineness is the perception of reliability and trustworthiness, sometimes enhanced by third-party endorsements, like VeriSign or money back guarantees. A solid personality demonstrates that the website is capable of conducting its business in a professional manner, as proved by the depth of selection, the ease of the process and the lack of mistakes. Finally, the only negative dimension, this of unpleasantness refers to anything that might irritate or annoy the user, from complicated features and processes to meaningless content and lack of support.

As we live in the experiential rather than transactional marketing era, one could say that the overall user experience is more important than the design itself; so, in the initial stage of the strategic decision making about the website, the personality question must be answered. Which personality is more compatible with our brand and our internet-related objectives? Obviously, we would all prefer to create a website that would be very enthusiastic, pleasant and sophisticated, yet genuine and solid, but this is not an option as some features are mutually exclusive (for example, either you will invest in fun aesthetical features that will enhance the enthusiastic aspect of the website or you will keep it plain and simple to communicate reliability). In that case, which personality traits should we sacrifice to keep our customers satisfied and our website effective? And, in terms of the bigger picture, what is the role of the website in our overall marketing strategy? Is it a channel of communication with existing audience (and therefore an extension of our existing branding rationale) or an attempt to attract new audiences that might call for added and new personality features? Again, as in the website objectives discussion, decision making should be objective and based on insights, not subjective based on personal preference and superficial aesthetic motives to provide for a positive customer centered brand experience.

Recent research found that different experiential values have a different impact on the manipulation of the personality dimensions and those findings can be used as a roadmap to building better websites and online experiences (Shobeiri et al., 2012). They tested four experiential values, namely playfulness, aesthetics, Customer Return on Investment (CROI- receiving maximum benefits with the minimum investment of time and energy) and service excellence and how each of them impacts the five personality dimensions. The major contribution to an improved understanding of online customer satisfaction was that service excellence has been found to strongly influence all five dimensions: we perceive a website to be more enthusiastic, sophisticated, genuine, solid and less unpleasant if the quality of the service is high. Contrarily, aesthetics is significant if we pursue an enthusiastic, sophisticated, pleasant personality but has no impact on genuineness and reliability, i.e. a clear indication on which experiential values to focus when developing a "reliable" personality, i.e. for a financial or insurance institution.

The Customer ROI factor leads to interesting conclusions as it has no significant impact on any personality trait. As explained by the researchers themselves, the industry's common focus on efficiency and affordability makes CROI fall short on being a distinguishing element of an e-retailer's website personality- it has become a hygiene factor. Due to the vast provision of CROI by many e-retailers today, this factor might not be sufficient to make customers really involved and interested in the website (Shobeiri et al., 2013). Actually, CROI had a negative impact on enthusism and sophistication revealing that users find no challenge or fun on the very standard/very easy to use websites. However, it could be a very well documented strategic decision of the marketing team, to sacrifice the distinctive, enthusiastic personality in order to focus on offers and simplicity. Finally, playfulness was the only dimension to have both positive and negative impacts on personality dimensions: positive ones on enthusism and sophistication, negative ones

Table 2. How to create a website personality

Personality Dimension	Determinants and tactics
Enthusiasm	Provide excellent services Focus on colours and design Use a friendly, welcoming tone of voice Add playful elements
Sophistication	Provide excellent services Select the colours and designs that create an upscale perception Add playful elements
Genuiness	Provide excellent services Keep the aesthetics simple, avoid playful elements that might be irritating Place prominently your security signs and all tactics and initiatives (like money back guarantees) that show you are trustworthy
Solidity	Provide excellent services Keep the aesthetics simple Add features that are meaningful for the user and helpful for the transaction
Pleasantness	Provide excellent services Focus on the aesthetics Avoid playful elements that might irritate users Create meaningful content, avoid superficial statements

on genuineness and pleasantness. This implies that, when looking for a straightforward, highly efficient online transaction, website users find the playful elements as annoying, superficial and unpleasant.

At this point, it is becoming apparent why marketers should focus on the decision and the trade-offs and remember, that it is not a "one size fits all" process. Consumers and visitors change their expectations based on their goals, and this is where our locus of attention should be: the fact that a fun website might be relatively successful does not imply that this approach would work in the context of other strategies. In the same vein, our personal preference for simple and plain websites is not a guideline for all kinds of audience responses. When we craft experiences, every detail is important as it influences the satisfaction level of those who are the most important stakeholders: our visitors.

LEVELS OF WEB DESIGN

After reviewing your brand values, your marketing goals and aligning your web personality with them, the next step is the development of the website, with the contribution of the technical team. As already mentioned, there are 7 features in your web developers' toolbox and the when and how to use them is a layered, evolutionary process, starting from basic company information sharing, proceeding to provision of customization and sharing tools and ending up to a total digitalisation of the service through online processing. As websites move through the stages of development from inception (promotion) through consolidation (provision) to maturity (processing) layers of complexity and

Figure 1. Layers of website development
Based on Doolin, Burgess, and Cooper (2002)

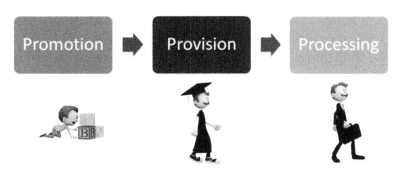

functionality are continuously added to the site (Doolin, Burgess and Cooper, 2002). This addition of layers is synonymous with the business moving from a static Internet presence through increasing levels of interactivity to a dynamic site incorporating value chain integration and innovative applications to add value through information management and rich functionality. And, as long as the ultimate scope of every website is to nurture a relationship with the brand, the users and a brand community, the "reason of why we need these levels of rich functionality" becomes self-explanatory.

The idea of the Extended Model of Internet Commerce Adoption (eMICA) was first expressed by Doolin, Burgess and Cooper (2002) expanding on a previous model presented by Burgess and Cooper (2000). According to their framework on website depth, there are three major tiers of website adoption: Promotion, Provision, and Processing. However, as we established earlier, as internet marketing principles are not written in stone, the elements constituting each level at the initial framework have become outdated in the present environment, and therefore we are attempting an update of this model here.

The general idea is simple: at their initial stages websites are merely informative and exist to provide the audiences with some very basic information. At the next stage, the website becomes more interactive, the quantity and quality of information are enhanced and two-way communication is introduced. Finally, the website provides the user with a seamless experience including all aspects of transactions, from A to Z, a complete digitalization of the process. If we could attempt a parallelism with retail marketing, the first level refers to a store with a sign and a simple catalogue of its collection. At the second level, stylists are hired as sales consultants with a focus on the merchandising and atmospherics and loyalty schemes to be presented. Finally, the store adds a made-to-measure department, where clothes can be tailored to the customers' preferences, while supportive services like home delivery, ironing etc. are offered.

Although the offering whilst moving further in the evolution chain is becoming of better value, it would be questionable to assume that actually being on the first or second stage is the result of a false management decision. First of all, something is better than nothing; so it's better to have a simple website than no online presence at all and second, every decision is related to internal and external circumstances that are not visible to the outside observer. Our premise here is that technological and marketing advancements provide companies with ample opportunities to grow, gain market share and thrive online and the website can be the tip of the spear on the battle for differentiation- in other words it is worth to climb high in the priorities lists.

Let's look closer at the website layers' approach and, while you read, try to evaluate the stage your website is currently on:

- At the Promotion tier, the website shares basic information, like a short 'about us' page, contact information, address and phone numbers. It can be a one-page website, with a short description of the company services but not much depth of information. The website can be easy to navigate but with low interactivity and usability, offering very limited marketing opportunities and no investment in services and innovativeness, let alone online processing.
- At the second layer, the orientation is still transactional but richer information is shared, as we have moved to the medium level of interactivity: customization features are introduced, with account management pages, feedback forms, downloadable material, e-brochures etc. At this tier, all 6 dimensions- apart from online processing- are potent to be used extensively, so the final mix is subject to decision. For a great amount of brick-and-mortar businesses, this is the stage where they are supposed to be before they alter their business model to incorporate online processing.
- At the ultimate third level of processing, services are fully digitalized and commercial transactions are processed throughout the website. At this point, the website can be a fully functional business tool, featuring online shopping, digital signatures and encryption, live communication, customization and supportive services. In terms of interactivity we have now reached the highest level, which is the locus of co-creation (Kaufmann and Shams, 2016), with discussion forums and community features, chat rooms, newsletters, virtual tours etc. A website at this level of interactivity can become the fountain of sense for a brand community, the source of a feeling of togetherness among the users and the brand; it can enable and nurture the relationships among the brand and the brand followers. Of course, when discussing online communities (see the following chapters), the website is essential but not sufficient if it is not supported and inspired by a coherent brand culture and updated marketing policies; still, it is a sine qua non element in the co-creation process.

As shown in Figure 3, all website features are in higher levels of use as we move towards the final layer.

Figure 2. Layers of website adoption and use of features
Based on Doolin, Burgess, and Cooper (2002)

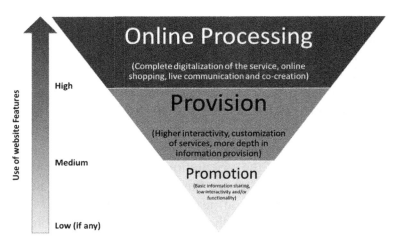

For a company to fully move to the processing stage, significantly more investment is needed than a website and technological excellence: we are facing a business model shift inside the company, backed up with strategic objectives, new roles and policies and a novel corporate identity that will allow the change adoption. Such a decision does not imply that traditional sales and communication channels will become obsolete, but as we monitor the latest customer trends and how they keep moving more and more of their activities online and mobile, it doesn't make sense for any company that plans for the future to oversee this persistent trend.

DESIGNING THE WEBSITE

What we have discussed so far, clearly shows that it is not only about the design, it's more about the experience, and the introduction of the "UX designer" as a job title is the best of proofs. A good website is one that users enjoy interacting with, one with useful content and pleasant environment, easy to use and with congruence between personality and behavior. Surely, colors, images, page layout are important but not from an artistic, graphic point of view; strategically, as building blocks and facilitators of the overall website or even brand experience. "But, how can we know the factors constituting a positive experience for our user", one skeptical marketer could ask.

First of all, remember Jakob's Law of the Web User Experience: users spend most of their time on *other* sites, so that's where they form their expectations for how the Web works. Hence, learning from the best and adopting excellent practices is recommended on the internet, when of course, they are aligned to our strategy and counterbalanced by innovativeness in services or supporting features; after all nobody likes copycats. For example, according to alexa. com, amazon.com is in the 6th place of the top websites in the world and the first in the online shopping category. Probably you don't have the resources to develop a new amazon.com, but understanding how it handles the user experience and trying to create a similar one- in terms of approach and mentality- could be a prudent marketing decision when developing an e-shop that does not demand to reinvent the wheel.

In this particular amazon.com case there have been loads of published case studies as an effort to understand this digital phenomenon that changed first the bookstore industry and then retail altogether. Before focusing on the insights that refer to the customer experience, it is interesting to take a quick look at the corporate culture behind it. From 1997 until today, the company has declared in multiple occasions its focus on the customer experience: The mission statement of 1997 specified that the focus on growth rather than profitability within the business model and that it could be achieved by focusing on customers in the long term (Amazon.com Investor Relations, 2011). In the Annual Report of 1998, the company's mission was already defined to be "the most customer-centric organization in the world" (Amazon.com Investor Relations, 2011). Later, the Amazon.com website states that the company's mission is "to be Earth's most customer-centric company where people can find and discover anything they want to buy online" (Amazon.com Investor Relations, 2013). Today, in the most recent annual report, they are talking about "customer obsession" (Amazon.com Investor Relations, 2015). The success of Amazon.com and the compelling numbers of 100 billion dollars in annual sales (A Amazon.com Investor Relations, 2015) combined with the academic evidence that online customer service experience impacts on sales (Klaus, 2013) can support a conclusion that amazon.com provides an online customer experience worth studying and learning from. In this vein, Philip Klaus in his insightful publication in 2013 studied in depth the case of amazon.com to end up with a framework on what he calls OCSE (online customer service experience). In his view, there are two categories of factors that determine amazon.com customers' satisfaction: functional and psychological. The first set refers to those characteristics that cannot be omitted otherwise the website will not function in a satisfying manner and they are: usability, product presence, communication, interactivity and social presence.

- "Usability relates to attributes that enable online customers to feel comfortable using the web site, such as perceptions of site speed, ease-of-use, and hyperlink design. These attributes are directly and profoundly influencing the online consumer's experience. Customers have clear expectations that the web site should provide users with basic features effective in helping them to achieve a specified goal.

- Product presence represents the requirement to assess products in virtual environments and subsequently stimulate purchase intentions, such as image interactivity, and additional access to content ("look inside" feature). This was evident from quotes such as "The option to 'click to look inside' is very nice and it actually makes me feel like I am in the store," and "If I cannot actually touch the book, I, at least, want to take a peak, and see if I like it." In order for customers to perceive the presence of a product, the web site will need to offer users options to interact and manipulate visual images of a product, an important aspect of OCSE.

- Communication describes attributes reflecting the customer's perception on how communication reduces the risks associated with e-commerce, such as follow-up and transaction confirmation messages, similar to what traditional service marketing literature describes as reassurance in customers' perception of service quality.

- Social presence, a previously unexplored dimension of OCSE, constitutes attributes reflecting the customer's virtual interaction with other shoppers through comments, product reviews, and social media linkages. This dimension was often cited with reference to its impact on the purchase decision process, in particular in the information search and alternatives evaluation stages, evident by quotes such as "Reading customer reviews is really helpful because it gives me more information about the book or product, but it is also interesting to know about the experiences of other people using the product."

- Interactivity describes the influence of the dynamic dialogue between the web site and its users, and vice versa." (Klaus, 2013 p. 448).

One might be surprised by the fact the that social presence, in terms of easy and immediate access to other users' reviews and evaluations is categorized under the functional dimension- the attributes that are considered "basic elements of the website" despite its intense emotional aspect (user generated reviews, as we will see later satisfy our need of belonging to a larger community of like-minded others). The explanation is that in this framework, the psychological factors are those who reduce the risk and fear of online transactions and make the environment more friendly and closely related to physical stores and services, context familiarity, value for money and trust, namely.

- Context familiarity refers to the perceived similarities between the physical and the online stores and these elements that make users feel more familiar and less uncertain within this new experience. In the case of amazon.com context familiarity is obtained by maintaining the same visual representation style throughout the website, so after some minutes of browsing the context does feel familiar. If we talked about the digital version of a physical store, customers would value if the organization of products was the same in both shopping alternatives- and this is a good practice to build seamless multi-platform experiences.
- Value for money reflects the perception that internet purchases are of "better value" in comparison with physical stores. Offers and value deals combined with services that save time and effort make the customers feel that buying from this e-shop is a smart decision (the benefits compensate for the potential risks).
- Finally, trust is a major determinant of OCSE, and it is the only one that it is omnipresent before, throughout and after the purchase, as illustrated in the figure below. The lack of personal contact and the physical distance need to be counterbalanced otherwise customers will evaluate the purchase as high risk and refrain. From one hand, signs and guarantees for the security of transactions have proven to be very effective. On the other hand, the brand is a source of trust itself: amazon.com is making constant and hard efforts to build and maintain a reputation as a reliable retailer and this reputation when backed up by positive customer word of mouth is a valuable source of trust, therefore an element of high quality OCSE (and ultimately sales).

Before leaving the amazon.com to go back to the web design discussion, let's see what dimensions are important in each stage of the customer journey.

So, even if the majority of companies are not in position to fund a project as huge as amazon.com there are some lessons to be learnt, applied and be useful. From this angle, when it comes to user experience, it is recommended to thoroughly investigate the benchmarks of the respective category and then do the same as everybody else: if the majority of the "big" websites in your industry do something in a certain way, then follow along, since users will expect things to work the same on your site.

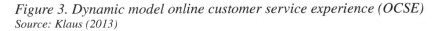

Figure 3. Dynamic model online customer service experience (OCSE)
Source: Klaus (2013)

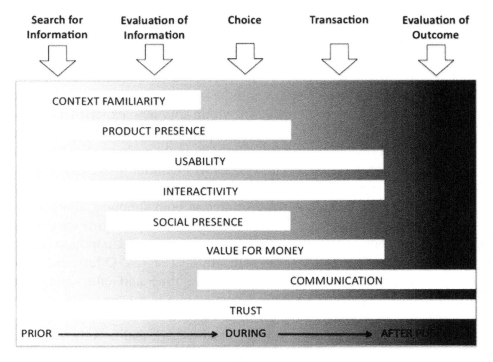

"Isn't this an argument against innovation?" one might wonder. Actually, it is not; it is, however, an indication of the delicate balance between the established and the novelties. As marketers, we need to understand that internet users have already developed habits and expectations that are formed outside our website, while browsing elsewhere- some of which are very significant and not following them can be a deal breaker. Let's take a simplistic example: in every online shop, you will find a prominently placed search box, because users have developed the habit of typing what they are looking for and then check the results. If you decide to skip the search box, for any given reason, you must be aware that it will disrupt the user experience, potentially in a negative manner. Whether you will decide to go on with this decision is a matter of strategic objectives, but as the quote says, you first have to learn the rules before you can break them. The meaning of Jakob's Law is that if you decide to remove the search box only in order to be different, then don't. First and foremost, you have to make sure that the user experience is immaculate, and then you can add and remove features, introduce new ideas and functions, even attempt to subtly break behavioral patterns. It is like deciding to turn the lights off in your retail store, although you know the impact of lighting to the shopping experience. If this action is aligned to a strategic objective and adds value to your brand, they you will most certainly do it. But, if it is just a thing you will do in an effort to stand out, does it really make sense to pay the cost of making shoppers that uncomfortable?

Since the goals and needs of the customers determine our decisions, creating personas (Schaefer & Klammer, 2016; Gartner.com, 2015; Chaffey, 2016) can be very useful, as a method to dive into the mind and psyche of the users, in relation to a specific product, service, and/or brand. In the case of the online presence of an established brand, marketers are already familiar with their key audiences while users have already formed their expectations from their previous encounters with the brand. By putting these expectations on a paper in the form of a persona, it is easier for the marketer to select the website personality dimensions and to provide the technical team with the appropriate guidelines. For example, a buyer persona type for an insurance company might be the 35-year-old male executive, with two kids that like things to be done quickly, without unnecessary hassle or time wasting. This behavior would guide us towards a solid website personality with good content and absence of playful elements. Given that this is also compatible with our brand image we know exactly what to write on our brief to the development team (in case our brand addresses different audiences with distance behavioral characteristics, our online marketing strategy should include mini sites developed to satisfy each group separately).

It is quite common, however, to underestimate the complexity of online user behavior and how even the smallest detail can change our website impact altogether. When the user experience is tainted, users abandon the website, somewhere in a stage of a process or immediately. When users visit one page only, i.e. the landing page and then exit the website, this action is called bounce and it is measured by Google analytics and other relevant tools as it is a very clear indication of whether users' expectations are met or not by the website. According to kissmetrics.com (2010) bounce rate on an average website is about 40%, a ratio that is almost doubled (70%- 90%) when it comes to simple landing pages with a call to action only (for example a sign up page or an add to card button). Reading between the lines, these numbers show that almost half of the users prefer to leave rather than stay on a webpage- a clear demonstration of their intolerance to loud marketing messages and low quality. Since data are overwhelming, thorough research has been conducted in order to demystify what makes visitors bounce.

Table 3.

Factors That Affect the Bounce Rate	Tips to Improve Bounce Rate
Elements of unpleasantness, disrupting the usability of the website (like pop-up ads and streaming videos that might slow the performance down)	Be essential by providing meaningful, useful and high quality content.
Traffic generated by search results that are irrelevant to the actual content of the website	Craft your SEO strategy in a way that you will rank high on branded and related terms.
The design of the landing page- too complicated or too busy	Select a design that will be clear, simple and easy to navigate.

Adapted from https://blog.kissmetrics.com/bounce-rate/

Both the quality of the content and the search engine optimization are factors influencing different stages of online marketing, thus, we will refer to both of them extensively, later in this chapter and throughout this book.

Apart from bouncing, another behavior reflecting unsatisfactory experience for the user is abandoning the website in the middle of some process. According to statista.com (2016), in 2015, 68.53% of digital shopping carts and baskets were abandoned and the purchase was not completed. The 80% of the users fail to complete their transaction for a reason related to the website experience, such as unclear return policy (23%), inability to check out because they don't remember their username/password combination (22%), lack of international payment and shipping options (20%) or any other reason that makes them choose to shop in the store (20%). The remaining 15 percent states that, although willing to proceed with the transaction, they don't do so as they get distracted- which can be interpreted in that the website and the process are not engaging enough.

Although at first, they might look different, a closer look on the findings of a similar survey published on clickz.com (2015), concludes, again, that confusing processes alienate users and combined with the insecurity that they might not get the best deal, they explain the 100% of the online shopping carts abandonment:

- 28% of the users abandon the shopping card due to unexpected shipping costs
- 23% because they couldn't check out without creating an account
- 16% because they were conducting research
- 13% because they are concerned about the safety of the payment
- 12% due to confusing checkout
- 8% because they couldn't find a coupon code.

Note that the industry with the highest abandonment rate is the travel sector with 80.1%, a phenomenon which has been explained as a result of the very complicated check out process where customer details and personal information are mandatory. Also, it is very interesting how "Insert coupon code here" prompts to send dual messages to users: if they don't owe a coupon they are indirectly told that they could get a better deal than the one they have. The action that follows is to leave the website, go to a search engine and look for a coupon code, but it is not a certainty that they will return to the website, as they might not find the coupon or get attracted by another deal, elsewhere.

All the aforementioned findings reinforce the initial premise of this chapter that it is the 'experience over the design', the 'essence over the impressions': in order to be successful on its purpose, as a means to a strategic end, the website has to provide excellent services in an easy-to-navigate manner that makes it useful and functional. Whatever disrupts the experience of the user, even if it initially seems as a good marketing tactics, like intrusive ads and persisting call-to-action; it significantly impacts the user behaviour, usually by sending them away from the website.

SEARCH ENGINE OPTIMIZATION- HOW TO WRITE COPY FOR THE INTERNET

Take a moment to reflect: how many times did you access Google or any other search engine during the past week? The chances are that the answer will vary from several to many. This is why one of the paramount important aspects of modern web design and online marketing today, in general, is search engine optimization (SEO): the extent to which a website and its content are friendly to the search engine crawlers. Of course, in the battle for traffic generation, we always have the option of paid advertising in any of the various existing forms; but, if you want to be a competent marketer and able to survive even in periods of budget drought, bear with us for some minutes to focus on the organic (unpaid) traffic. Before going any further it is useful to shed light on two significant subjects:

- First of all, SEO is more of an architectural blueprint than a set of tactics, because it is related to all aspects of a website, from the managerial decision making to the technology used, the structure, and the content and marketing initiatives. And, given that the majority of traffic is generated via search engines, SEO is, in a sense, a central determinant for the viability of any online project. On the other hand, the very nature of the SEO, which is based on users' behavior and search patterns, bonds it tightly to segmentation and targeting, the selection of the audiences. Thus, for all the above reasons, SEO is a matter of strategy.

- Albeit very important for the past years, there is a notion that the beginning of the end for SEO has already been heralded. Leaving aside how ephemeral everything on the internet is, today there is an immense focus of attention towards really good content: if you work well in producing and disseminating relevant and high quality material, your audience will *eventually* respond. Against this backdrop, investing resources to craft SEO tactics and practices to attract users, while failing to produce good content in the first place can end up to a waste of resources. The repeated message here is: First make sure that you do your job well, and then use the available boosting tools, engendering success.

For us, SEO is still very useful and mandatory to create a conditional online mentality: when you write for the internet, you have to remember how the internet works. Algorithms and rules might (probably will) change constantly, but the need to know your audience will remain quintessential; so, this is a good opportunity to adopt a new "search engine optimized" mindset that will probably make you a better digital marketer.

For starters, it is important to realize that search engine crawlers are basically software programs and, like all software programs, they come with strengths and weaknesses. Publishers must adapt their website to facilitate the job of these software programs, in essence, leverage their strengths and make their weaknesses irrelevant. The scope of search engines like Google, Bing.com, Ask.com etc. is to provide the users with the most accurate and relevant results for their searches, in the fastest possible way. But, given that users don't always form their questions in the most comprehensive and focused manner and they are looking for quick access to information, a search engine actually interprets the words typed by the user, in an effort to relate them to known meanings, provides results that seem satisfactory and then track the behavior of the user in order to evaluate the quality of these results for further reference (Enge et al., 2012).

Figure 4. Google.com search results for Barack Obama

For example, if you type "Barrack Obama", most search engines will relate the term Barrack Obama to the taxonomy "person" and provide mixed results, including a short biography, news and social media accounts and a set of related search terms (see Figure 5 for an example). Similarly, if you search for an "Italian restaurant", the search results will include maps and nearby recommendations, along with reviews and images.

Does it sound too simple? Well, it's not. Let's look at a different example, to further showcase how complicated a search can be, especially as voice commands become more popular. Consider the following search string:

Voice: Empire State Building

Search engine results include the map and address, an excerpt of basic information, always with a "more" button that directs to the source of the information and a list of websites related to the Empire State Building, that are listed based on how optimized they are, as we will explain later.

Voice: Find Me Tickets

Search engine results include ticket information about the Empire State Building although the specific text is not included in the initial search term. If you look at the search box in Google, the engine interprets the "Find me tickets" to "Empire State Building tickets" through a process of semantic connectivity retrieving information based on connections made by the software as a result of previous searches.

Therefore, while scanning trillions of webpages, the search engines need some clear indications that the search term- the keyword- is included in a specific page, to qualify it as a relevant result. This is the marketer's and web developer's task, to make the website easy for the search engine to crawl and explore. In other words, the website visit should be an engaging user experience- otherwise, users will abandon. Although some SEO aspects are technical and better understood by your web developer, here is a list of some elements that can be read by the search engine and others that can't be read:

- The HTML code is where the search engine crawler is primary looking for information to be retrieved. Although the coding part is technical, you can see what we are talking about by right clicking in almost all browsers and select the "view source" from the menu. Inside the code, there are some areas that are critical for the optimization, such as the title, and the meta-description. Below you can see a short part of the Huffington Post (huffingtonpost.com) code with the title and meta-description parts in yellow.

The title is used as the header of the search result while the meta-description is the short description underneath it. Apart from the SEO purposes, the keywords included in both elements signal that it is a news related website; those two elements will help the user decide whether to click on this webpage or look further.

Figure 5. HuffingtonPost.com code excerpt

```
<head>

    <meta http-equiv="Content-Type" content="text/html; charset=utf-8" />
    <meta http-equiv="X-UA-Compatible" content="IE=Edge,chrome=1" />
    <title>Breaking News and Opinion on The Huffington Post</title>
comedy  Huffington Post" />
    <meta name="Description" content="The destination for news, blogs and original content offering coverage of US politics,
    <meta name="Keywords" content="news, breaking news, news blog, business, sports, politics, technology, entertainment, liv
    <meta name="robots" content="noodp,noydir" />
```

Figure 6. The title and meta-description as a part of the search result

In the past, the field "meta-keywords" was also valuable for the optimization but after severe manipulation from spammers, search engine crawlers today ignore it, so it doesn't really have any SEO value.

In the same manner, the crawlers read the plain text content that is included on the website. The process to optimize a text will be explained later; so for now, it is important to understand that if we want our content to be searchable, having it in plain text format is a good practice. On the other hand, text written on images, or hidden behind forms cannot and will not be accessed by the search engine crawlers, so this practice should be avoided. When it comes to images, the software can read an attribute called 'alt', a tag that briefly describes what the image is about. The image alt is a part of the code (as seen below), so it is a technical aspect but to select the text and keywords included there, is the marketer's job.

On the images area in general, search engine crawlers cannot yet read them, apart from the alt field. However, there are some initial steps taken towards this direction, as Google already has the ability to perform searches based on images. The same is the case with flash files, where some information can be excerpted by the software, but since it is difficult and complicated, flash is not considered an optimized selection. Video and audio content are also challenging to read, although some embedded tags in MP3 files can be accessed. Finally, search engines cannot read content inside a program, like in the case of JavaScript and AJAX; readable content in this context is anything written on the code in a manner visible to the human eyes.

Remember that search engines are aiming to provide results that are of high quality and related to the search terms. To measure quality of content, some more aspects are evaluated by the crawlers (e.g. Enge et al, 2012; Moz. com, 2015; Google, 2010)

- **The Length and Reading Level of the Document**: A 100 words text seldom is really useful and informative, so texts smaller than 400-500 words are missing out on the quality factor. On the other hand, by counting the words per sentence and the average word length, crawlers estimate the educational level needed for the content to be understood. For example, if an article that seems childish- in the aforementioned terms- is posted on a financial portal, there is a high probability that the crawler will overlook it.
- **Spelling and Grammar Mistakes**: If a text is poorly written, it cannot be considered as quality content as it will probably dissatisfy the user.
- Finally, the behavior of the users is monitored and reflected on the quality evaluation of the website. For example, if users tend to click on a specific search result and then immediately click the "back" button, it is counted as a poor performance of the result that will consequently impact its ranking position. Remember that earlier we referred to this case as a bounce rate cause. So, in simple words: if you try to bait visitors to your website not only you will probably end up with skyrocketing bounce rates but search engines will also poorly evaluate your quality and, thus, tank you by high rankings.

When ranking the different webpages, the search engine is looking for signals of relevance for the searched term and importance of the displayed website. These are the two terms that best explain the essence of Search Engine Optimization. Relevance refers to how proximate the content of a webpage is to the searcher's intention. To put it in a nutshell: the crawlers are trying to find if the keyword(s) typed into the search box exist on a webpage, literally or as a result of the semantic connectivity, an effort of the latest search engine algorithms to decipher the intention of the writer and to understand the text as meaning not as a set of keywords.

In any case, the role of keywords is central to SEO strategy and it is a creative and analytical process closely related to the marketing objectives. Keywords is the conjunction between what a company / brand pursues and how users/customers have it in their mind. Every keyword list is idiosyncratic, but it is completely useless if it only reflects the inside of the company and not the customer perceptions. Let's take the example of a financial institution launching an innovative service for low cost online transaction, followed by a new terminology for the project and its key functions, like "easylification" and "lowcostability". Although those new word creations are significant for the project itself, the marketing team has to ask themselves: is there anyone in the world that will actually look up for these words, at this stage, when they are not yet presented to and understood by the public? Are there any other words that people could search for and yet be satisfied to find our page (and service) as a result? In this fictional case, words and phrases like "online transactions", "Ripple", "Low-cost transactions", "e-wallet" etc. should definitely be named as keywords, along with the more specific ones, both in organic and paid results as otherwise the crawlers will find no match for the webpage until someone is actually looking for the newly launched terms; or, in the case of a scent marketing company, selling diffusion systems for professional scenting, perhaps the use of the word "aerosol" would be an effective keyword for the markets where aerosol scenting systems are still leading the market. The brand may not sell aerosol systems, but the user looking for it might be satisfied by a substitute solution.

Populating a list of keywords is half creative, intuitive teamwork and half analytical research. The first part includes a brainstorming among different stakeholders, to capture the words that best describe in their minds the promoted industry/ category/ product/ service. From this process, in which potential customer participation is priceless, the marketing team might end up with hundreds of keywords. The next part will be the sorting process, with the use of tools like Google Keyword Planner or other paid services that give us the insights on the potential performance of each keyword, its popularity among the groups we are targeting and the competitiveness of the market for this specific keyword, while suggesting new keyword ideas. The uploading of the keyword list is generated by the brainstorming. Evaluating each word based on the Planner data will allow us to craft a strategy that will be effective and competitive.

The following step relate to matching each page of your website with some specific keywords to facilitate that the search engine crawlers understand exactly which webpage should be included in the results. Using all the keywords everywhere in the website definitely reduces the relevance factor, as although the website as an entity might seem relevant to a term, no specific page is. Make a list of your keywords and match them with your pages, in a way that everything, in both categories is matched. If you find yourself with a keyword with no matching page, then you should create a new one; if you find a page with no keyword, either rewrite the content or add a keyword to your list. If your website has limited pages and you find yourself with too many keywords per page, a good way out is to build a blog, inside the website, and target posts to the remaining keywords. This is a very practical way to build the website architecture and, at the same time, the solid evidence that the keyword strategy related decisions should be made early in the website development process. As soon as you finish this part of the project, you are also done with the sitemap and website architecture. The next step is to incorporate the keywords into the content of the page, starting with the title and description, image alt and the text. While composing your texts, please, keep in mind the golden rule: quality is more important than quantity. That means that search engines will not reward sketchy writing, promotional but useless content or keyword stuffing (overusing keywords). Therefore, a copywriter should write meaningful content, insert the selected keywords where appropriate but also take advantage of the semantic connectivity and make use of the other words that are closely related to the main theme; this will lead the crawlers to the conclusion that the content is relevant. For example, if we are writing an opening paragraph for a biography dedicated to Freddie Mercury and we have decided that our keywords for the page will be "Freddie Mercury biography", here are two potential excerpts:

"A Freddie Mercury Biography"

A Freddie Mercury biography, dedicated to his exciting life and his musical legacy: a life that has been intriguing, full of extravagant moments, those that this Freddie Mercury biography will capture, as a tribute to the great man and artist. This Freddie Mercury biography is a "kind of magic".

"A Freddie Mercury Biography: It's A Kind of Magic"

For those looking for a Freddie Mercury biography that delves deeply into the mind and soul of the talented front man of the famous rock band "The Queen", this book will rock them. Diving in the mind of Freddie Mercury, the father of legendary songs as Bohemian Rapsody, Another One Bites the Dust and We are the Champions, this book will capture the life, the passion and the inspiration behind this great man. This is not just another Freddie Mercury biography. This one, it's a kind of magic.

In general, both texts explain the same thing that this is a biography for a person named Freddie Mercury. The first excerpt is written with a narrow focus on the keywords that are used 4 times in 55 words. For the crawler, this is keyword stuffing and for the reader, this is bad copywriting. The second excerpt uses the keyword 3 times in 95 words but it takes advantage of the semantic connectivity, introducing other terms that are semantically related to the keyword: singer, Queen, song, Bohemian Rapsody, Another One Bites the Dust, We are the Champions, tribute, life, book. By inserting all these words in our copy, we create a grid of meaningful content related to Freddie Mercury, while avoiding to exhaust the reader with repetitions that are too obvious. Note, that in both cases the keyword is included in the title and in the first words of the first paragraph, as both placements are very important for the search engines.

The final step to a good score in relevance is to work over your internal links, in order to make navigation easier both, for the user and the website crawler. Make sure that you put keywords as anchors rather than "Click Here", "Read More" prompts. Proper internal linking will make the experience of the user easier and more comprehensive and will upgrade the overall quality of your content, when used wisely.

Having taken care for all the keyword related aspects of SEO, the next challenge is to show to the search engines that your website/ webpage is important. But how one can measure importance? Let's consider the following aspect first: if we are looking for a cardiologist and we ask our friends for recommendations, what would make us consider one cardiologist being more important than others?

- If more than one of our friends referred to him
- If the friend that referred to him had a personal positive experience with this doctor (we consider this friend as more "relevant" to our situation)
- If a friend that we respect a lot refers to him and previous recommendations of the same friend have always been valuable.
- If they refer to a doctor that is already famous.

Transferring this example to the search engine environment, the crawler is looking for recommendations from other websites in order to decide which website is more important than the others. Thus:

- It is a good sign that the website is important, when a website has a great amount of links from other websites to it.
- It is also conducive for SEO, when a website has been referred to (through a hyperlink) by a leader in the industry/ field.
- Obtaining a link by one of the "big" websites, the ones that are considered to be very trustworthy ones in general, is very significant for the optimization (and ranking) of a page.
- Finally, the analytics of the website itself signal its importance: the traffic, the page views per user and the bounce rate are interpreted as indicators of importance.

It is pretty straightforward that the most significant parameter here is, again, good content (as in the example with the doctor, first he has to be a good one): meaningful, well written, high quality information, distributed in a consistent manner that will attract the attention of users (and therefore boost the website analytics); this will also establish the website as an authoritative source of content worth sharing. As we said earlier, first you have to do your job well.

For well-established brands, getting referrals and higher rankings both in branded and unbranded searches is easier, due to their popularity in the offline world; but they still have to earn the online visitor's loyalty through good content. For smaller brands, encouraging brand representatives to produce and distribute content to portals and other websites, such as guest bloggers or article writers, and always accompanying the post with a link to their website is a good method to gain visibility and links; at the same time, they build a reputation as being knowledgeable and influencers, which in turn, comes with extra benefits for the brand itself. Note, that link building requires planning in terms of identifying potential influencers that could share our content, research common keywords etc. Repeatedly, we cannot overemphasize the determining significance of the quality of the content itself.

Although, so far, it hasn't yet been entirely clear if social media sharing directly influences the importance factor, there is enough evidence that, yes, social media can contribute to our search engine optimization efforts. On a recent article published in Forbes.com (Demers, 2015) the author identifies 6 different ways as to how social media support SEO:

- The number of followers is an indication of importance for the search engines. A company/ brand with 500 followers is considered as "less important" than a mega brand with millions Facebook Likes and Twitter Followers. Again, quality matters: 10.000 organically obtained followers are much more valuable than 100.000 proxy followers, therefore, there is no other way to succeed than being consistent and patient (also buying fake likes will lead you to nowhere).
- Being active in social media provides your content with more visibility and, therefore, with more chances to be linked to. Needless to say, that the more engaging and interesting the content itself is, the more successful of your efforts will be as social media, as a broadcasting channel, can be great multipliers for the appreciation of good content.

- As social media posts find their way in search engine result pages, optimizing social media content- by the use of headers, keywords, and eye catching images/ videos- is a good and helpful strategy. This is not flashing news, however, it is an extension of your existing SEO strategy, so make sure you use the same keywords and targets both, on the website and in the social media.

- Social sharing and engagement are equally important as external links, as they indicate authoritative content. Today, however, the extent to which practices like "Like and Share" contests have a positive impact on the overall online marketing performance is questionable: they used to be considered as best practices and, still, they make sense in terms of extending organic reach and creating awareness but they hurt the image of the brand and attract "free riders" rather than loyal followers. We will elaborate on this later in the book.

- Sophisticated targeting mechanisms provided by most social media platforms allow marketing practitioners to locally optimize their posts and to get better rankings on local searches. Posting updates on local activities that the company/ brand took part or creating campaigns of local interest and developing a network with local social media influencers, being visible among the community will be beneficial not only for the brand image but for SEO as well.

- Being active on social media starts a virtuous circle of benefits for the brand and SEO: the more visible a brand is, the more awareness it gets. Therefore, users will initiate branded searches, and this will lead to a higher ranking for non-branded searches as well. In turn, being among top results on the search engine will enhance awareness, and direct more users to social media brand pages, resulting in higher engagement and so on…

To sum up, SEO is a fundamental element of any modern online marketing strategy, let alone websites, and a conscious and structured approach should be crafted very early in the website development process. There are good practices and marketing tactics, and you can also buy your presence on the result pages through PPC (pay per click) advertising but nothing will substitute the value of good content. From this angle, the internet can be a very fair, democratic and equal opportunities enhancing context where every brand- small or big- can gain their place under the sun by committing to high quality content.

METRICS IN A NUTSHELL

As you will read this book you will notice that it's our premise how each organization has its own objectives therefore different ratios and metrics to quantify success. However, since it is a common belief that digital marketing's comparative advantage is this very ability to monitor and measure everything and given that most of us have seen or experience the "paralysis by analysis", we are summarizing here some key metrics that you might find useful in your digital marketing practice.

The figure below, taken from PWC's report on measuring effectiveness illustrates the main areas of performance that can be related with marketing objectives:

As you can see and understand, this is a pool of indicators that if not combined with strategic objectives, they remain deprived of meaning. The first area, display is used to count the number of impressions a banner had but can also be expanded to reach, in the social media context. When we are aiming for engagement or exposure, having our message placed in front

Figure 7. Nine categories of indicator to measure online performance
Source: PWC (2011)

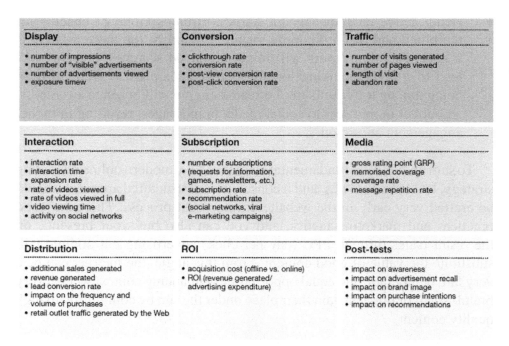

of the customer is the first step of everything. Even if you are not running paid campaigns, still, always keep reach under your radar because it might not be the more useful measure (you will see why in a moment) but it is the denominator of many. The second area is conversion. We will talk about conversions a lot in this book, because one can say that this is the bottom line of a marketing campaign. Conversion is related to the expected reaction to our message- e.g. to click a banner or an AdWords text, to follow our Call-To-Action button etc. Comparing your CTR (click through rate) with industry benchmarks, or even better, with other versions of your campaigns is a good practice to evaluate the effectiveness of your messages. Needless to say, that low conversion means further investigation and immediate intervention. Traffic is related to your website and it is a number you should know at any time, by heart. How many people visit your website monthly, how many page views do you have in total. Also, what is your bounce rate, how long do they stay in the website and all these behavioral and demographic data that are effortlessly provided by analytical tools and are the bread and butter of the digital marketer. Interaction is an equivalent to social media engagement and it measures the extent to which our audience gave us some kind of signal that they liked our content. It could be the likes, comments, shares, retweets or the times our videos were viewed, it could be anything that makes sense in the context of our marketing strategy, but, engagement is possible the most important measure of all. In the following chapters we will elaborate in the power of like or share and why having a limited but engaged audience is much more valuable than having a large but indifferent one. The following areas of the PWC propositions are more specific to objectives that are related to newsletter signups, online or offline sales or specific areas like impact on brand image. The variety of these measures is a great indicator that we can measure whatever makes sense to us, as long as it is bound to a strategic objective. What is useful to remember is exporting reports and statistics is not what measuring digital marketing is about; making meaning out of them is. These metrics are the keyhole to the minds of our customers, the greatest way to trace and decode their behavior. When reasoning, experience and knowledge are combined with these metrics, then you have the perfect recipe for effective decision making.

Answers

- Designing a website is a matter of cross functional collaboration between strategic, marketing and technical thinkers. The final outcome is the translation of decisions (like the role of the website in the overall marketing strategy and the very objective of the website itself) into technical and design features that will engage the targeted audiences. No part can be successful on its own as internet marketing is a team project, by default.

- Interactivity, navigation, functionality/ usability, marketing, service, innovativeness, online processing: Each of the seven dimensions will be exploited accordingly to contribute to a result that is compatible with the strategic purpose of the website.

- Internet marketing rules are not written in stone and they change rapidly. What is today's innovation, will be tomorrow's prerequisite. Therefore, the marketer should be alert at any time for advances and closely monitor her/his audiences' goals, values and needs in order to accordingly adapt their strategy.

- The human characteristics attached to our website, namely, its personality, determine its main features and elements. There is one standard demand regardless the chosen personality, and this is service excellence. Apart from this, colors and designs, simplicity versus playfulness, rich content, and supporting features etc. are elements that should be examined separately, in relation to the selected personality.

- Search engines evaluate potential results versus their relevance to the searched terms and importance as sources of information on the field. Crafting a keyword strategy that captures the cognitive and emotional schemata of your audience and supports it with good content, would be a "best practice" to build on the relevance aspect. On the importance angle, websites with high traffic and indications that are authoritative sources of information are considered as more important by the search engines.

- The golden rule of SEO, given the latest advancements on the internet, is "Do your job well and the rest will follow". This means that if you spend too much time finding ways to manipulate the search engine crawlers at the expense of the quality of your content, you will probably end up empty handed. First and foremost, make sure that your content is worth it and then consider anything else.

REFERENCES

Aaker, J. L. (1997). Dimensions of brand personality. *JMR, Journal of Marketing Research*, *34*(3), 347–356. doi:10.2307/3151897

Amazon.com Investor Relations. (2011). *Annual reports and proxies*. Retrieved from http://phx.corporate-ir.net/phoenix.zhtml?c=97664&p=irol-reportsannual

Amazon.com Investor Relations. (2013). *Company facts*. Retrieved from http://phx.corporate-ir.net/phoenix.zhtml?c=176060&p=irol-factSheet

Amazon.com Investor Relations. (2015). *Annual report*. Retrieved from http://phx.corporate-ir.net/phoenix.zhtml?c=97664&p=irol-reportsannual

Chaffey, D. (2016). *An introduction to best practices for using buyer personas to create more customer-centric websites*. Retrieved from http://www.smartinsights.com/marketplace-analysis/customer-analysis/web-design-personas/

Clickz.com. (2015). *Why do customers abandon online shopping carts?* Retrieved from https://www.clickz.com/clickz/column/2435488/why-do-customers-abandon-online-shopping-carts

Cooper, J., & Burgess, L. (2000). A model of internet commerce adoption (MICA). In Electronic commerce: Opportunity and challenges (pp. 189-201). Hershey, PA: IGI Global.

dAstous, A., & Levesque, M. (2003). A scale for measuring store personality. *Psychology and Marketing*, *20*(5), 455–469. doi:10.1002/mar.10081

Doolin, B., Burgess, L., & Cooper, J. (2002). Evaluating the use of the Web for tourism marketing: Case study from New Zealand. *Tourism Management*, *23*(5), 557–561. doi:10.1016/S0261-5177(02)00014-6

Enge, E., Spencer, S., Fishkin, R., & Stricchiola, J. C. (2012). *The art of SEO*. Sebastopol, CA: O'Reilly Media.

Forbes.com. (2015). *6 Social Media Practices that boost SEO*. Retrieved from http://www.forbes.com/sites/jaysondemers/2015/01/27/6-social-media-practices-that-boost-seo/#272d21012720

Gartner.com. (2015). *What's in a Name? Creating Personas for Digital Marketing*. Retrieved from http://www.gartner.com/smarterwithgartner/whats-in-a-name-creating-personas-for-digital-marketing/

Google.com. (2010). *Search Engine Optimization Starter Guide*. Retrieved from https://static.googleusercontent.com/media/www.google.com/el//webmasters/docs/search-engine-optimization-starter-guide.pdf

Kaufmann, H. R., & Shams, R. (2016). *Entrepreneurial challenges in the 21ˢᵗ century. Creating Stakeholder Value Co-Creation*. Hampshire, UK: Palgrave Macmillan.

Kissmetrics.com. (2010). *Bounce rate demystified*. Retrieved from https://blog.kissmetrics.com/bounce-rate/

Klaus, P. (2013). The case of Amazon.com: Towards a conceptual framework of online customer service experience (OCSE) using the emerging consensus technique (ECT). *Journal of Services Marketing*, *27*(6), 443–457. doi:10.1108/JSM-02-2012-0030

Livestats.com. (2016). *Internet users*. Retrieved from http://www.internetlivestats.com/internet-users/

Moz.com. (2015). *The Beginners Guide to SEO*. Retrieved from http://d2eeipcrcdle6.cloudfront.net/guides/Moz-The-Beginners-Guide-To-SEO.pdf

Poddar, A., Donthu, N., & Wei, Y. (2009). Web site customer orientations, Web site quality, and purchase intentions: The role of Web site personality. *Journal of Business Research*, *62*(4), 441–450. doi:10.1016/j.jbusres.2008.01.036

PWC. (2011). *Measuring the effectiveness of online advertising*. Retrieved from http://download.pwc.com/ie/pubs/2011_measuring_the_effectiveness_of_online_advertising.pdf

Schäfer, A., & Klammer, J. (2016). Service Dominant Logic in Practice: Applying Online Customer Communities and Personas for the Creation of Service Innovations. In *Managing Innovation and Diversity in Knowledge Society Through Turbulent Time: Proceedings of the MakeLearn and TIIM Joint International Conference 2016*. ToKnowPress.

Shobeiri, S., Laroche, M., & Mazaheri, E. (2013). Shaping e-retailers website personality: The importance of experiential marketing. *Journal of Retailing and Consumer Services*, *20*(1), 102–110. doi:10.1016/j.jretconser.2012.10.011

Smith, P. R., & Chaffey, D. (2005). *E-Marketing excellence, the Heart of Business* (2nd ed.). Elsevier.

Statista.com. (2016). *Online Shopping cart abandonment rate worldwide from 2006 to 2016.* Retrieved from http://www.statista.com/statistics/477804/online-shopping-cart-abandonment-rate-worldwide/

Tarafdar, M., & Zhang, J. (2008). Determinants of Reach and Loyalty — A Study of Website Performance and Implications for Website Design. *Journal of Computer Information Systems*, *48*(2), 16–24.

Ting, P., Wang, S., Bau, D., & Chiang, M. (2013). Website evaluation of the top 100 hotels using advanced content analysis and eMICA model. *Cornell Hospitality Quarterly*, *54*(3), 284–293. doi:10.1177/1938965512471892

Chapter 3
Consumers and Communities

ABSTRACT

The Internet has transferred the power from the brand to the customer, evolving the latter to a "prosumer" (pro-active consumer) that demands more access to the brand decision making process. This change calls for new politics inside the marketing department and introduces a new challenge for the strategic marketer: to invite and involve consumers in brand communities populated of like-minded members, in order to fulfill their fundamental psychological goal for belongingness. In this chapter we discuss the characteristics and the specifics of community building, as it emerges as a great means to the end of loyalty building. Additionally, we attempt to decode the consumer behaviour online, in order to develop useful tools for segmentation and targeting, adapted to the new elements of what consumer perceives as value.

Questions

- How does the internet facilitate the "revenge of the customer"?
- Why are brand communities more useful for marketers than sales promotions?
- Has the way we shop changed due to the internet?
- What are the main factors of online consumer behaviour?
- Why are personas, the secret ingredient of good marketing strategies?

DOI: 10.4018/978-1-68318-012-8.ch003

INTRODUCTION

Did you ever wonder why the internet is so important after all? A quick answer is: "because it has changed the way we behave, as individuals and as consumers". In the online world, traditional concepts like groups, communities and socializing have found new meanings, re-defining antecedents and consequences of our marketing efforts. Therefore, in an attempt to decode those new behavioral patterns, we will discuss how lifestyle and buying behaviors have been re-shaped by the new digital world in this chapter. We aim to provide the reader with a 'helicopter view' on Consumer Behavior with a focus on probably the most prominent concepts affecting digital branding today: communities and co-creation.

First of all, in marketing everything roots in the hierarchy of values, what we really want and need, what is important to us, what motivates us to behave in a particular manner? In their recent Harvard Business Review article, Almquist, Senior and Bloch (2016) proposed an evolution of the Maslow pyramid, the "universal building blocks" of value that may explain the complicated psychological mechanism that leads to product selection.

According to the authors of this article, that have conducted extended research in order to understand what really drives consumers, the higher the level on the pyramid, the more powerful the values are- although quality is the one product/service value that cannot be traded off, despite its place on the lowest, functional level. Also, it occurs from the illustration, that belonging is amongst the very powerful values, in the "life-changing" segment. This means that, when presented with multiple options, we might prefer one brand from another, and ultimately become loyal to it, because on the top of its functional benefits, it promotes us to members of a community. From this perspective, and in an effort to find the practical implications of this conclusion, for the marketers that struggle to differentiate and to provide additional value to their offerings in order to engage their targeted customers, adding the strong benefit of belonging to a like-minded community, could be a fruitful addition. Having said that, we can now see how online communities function and what makes the valuable- or not.

Figure 1. The elements of value
(Almquist et al., 2016), Source:hbr.org

The Elements of Value Pyramid

Products and services deliver fundamental elements of value that address four kinds of needs: functional, emotional, life changing, and social impact. In general, the more elements provided, the greater customers' loyalty and the higher the company's sustained revenue growth.

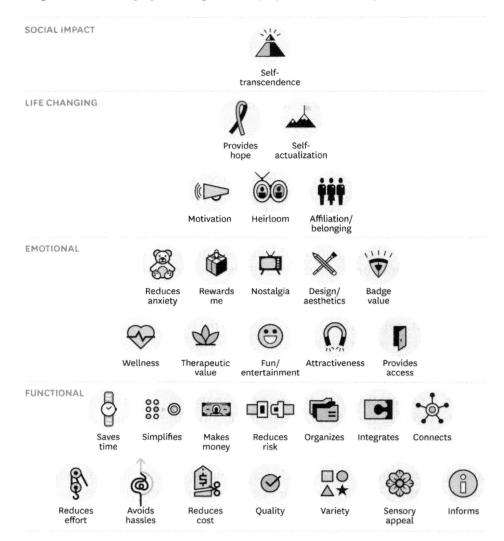

Figure 2.

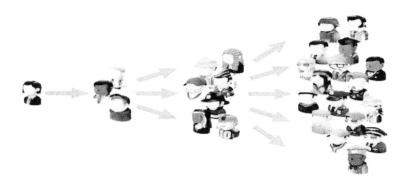

THE ONLINE COMMUNITIES

Undoubtedly, the new technologies have changed to a great extent the way we live, communicate and work. New behaviors have been developed due / thanks to the new media, and our fundamental human needs have found new outlets. According to an interesting survey on consumer behaviour, defined as how and why people react/behave in certain manners in certain environments, due to the social media and the new values that have emerged, consumers' preference has shifted from the logo-heavy, luxury products to more meaningful yet subtle ones, as they refrain from showing off their wealth (The Washington Post, 2015). In other words, old rules are re-written as the digital consumer demolishes established patterns and perceives value and price in different ways; it is quite accurate to claim that the digital revolution has created a new type of consumer behaviour that is, however, demonstrated, both in the online and offline contexts. To put some factual numbers behind this claim, let's see how much time US citizens spend using major media types.

As you can see, we spend half of our day consuming content, equally shared between traditional and online media, with a significant rise of the mobile use. From comparing the fluctuations of time spent per medium throughout the years, it is clear that digital content has replaced print but it hasn't influenced much the television and radio consumption, as they face only slight decreases. From a behavioral perspective, the findings, in general, confirm that consumers in the digital age are multi-taskers (Deitchman, 2010), as they obviously combine two or more media uses at the same time, and consequently split their attention, otherwise they would be left with no time to work and live. It is intelligible that our lives as consumers have

Figure 3. Average time spent per day with media
Source: eMarketer (2015)

Average Time Spent per Day with Major Media by US Adults, 2011-2015
hrs:mins and CAGR

	2011	2012	2013	2014	2015	CAGR (2011-2015)
Digital	3:40	4:20	4:51	5:15	5:38	11.4%
—Desktop/laptop*	2:33	2:27	2:19	2:22	2:22	-1.8%
—Mobile (nonvoice)	0:48	1:35	2:16	2:34	2:51	37.2%
—Other connected devices	0:18	0:18	0:17	0:19	0:25	7.8%
TV**	4:34	4:38	4:31	4:22	4:15	-1.8%
Radio**	1:34	1:32	1:30	1:28	1:27	-2.0%
Print**	0:44	0:38	0:32	0:26	0:21	-17.0%
—Magazines	0:18	0:16	0:14	0:12	0:10	-13.5%
—Newspapers	0:26	0:22	0:18	0:14	0:11	-19.8%
Other**	0:39	0:38	0:31	0:26	0:24	-11.7%
Total	11:11	11:46	11:55	11:57	12:04	1.9%

Note: ages 18+; time spent with each medium includes all time spent with that medium, regardless of multitasking; for example, 1 hour of multitasking on desktop/laptop while watching TV is counted as 1 hour for TV and 1 hour for desktop/laptop; *includes all internet activities on desktop and laptop computers; **excludes digital
Source: eMarketer, April 2015

188127   www.eMarketer.com

embraced new habits, like researching online to compare value and prices, look up everything and becoming more curious, demand and gain access behind the closed doors of the corporations and press for transparency, and shop instantly from our mobile or computer. In other words, we are living in a new era where consumers have multiple means to use so that they ultimately have more power and control than ever before. It is, one could say, the revenge of the customer, as, thanks to the digital environment, that allows and encourages user generated content, consumers don't have to be passive recipients anymore; vice versa they contribute and they co-create (or co-destroy), they are transforming to "prosumers" (proactive consumers) or even "persumers", as apart from consuming they are also looking for personal benefits, like self-actualization and self-fulfillment (Marino, 2015). Since digital marketing is no exception to the strategic thinking path we follow, let's start with the fundamental question: "What do these prosumers expect, need and want"?

As we will discuss later in chapter 5, the digital context and the social media have become the answer to our need for enhanced togetherness, acceptance, and belonging. In fact, the idea of the user generated content and prosumers implies the existence of a community: the content is created to be shared; reviews are written to be read; it is a joined action of sharing and exchanging among the members and the brand. Sharing, in particular, is an inherited trait of the social media and a popular subject of research and extensive analysis. Consider the search findings that highlight the difference between the psychologies of 'liking' a piece of content and 'sharing' it (Schaefer, 2015): while liking is a typical, low-involvement sign of approval, sharing means to endorse and adopt, as a part of our own mentality and identity: What we choose to share and, even, what we choose not to, signifies who we are or, at least, we want to be, our perception of our ideal selves.

Regarding sharing as a psychological phenomenon makes it easier to understand why users do not engage in brand-promoting and sales related content and why financial rewards are not nearly enough to support an evergreen brand community (Ind et al., 2013). Prosumers are seeking for communities of like-minded members, to fulfill their goal for belongingness. Being a part of a distinctive group that we trust and feel committed to (Casalo et al., 2008) bears emotional benefits while enhancing our social identity with the traits related to the group. In an online community, members have a great tendency to transcend their personal identity (i.e. identity related to a person's individual sense of self) and to develop a social identity that is an individual's self-concept that derives from the knowledge of being part of a social group (Facebook brand fans). Research findings show that social identity also includes the emotional significance involved in such a membership –i.e. attachment to the group and feelings of belongingness (Vernuccio et al., 2015) and, ultimately, enables stronger emotional ties with the brand itself. So, if we are aiming for long term loyalty as a result of the emotional connection with the brand, tactics like giveaways and promotions likely fall short: prosumers are looking for those intrinsic rewards that will keep them involved in the co-creation process for a long time (Cherif et al., 2016; Ind et al., 2013).

A review of recent literature in the field of online communities primarily reveals that they behave in the same manner as offline communities (Dessart et al., 2015; Semenik et al., 2012). A brand community is essentially constructed on a set of relationships that community members develop with the brand, the product, the company (marketers and representatives) and other customers. This perspective, opposed to initial models of brand communities which assumed

Figure 4. Lego users are among the most active communities with the Eurobricks and Lugnet networks
Source: www.eurobricks.com

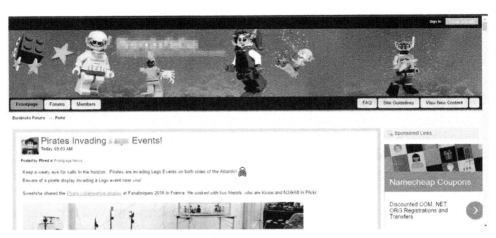

only relationships between consumers, highlights the role of the brand staff in the community, and provides the marketers with ample opportunities to differentiate and create value for their brands. Members of the community can play the role of the support service department of their companies, essentially by helping each other and fixing each other's problems with the brand. They can also be the brand's advocates in defending the borders of the brand as well as evangelists trying to make a desirable impression on outsiders. Members of a brand community can be an excellent source for innovation and product improvement because they are highly attached to the community and the future prospects of the brand matters to them (Habibi et al., 2014).

Thanks to the intrinsic, participatory benefits of belonging to a community, engagement is equally induced by utilitarian or hedonic brands (Vivek et al., 2014). In fact, being a part of the community is hedonic per se and it directly impacts the loyalty to the brand (e.g. Cova et al.,2007; Casalo et al., 2008; Dessart et al., 2015; Kaufmann et al., 2012) representing the holy grail of every marketing effort. Therefore, since online brand communities are related to brand loyalty, strong emotional brand relationships and positive word of mouth, they become a desirable asset for the brand and an outstanding target to pursue. This is the reason why new marketing roles, like the community manager, have lately emerged as an answer to this new challenge imposed to marketers by the new digital world.

A relatively new trend in Marketing is to 'build a bridge' connecting the individual and social identity of the customer and other stakeholders with the identity of the brand, a process termed 'identity congruence' or 'consonance'. Kaufmann et al. (2012) researched the increasing dynamics between consumers, the social groups they belong to, and brands emphasizing the condition of 'resonance': "In a brand community a consciousness of kind, shared rituals and traditions and moral responsibility exist among their members. Rituals and traditions function to maintain the culture of the community. The condition of resonance depends on continuity and proactive attitudes due to the frequency of the relationships and the quality of exchange of emotive as well as cognitive information. Furthermore, when reaching this condition a progressive development is put into action, which allows the gradual blurring of boundaries between firm and consumer, as shown in Figure 4. Consequently, achieving this state of resonance is the expression of reaching ever greater levels of sharing and trusting on trends and perspectives (Kaufmann et al., 2012, p. 407/408).

Figure 5. Conditions of resonance
(Kaufmann et al., 2012, p. 408)

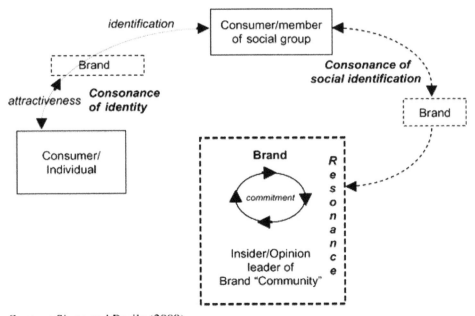

Source: Siano and Basile (2009)

Simply put, when consumers actively and systematically participate in a brand community, e.g. regularly visiting the community's forum and posting questions and answers, they progressively embrace the brand values and the values of the group as their own. As they continue to participate, they feel a stronger bond with the community and the brand, a feeling of 'commitment' that will not allow them to refrain from visiting the forum for a long time, neither to select a competitive brand.

Lately, there have been voices in the academia (e.g. Christodoulides, 2008; Merz & Vargo, 2009; Hatch & Schultz, 2010) and inside the marketing departments claiming that including consumers, and stakeholders at large, in the brand value creating process is the branding perception of the future, as it provides the context for strong and meaningful brand-consumer relationships. As we have suggested recently, we are moving beyond the Service-Dominant Logic (Vargo & Lusch, 2008) where focus was in the excellent service provision, towards the Co-creation Dominant Logic (Kaufmann & Manarioti, 2016), where all marketing efforts are oriented to inviting customers in. Simply put, this means that companies and brands create and introduce new channels and practices- and therefore adopt the much needed mindset shift- in order to initiate a two-way communication and allow the customers to access, in some extent, the decision making processes. Forums, chats, discussions, newsletters etc are only some of the channels provided by the digital advancements that enabled co-creation. However, the underlying idea here is that companies need to abandon some of their existing processes and perceptions, in order to create the conditions for co-creation to occur. As Prahalad and Ramaswamy (2004) suggested, there are four building blocks of co-creation:

Figure 6. Building blocks of co-creation
Based on Prahalad and Ramaswamy (2004)

Dialogue refers to the open communication with customers and stakeholders, in order to obtain useful insights, ask their feedback, share considerations etc. Of course, dialogue implies equality that both parts of this conversation are equal and equally willing to talk, to listen, to trust and to share. On the same token, it dictates a selection of subjects that are interesting for both parts- a great challenge for traditional marketers that are used to only talk about their brands and a useful tip for content creation (Chapter 6).

Access means allowing consumers to look inside the company, learn and understand some decision making mechanisms, and being able to participate in the value creation process. Access is in the heart of co-creation but it is a common pitfall, as well, as companies are reluctant to put their secrets out in the open. Obviously, this is kind of contradictory, as, if you want your prosumers feedback about a product that your brand is currently designing, you have no other option than disclosing some information about it.

Risk was initially about the responsibility of the company towards engaged consumers and a stance of reliability and trustworthiness. When consumers are asked to participate in the product development process or provide ideas about a new marketing campaign, the company must address intellectual property rights in a decent and trustworthy manner- otherwise it can all turn into a reputation disaster. Later, when the initial model was infused with branding concepts (Hatch and Schultz, 2010) risk also took the meaning of losing credibility as a result of extended exposure, or losing control of the community and suffer from negative word of mouth, or even lose distinctiveness as competitors gain access as well.

Finally, Transparency is a very proximate to access and it refers to the company's determination to disclosure and adopt an open-door policy. Social media can really enhance the transparency perception, but the important factor here is the managerial commitment to this.

Bring all together, to a comprehensive and more practical model, Hatch and Schultz (2010) studied the LEGO community (Lugnet) and conclude in a matrix bringing together Dialogue and Access, under the term Company/ Stakeholder Engagement and Transparency and Risk as Organisational self-disclosure. The matrix, illustrated below, will also help you evaluate your company's performance and the level of readiness, in terms of co-creation.

In the low-low frame, the company adopts a traditional perspective that is not quite open to suggestion or invites consumers and other stakeholders to co-create. This is a common status for many corporations that either have not yet been persuaded about the value of co-creation, or they are too secretive to disclose. On the other hand, the company that, for some reason, is high

Figure 7. A framework for brand co-creation
Source: Hatch and Schultz (2010)

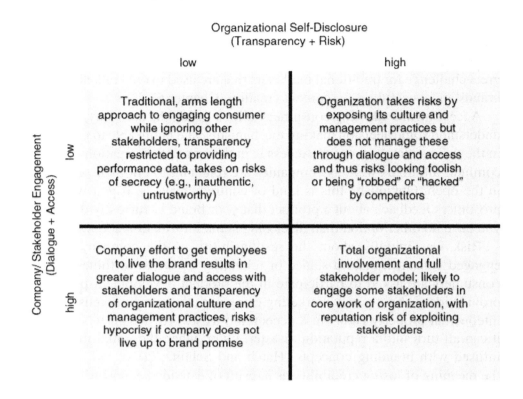

on self-disclosure but low on engagement is on the verge of being exploited. Too much information is shared but either because co-creation efforts have failed or because no efforts were made at all, stakeholders and consumers remain alienated. Hatch and Schultz insist a lot in the role of the personnel in co-creation, therefore in the high engagement/ low self- disclosure frame they focus on the success to make the employees live the brand and therefore succeed in initiating a dialogue with consumers and other stakeholders. As employees are the access points to the company, having them involved in the community gives the perception of greater access. However, scoring low in transparency and risk creates a gap between the two the community and the "inside" of the company and it might result to a verdict of hypocrisy- as the company asks but doesn't share. Finally, the high/ high frame includes those companies that have manage to build a strong, two-way communication with their stakeholders, and they practically are parts of the company. The only risk here is to maintain a balance, in order to avoid accusations about exploiting stakeholders. Maintaining a culture of reciprocity is a good practice and it is among the behaviours that make consumers feel rewarded for their decision to co-create- therefore, engage even more.

In one of our recent publications, in the Journal of Product and Brand Management, we have proposed a framework that explores how the emotional connection with a brand impacts the consumers' commitment to community and in turn, how it triggers co-creation and ultimately, loyalty. What we have posited is that consumers tend to emotionally connect with brands in a passionate way, that resembles love and it is termed as "brand love" when brands are self-expressive and when there is a prior attachment with the brand (Carroll and Ahuvia, 2006). In that state, they become more committed to communities and they trust the brand more. As they get more involved in the community and since they care for the brand, they start to participate in the value co-creation process, they become active members of the brand community. All this engagement, makes the brand their "safe place" and, therefore, leads them to higher levels of loyalty. Of course, this psychological mechanism is put in action when consumers are involved with the product/ service category- otherwise they don't bother to co-create or approach the community. In fact, there is evidence that some product/service categories are more "loveable" than others, as they are perceived as more hedonic (Carroll and Ahuvia, 2006), or as discussed earlier, their value comes from the higher levels of the pyramid, not just from functional elements. But, this separation is not valid when we discuss about communities and co-creation: all brands, regardless their categorization, can bring their audiences together, in a participative context of discussing, sharing and acting as a community. Note that, and here comes the idea of integration again that we already discussed in Chapter 1, the role of the customer-contact personnel is paramount. As brand representatives personify the brand, their behaviour determines the brand experience, thus the level of customer satisfaction and emotional attachment. When our staff bears the same values with the brand, they are actually active members of our community, they co-create and they set the pace for other members to do so. In other words, structure they will use to the company's relationship to brand communities should not reside only within the marketing function because it is a strategic involvement that potentially involves every employee in the company (Fournier & Lee, 2009).

Marketers, when designing brand experiences and make plans for online communities, they have to take into consideration how internal customers are going to be approached, with appropriate leadership tactics, in order to be the initiators of this community.

Figure 8.
Kaufmann et al. (2016)

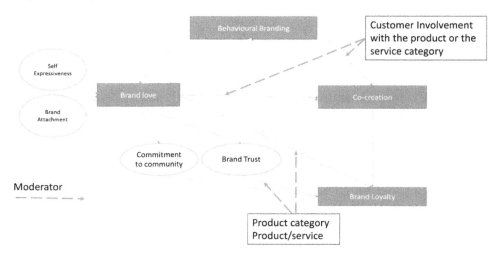

Confirming the importance of communities in modern marketing, PwC's Total Retail Report (2016) suggests that community building can be a great marketing tool when it goes beyond the simplistic extrinsic rewards loyalty program mindset, which can be very effective in the short term but wastes the opportunity of a deeper, meaningful, strong relationship. Whilst loyalty schemes and bonus point systems are very established practices to make a customer loyal, the question arises if they are able to transform them to active members of a community and to provide them with intrinsic participatory benefits? The obvious answer is that they are not, and here waits a great opportunity as well as challenge for the new generations of marketers to take traditional practices a step further.

Of course, communities also have their dark side, as they cannot be controlled by the brand when for any reason disappointed community members would react negatively. So, inviting customers to post reviews of their experience might be a good way to create a sense of sharing, but only if you are confident, that your brand will benefit from the reviews. As we said in chapter 2, again, first and foremost, you have to do your job well.

Let's take the example of a successful community, that of Sears (https://community.sears.com/).

The store has encouraged the customers to share their ideas or complaints but also their expertise on a webpage dedicated to the users. Here, the brand posts tips, asks for feedback and also invites users to vote among user proposed

Figure 9. Sears online community

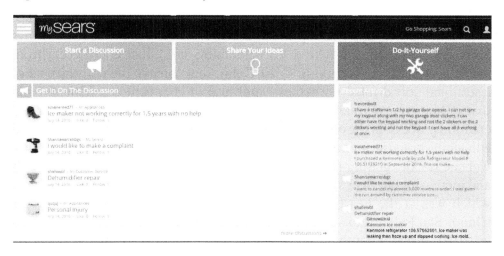

ideas for the one that Sears will proceed with. This community might be initiated by the brand itself but a visit will show you that the users are in control, as they are allowed to post their complaints, discuss malfunctions and problems. Through this process, however, they are becoming members of something bigger, of a community of consumers with the same interests and concerns. When they will need information or guidance, here is where they will turn to, because trust exists. Needless to say that just being around a brand for a long time, let alone discussing and having transactions with it in a humane and personified way, triggers emotions for it that are the foundation of long term loyalty (more about online brand communities and the role of social media in their formation in Chapter 5).

Building and maintaining an online community is a demanding task with strategic implications and it mandates the alignment of brand and consumers values and their translation to meaningful benefits. There is a useful example of an online community fail, as described by Rosella Gambetti and Guendalina Graffigna in their publication, in 2015. The case they have studied is Chino Sanpellegrino, an Italian cola brand owned by Nestle. In their words:

"Chino Sanpellegrino brand decision-makers focused on the online brand community as both the key asset of its entire marketing strategy and the true expression of its brand positioning aimed at creating an enduring and empathetic consumer–brand relationship and, ultimately, encouraging value co-creation between brand and consumers. In particular, Chino` Sanpellegrino brand decision-makers in their marketing communication plan intended to use the online community as a virtual interface to engage both consumer and brand in a co-creation process. They nurtured co-creation of ideas, values and contents with the 'free spirit' philosophy of the brand that has always epitomized 'the other way to drink something dark', that is 'different from the mainstream' (i.e. drinking Coca-Cola), that 'breaks the conventions of traditional soft drinks' (sweetness, high use of chemical components) and that is 'not to everyone's taste' ('you either love it or you hate it'). A co-creation process, in the online community marketing objectives, was aimed at enhancing brand awareness and product revenues by increasing the community website traffic, getting more active members, generating social networking and increasing product sales by boosting the participation in the online game which was at the heart of the community offering. Created in 2005, the Chino` San Pellegrino's online community had achieved 110,000 members by 2010. It had a complex, varied structure that offered social networking (forums, chat) and personal pages, allowing participants to assemble their own content (i.e. blogs accompanied by images, multimedia materials and personal commentary). Finally, it had a section with banners and pop-ups offering consumers constant updates on the brand, social events, gossip etc.

The online brand community, however, suffered a severe downturn between 2008 and 2010, losing website visits, active members and consumer participation in the online game that was accessible only after buying a Chino` Sanpellegrino item. That also meant a slight decrease in product sales, as brand managers acknowledged. Moreover, these negative events were accompanied by the almost total absence of consumer social exchanges in the dedicated areas of the website. All these aspects drove brand decision-makers to explicitly consider their online community a failure, in that it failed to achieve its marketing objectives. This downturn led brand decision makers to first strategically rethink he community concept in 2011 and [...] to finally close down the website in 2013" (p.160).

In their analysis the researchers revealed that the failure of the community was a result of poor management by the decision makers, as they failed to stipulate a coherent set of marketing objectives and vision for the community. Their inner tensions were translated to an ambiguous community identity, with complicated orientation that ultimately focused on an opportunistic relationship with the consumers (they came only to play and win but completely ignore the forums, chats and other co-creation prompts). Consumer, on the other hand, had perceived the community as something completely separated from the brand, as the brand managers didn't actually manage to clearly communicate the brand values and key messages inside the community. As a result, the project failed altogether, not because consumers didn't care about the brand or due to any technical problem, but merely because of inadequate planning and managerial backup.

This final example is just a reminder that some online marketing decisions are not tactical, but strategic and that- vice versa- the answer to some strategic questions can be found inside the online marketing function. This is one more reason why highlight the multifaceted role of the digital marketers and how determining it is for them to maintain a strong strategic and integrating viewpoint.

ONLINE SHOPPING BEHAVIOUR

People increasingly buy online and we are just stating the facts. There is nothing to argue here, and the only decisions on stake for the marketer are how to enter the game and thrive: either as an exclusive online retailer or as a brick-and-mortar one that needs to move forward. According to statista. com, in 2019, 32.8% of the total world population will have adopted online shopping, a percentage which translates into 57.6% of the total internet users' headcount.

Figure 10. Online shopping penetration
Source: statista.com

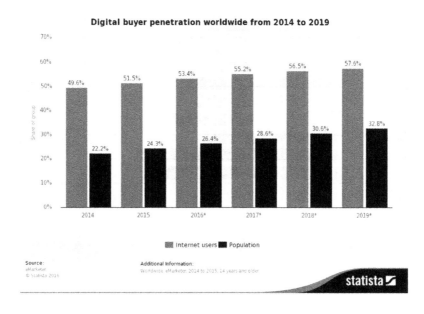

An even more groundbreaking trend, however, is how users have already moved to the second era of online shopping, buying more and more from their mobiles and, mostly, using them to research products, even while being in the store (Forbes, 2014). The role of mobiles is also illustrated in PwC's retail survey (2016) being reported in some countries as expected to be the main purchasing tool, while even in those, where it will not be the main purchasing tool, the penetration is still significant.

Figure 11. Mobile phone in online shopping
Source:www.statista.com

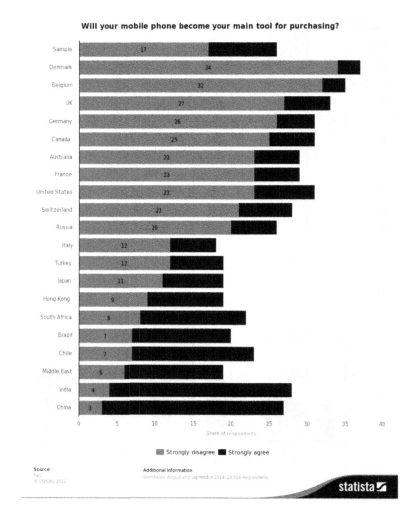

Summarizing, in depth research and price/ value comparisons make the online consumer or, better, the prosumer a serial searcher, a navigator that uses computers and mobiles to look for information, with Google holding 89.44% of the market share in April 2016 (Statcounter, 2016). The ease of access to vast information and the pursuit of the greatest deal have created this new type of behavior characterized by higher price sensitivity. Prosumers have the feeling that somewhere on the internet there is always a better deal and this can be found in no time! But even a correct price might not be a sufficient condition, if the brand's reputation is tainted. In the past, company decisions were made and protected behind closed doors and the public knew mostly what the board decided to share. This is not the case anymore today: every employee can tweet about their managers' bad behaviour or a doubtful corporate policy; they might even upload a video of their own bad behaviour that will become viral and will provoke a PR catastrophe (like the Domino's Pizza case). Or, a scandal can burst in a second when leaked to the internet and jeopardize decades of marketing efforts, as shown by the example of the Volkswagen emissions scandal. All this and so much more information is out there, to be found by the customers during their research to shop, waiting to impact their purchase decisions.

Precisely due to the complexity of online shopping, we have dedicated a whole chapter to it, later in the book. However, since this subject it is very closely related to the consumer behavior discussion; let's see here, at a glance, the major determinants of the online consumer behavior and their

Figure 12. Nielsen Report on apparel consumers' behaviour
Source: *Nielsen Retail Channel Track (2016)*

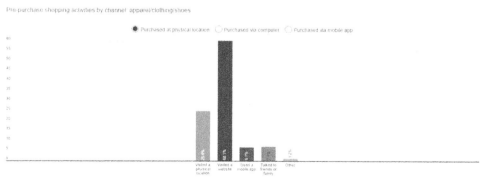

SHOPPERS ARE MOST LIKELY TO VISIT A WEBSITE BEFORE BUYING

implications for the marketer. According to a recent Nielsen's (2016) report on consumer behavior on apparel and clothes, they have included the website browsing to their decision making process although American shoppers still prefer the physical stores.

In a 2013 survey, again from Nielsen, it is reported that the Internet has a significant influence on consumers interested in buying new products in categories like electronics (81%), appliances (77%), books (70%) and music (69%). The trend is catching up in consumption categories too, such as food and beverages (62%), personal hygiene (62%), personal health/over-the-counter medicines (61%) and hair care (60%). Respondents in the Asia-Pacific region, Latin America and Middle East/Africa are most engaged in online decision-making. More than half of all global respondents consider the Internet important when it comes to purchasing new clothing (69%) and cars (68%).

Figure 13. Top 10 new product categories ranked by percent of claimed Internet importance in decision-making process

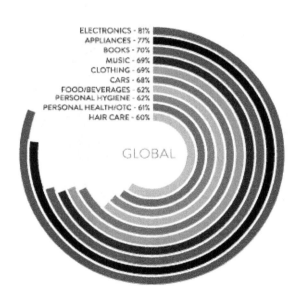

Based on respondents with online access only. New products are defined as any product not purchased in the past.

Source: Nielsen Global Survey of New Product Purchase Sentiment, Q3 2012

U.S. respondents state that the Internet is very/somewhat important when making a new product purchase decision for electronics (73%), appliances (63%), cars/auto (62%) and music (59%). Sixty-one percent turn to the Internet to help them make a new product purchase decision, when it comes to books, and 51 percent consult the Internet when considering new food and beverages.

Regarding the question as to 'what influences online behaviour', a great body of research resulted in a specific set of policies that encourage online shoppers to make purchases. Globally, 'best price' and 'free shipping' remain the two most powerful ways to encourage consumers to make online purchases. Those in Australia are more influenced by best price (68%) than free shipping (43%), whereas UK consumers are just the opposite: 90% are much influenced by free shipping versus 74% by best price. Results in the US are higher even, separated by only a few percentage points. France and Germany follow the global trend closely, but also cite 'trusted seller status' and 'return policies' as influential factors. In addition 'Recommendations from friends' was also mentioned as an influential factor across the globe (ChannelAdvisor 2011).

On this infographic, compiled by www.invespcro.com and based on a series of surveys and research, we can see the key factors that influence online consumer behaviour and the opportunities that arise for the digital marketer. First of all, the majority of US consumers are satisfied with their online shopping experience, overall and in the most important individual parameters, with the exception of mobile integration, obviously as a result of the aforementioned consumer trend to use their mobile for shopping that online retailers haven't caught up with yet. As you can see, consumers want two things: control and alternatives. They value the variety of products and brands, the multiple shopping and payment options, while they demand an easy, seamless experience and a "no strings attached" mindset with services that allow them to buy from any device and to return and exchange easily.

There is compelling evidence that the first reason for abandoning online purchases is high shipping costs (Shopify.com, 2013; Kissmetrics.com, 2015; B2CEurope.com, 2015) and the infographic confirms it: the 80% of online customers would prefer buying the products from a retailer offering free shipping. This is a rational behaviour as the consumer looks at the final price she/he will pay rather than the individual product price; therefore high shipping costs alter the value of the offering. For the online retailer, however, this evidence is crucial for strategic decision making on cost and profit structure and commercial policies in order to satisfy the consumers demand for free shipping.

Figure 14. Online customer satisfaction
Source: www.invespcro.com

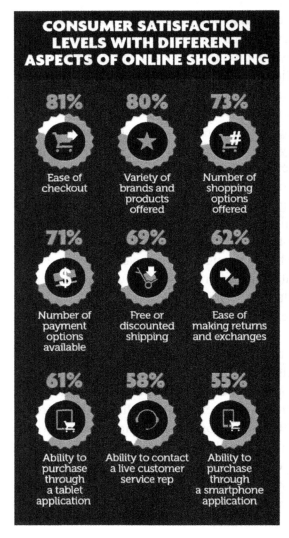

Figure 15. About shipping and returns
Source: www.investpro.com

80% of surveyed consumers are more likely
to purchase a product online when
offered free shipping

Furthermore, online customers are looking for some kind of reassurance that, if they change their minds, they can fix their mistakes, in an easy and not costly way. Note that, for specific product categories like clothing and apparel, that are very commonly purchased online (63% of the survey responders have bought clothes online, according to the same source) customers are not able to try the product on before purchase and are deprived of the opportunity to return it to a no questions asked manner. This can be the reasons for customers not to proceed with the transaction, and it may explain why consumers still prefer the physical stores for clothes' shopping (Nielsen, 2016).

Earlier, we referred to millennials having the habit of searching products online through their mobiles while being in the stores, in order to compare. Interestingly, this behavior doesn't go the other way round: online consumers

Figure 16. About incentives and influencers
Source: www.investpro.com

Figure 17. Social media influencing online shopping
Source: www.investpro.com

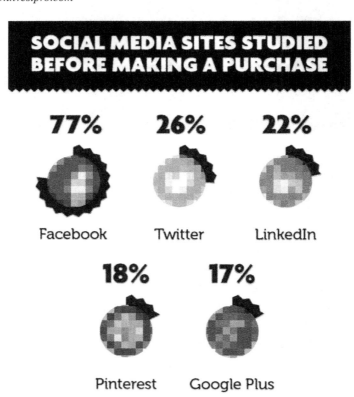

do not need to see a product "live" at a store, before buying it online. Therefore, the perception that we tend to we shop online only the things we have already seen offline can be labelled as outdated and marketers are ready to change their mind. Since consumers are willing to buy without touching and feeling the products, it's in the marketers' hands to make it happen, via the detailed presentation of the product and the policies to answer questions quickly (like a live chat or a FAQ area). Depending if the product is a low or high involvement product, a number of photographs, technical characteristics and detailed descriptions featured on the product page might prove very effective.

Finally, the power of social recommendation over marketing promotion is highlighted by this survey (www.invespcro.com), as 84% of online shoppers will look for reviews and suggestions on the social media, Facebook in particular. Therefore, crafting strategies to encourage online opinion sharing and reviewing is a key factor to online performance success, an understanding that takes us back to the community building and its participatory benefits.

Other Factors of Offline and Online Consumer Behaviour

Despite the major paradigm shift brought about by the www revolution, the foundation still rest on the traditional marketing models, like Kotler's (2005) framework on consumer behaviour. According to this model, the buying behaviour is the combined outcome of a complex set of parameters, drawn from different areas, starting from the cultural input and getting to idiosyncratic psychological needs. Kotler's (2005) model (see figure 3-13) is described in the following paragraphs in detail:

Culture refers to the set of basic values, perceptions, wants and behaviours learned by a member of society from family and other important institutions, while subculture is used to describe a group of people with a shared value

Figure 18. Kotler's model on consumer behaviour

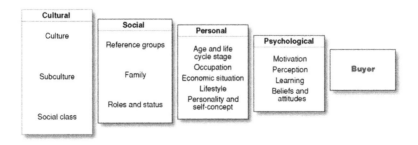

system based on common life experiences and situations, a community with norms and patterns that influence perceptions and behaviours. Social classes are relatively permanent and ordered divisions in a society whose members share similar values, interests, and behaviours.

Regarding the social factors, the Reference groups are those that have a direct face to face or indirect influence on the person's attitudes or behaviour that can -among others- be defined by brand preferences. On the other hand, the family remains a key influencer, as a very close reference group with lifelong patterns and habits. Finally, the role and status is more circumstantial and subjective and refers to the activities a person is expected to perform according to the people around him or her, as a result of the general esteem given to a role by society.

On a personal level, the demographic characteristics determine significantly the consumer behavior, as, for example, people change the goods and services they buy over their lifetime, e.g. taste in food, clothes, depending on their maturity and stage in their lifecycle. Occupation and economic circumstances are also determinant factors, as they affect the goods and services bought, the purchase power and price sensitivity, i.e. blue collar workers tend to buy more work clothes, whereas office workers buy more smart clothes. Also, the choice of Lifestyle, meaning a person's pattern of living as expressed in his or her activities, interests, and opinions, will determine the purchase behaviour in terms of consumerism mentality, brand preference, the share of wallet allocation etc. Finally, the person's distinguishing personality, as the set of psychological characteristics that lead to relatively consistent and lasting responses to their own environment and their self-concept, meaning the mental pictures that people have of themselves, are both very relevant for the marketers: If we are trying to build brands that targeted consumers will identify with, knowing and understanding their goals, needs and value systems will show us the way.

Finally, developing consuming patterns is an idiosyncratic process, in the sense that generalized factors that might be common for large groups don't necessarily dictate a unified behaviour for all, due to their individual needs and ideas. Motivation (drive), for starters, is a need that is sufficiently pressing to direct the person to seek satisfaction of the need, i.e. the drive to belonging to a likeminded community. Perception and learning refer to the process by which people select, organize and interpret information to form a meaningful picture of the world and how they can be changed due to experience. Finally, Belief is the descriptive thought that a person holds about something, for example, how trustworthy a brand is. This is translated into

Figure 19. Online consumer behavior
(Laudon & Traver, 2014, p.335)

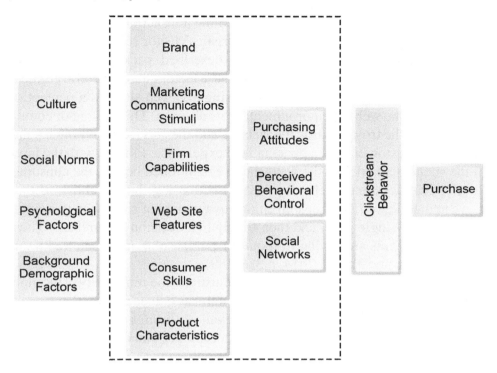

Attitude, as the consistently favorable or unfavorable evaluations, feelings, and tendencies towards an object or idea.

Naturally, since there are some very obvious differences between online or offline shopping, the traditional consumer behaviour models need to be amended accordingly. New factors like Web site features, consumer skills, in terms of technological literacy, product characteristics, attitudes towards online purchasing, and perceptions about control over the web environment come to the fore. In their attempt to trim traditional offline models online, Laundon and Traver (2014) took Kotler's established model a step further, enhancing it with a set of new factors:

From this point of view, in addition to the cultural, social, demographic and psychological factors, purchase behavior is also influenced by the brand and its marketing efforts and the firm as a whole. We have already mentioned how the reliability of the firm and the trust in that it can deliver high quality in an ethical and responsible manner have become important factors in the brand selection process, especially since the social media have set new standards to corporate information access. Additionally, the website itself, in the terms described in Chapter 2 will shape the consumer behaviour, in conjunction with their literacy about how to conduct online transactions (which increases with experience). The 'product characteristics' factor refers to how easy a product category can be handled online (described, packaged and shipped, such as books, software, and DVDs). All these factors shape specific attitudes (favorable or unfavorable) about purchasing at a web site and a perception of control of the website environment, or its absence. This feeling of control is a result of the trust towards the website and the services and policies that provide the customer with a personalized experience. Finally, with the input of the social networks, in the ways that we mentioned before, the consumer develops a clickstream behaviour, a transaction log they establish as they move about the web, from search engine to a variety of sites, then to a single site, then to a single page, and then finally to a decision to purchase. These precious moments are similar to 'point-of-purchase' moments in traditional retail (Laudon and Traver, 2014, p.388-389).

The online consumer behaviour model illustrates the complexity of the times we are living in, as it reveals the necessary delicate balance the marketer needs to maintain: to build brands and to present value offerings that can address the deep psychological individual needs for acceptance and belonging, in a user friendly way that is adjusted to new habits and inputs. As the model adds a number of new parameters on the top of an, anyway sophisticated, complex model, even existing factors, like cultures and social norms are transforming and psychological needs find new expressions online. Moreover, elements like the website design and the social media emerge as the areas the digital marketer needs to understand deeply, in order to handle a delicate decision making process in a highly competitive environment where the competitor is always just one click away.

Figure 20.

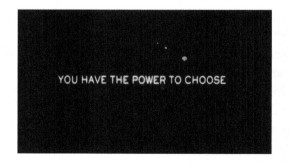

Today, consumers have both bigger quantity and better quality of information as ever before at their disposal, along with unhindered access to the opinions and word of mouth recommendations of hundreds or thousands of citizens about any product or service. Users like to share their opinions and at the same time, they have more trust in the experience of another user that in any marketing message. This in a way explains the overwhelming success of websites like www.tripadvisor.com/ and why large websites like amazon. com include a "Give your review" field everywhere. In fact, it is a good practice, and it is included in every well-crafted digital marketing strategy to motivate users to share their experience, as a brand capitalizes on the persuasive power of a good review while giving to the customer the much wanted power. Interestingly, the positive (negative) online customer reviews increase (decrease) the sales of weak brands (i.e., brands without significant, positive brand equity) but have no effect on strong brands. In turn, higher sales lead to more positive online customer reviews, which in turn strengthen the brand and aid its transition from weakness to strength (Ho-Dac et al., 2012)

Before progressing to customer profiling, let's spend a minute to understand the power of reviews, as documented by recent research findings:

According to emarketer (2015), since 2010 consumers' behaviour has completely altered towards online reviews: from 45% stating that they don't pay attention to the online reviews back in the day, the same percentage has fallen to 32% in 2015, signaling the higher significance of online reviews in the decision making process. What is also very interesting is what we do next, after reading a positive review: we go straight to the website. Note that we do not contact the company directly, we select to stay online and seek for more proof to back up the good review, this time on the website. Whether the proof will be found or not depends on the website design, but hopefully, you have read chapter 2 and now you know the rules of the game.

Having said that, we can now admit it: we are in a marketing era where, more than ever before, the consumers are in the driving seat. From user generated media, like YouTube that "gives users power and control to upload, download, post, and share videos to inform, persuade, educate and entertain others" (Reece and Blanchard, 2010, p. 235) to the deal-proneness, "which is the ease with which a consumer can get a deal, know what a good deal is, operate with knowledge of what a good price would be, and know a seller's cost" (Semenik et al., 2012, p. 434), one can say that consumers lead and marketers follow. The more we know of our consumers and decode their online behavior, the better we can tailor our online strategy to their needs and

Figure 21. Levels of trust in online review
Source: www.emarketer.com

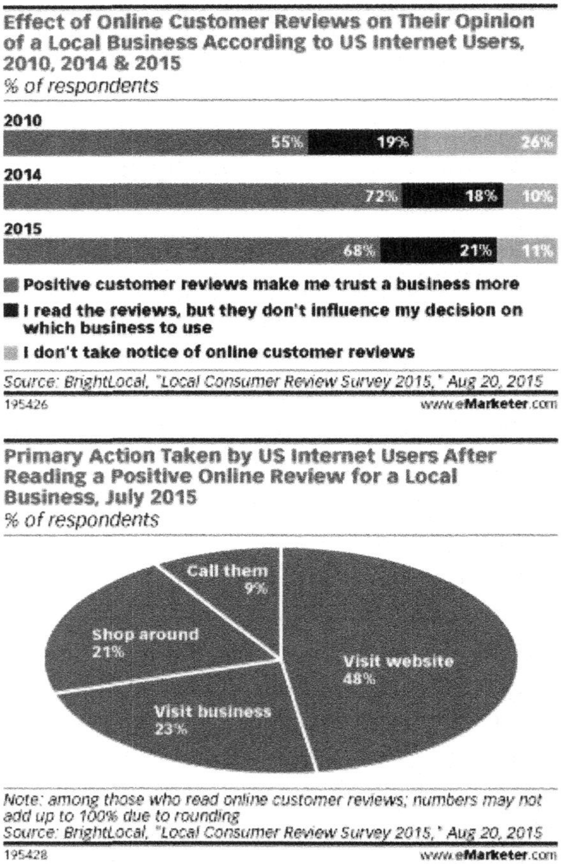

Effect of Online Customer Reviews on Their Opinion of a Local Business According to US Internet Users, 2010, 2014 & 2015
% of respondents

2010
55% 19% 26%

2014
72% 18% 10%

2015
68% 21% 11%

- Positive customer reviews make me trust a business more
- I read the reviews, but they don't influence my decision on which business to use
- I don't take notice of online customer reviews

Source: BrightLocal, "Local Consumer Review Survey 2015," Aug 20, 2015
195426   www.**eMarketer**.com

Primary Action Taken by US Internet Users After Reading a Positive Online Review for a Local Business, July 2015
% of respondents

Call them 9%
Shop around 21%
Visit website 48%
Visit business 23%

Note: among those who read online customer reviews; numbers may not add up to 100% due to rounding
Source: BrightLocal, "Local Consumer Review Survey 2015," Aug 20, 2015
195428   www.**eMarketer**.com

identity. And, since we are trying to look into the psyche of the consumers, traditional old school methods might not be sufficient enough.

DEVELOPING E-CUSTOMER PROFILE

One of the most amazing characteristics of the internet is the volume of available insights. In one way or another, every click is monitored and very sophisticated tools are launched in order to explore and use them. Knowing where to find these data and how to make use of them is a key skill of the digital marketer. However, a lot of technical support is needed also, so let's familiarize us with some important concepts and tools.

Figure 22.

Databases

A database is "a software application that scores records of individuals and their attributes such as names, addresses, and phone numbers. A database management system (DBMS) is a software application used by organizations to create, maintain and access databases. Databases are very practical for several applications as indicated by Smith and Chaffey (2005, p. 179):

1. "Enquiries coming in from offline mail-shots or online from the web site should be recorded centrally on the database and subsequently followed up carefully.
2. An integrated database can help sales reps know which web visitors have requested a real visit or a telephone call.
3. The database and the actual design of the web site can also help to nurture marketing relationships. The database remembers customer names, preferences, and behaviors.
4. An integrated database can personalize the experience and make relevant offers that match the needs of particular customer type.
5. The web site needs to be integrated with databases to deliver facilities such as transactional e-commerce, personalization and customer relationship management".

    Databases allow us to target specific segments of our audiences based on their behaviour and their preferences, for example, to show an advertisement only to people that haven't visited our website during the last month or to send a newsletter only to those that live in a specific zip code area.

Data Warehouse

The key purposes of a Data Warehouse are explained by Laudon and Traver (2014, p. 415): "A data warehouse is a database that collects a firms' transactional and customer data in a single location for offline analysis by marketers and site managers. The purpose of a data warehouse is to gather data into one logical repository where it can be analyzed and modelled by managers without disrupting or taxing the firms' primary transactional system and databases. Data warehouses grow quickly into storage repositories containing terabytes of data (trillions of bytes) on consumer behaviour at a firm's stores and web sites. With a data warehouse, firms can answer such questions as what products are the most profitable by region and city, what regional marketing campaigns are working, how effective is store promotion of the firm's web site etc."

Data Mining

Having an avalanche of data but not knowing how to convert them into intelligence is useless. Here comes data mining into the equation, "a set of different analytical techniques that look for patterns in the data of the database or data warehouse, or seek to model the behaviour of customers. Web site data can be mined to develop profiles of visitors and customers" (Laudon and Traver, 2011, p.415). Again, data mining is quite technical but its contributions are priceless for the marketer, as shown in the following figure:

As you probably understand, working with personal information and monitoring consumer behaviour click-by-click mandates for strict boundaries-legal but mostly ethical. During time, there have been many occasions where personal data were mishandled- from getting in the hands of spammers or frauds, to introducing intruding marketing strategies and much more. Besides legislations, that are now valid in most countries around the world, to protect personal data, it is the marketer's and the company's obligation to adopt an ethical stance towards their customers, and society, as we will discuss in a later chapter.

Figure 23. Data mining and personalization
Adapted from Laudon and Traver (2011)

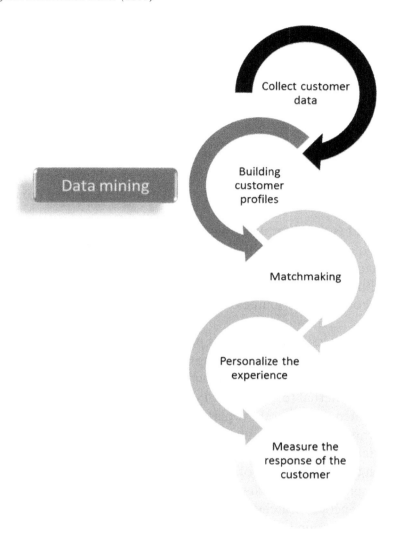

Creating Personas

Lately, the interesting concept of personas has been gaining ground in the marketing literature, describing the use of the insights collected through the aforementioned methods to build different virtual characters equivalent to target groups. What is different about personas is that they are personalized, individual-like types of consumers developed in an effort to capture their demographic characteristics, their goals, and fears, their online and offline behaviours, their motivators and deal-breakers. Although very detailed, it is even recommended to give a name to each persona, in order to make it more lively and intimate. Personas represent larger groups of customers that tend to behave in the same manner, to search for the same keywords, prefer a specific web design, looking for particular services, are more or less price sensitive, etc. Needless to say that developing and understanding our key personas is the cornerstone for good marketing strategies, potent to skyrocket our conversions.

When building our marketing personas, according to Gartner (2015) the starting point is to define our goal based on the following framework for positioning internal/ external customers and strategic/ tactical goals:

- **Internal (Customers):** Focus on customers or others who have some engagement with your products, for example, visitors to your website. Primary uses include improving customer experience and retention, upselling and cross-selling, and gaining a greater share of wallet from competitors. Data sources include CRM, web analytics, point-of-sale systems, etc.
- **External (Customers):** Treats people who are not existing customers, generally targeted for prospecting or growth. The outcome is often to find new prospects and leads for growth, or for new products and launches. Lacking internal (e.g., first-party) data, external segmentations rely on syndicated and other third-party data, media vendors, market research, government and other outside sources of information.
- **Tactical (Goals):** Tactical segmentations have the goal of determining which types and groups of people are more or less likely to buy product X or service Y. For example, Kraft segmented its customer base by whether people searched for recipes and were interested in Easter for a promotion around its Easter Bunny Cake recipe.
- **Strategic (Goals):** Strategic segmentations are more interested in exploration and discovery among groups of customers or prospects and often used by marketers who want to discover new insights for targeting, messaging or product development. This was the goal for tax preparation company H&R Block when it performed clustering analysis that identified three broad groups of customers: "Do-it-yourselfer," "do-it-for-me," and a previously unknown hybrid group it called "do-it-with-me," who preferred some help but not full service.

Having decided the nature and purpose of our segmentation, we are ready to turn to our data and mine information related to three sets of attributes:

- **Who They Are:** Demographics, stage of life cycle etc.
- **What They Do:** What products do they buy, which devices do they use, which sources of information do they trust, what media do they prefer
- **What They Think:** Attitudes and values, like if they are price sensitive or value oriented, if they tend to be loyal, if they engage in reviewing etc.

Having this information in hand, we can now develop a persona, describe a person like we know them and try to understand how they feel, what they want, what they really expect from a brand, a product, and a service. Working on the individual rather than the group level allows us to pinpoint differences in goals and motivators, that later will be generalized to shape a larger group of targeted audience. Marketing personas can be built using an existing template, like the one below, by developing a new one or with the use of a service like Hubspot's www.makemypersona.com. In any case, the final outcome will look a lot like this:

Note that some information is very explicit and detailed although fictional, in order to make the persona look and feel like a real person and make their character coherent and deep. Also, in the challenges and common objections sections the data input is related to the service/ product category we are promoting, here website development services. Therefore, if we try to bring together a marketing strategy, solely digital or integrating all channels, isn't it easier now that we have this specific person in mind? You can think in which networks and websites she/he can be easily approached (either by content or by paid advertising), what kind of content would engage her/him, what articles could nurture her/his need for personal growth and development, what tone of voice to use, how to approach her/him in order to emphasize her/his need to look professional, what are the intrinsic and extrinsic rewards we will be motivated by etc.

To sum up, the marketing persona is the evolution of the target group, a new, more insightful and detailed tool designed to capture the complex consumer behaviour in the www era. Although they can be found under the term "buyer personas" or "digital personas", implying that they are different versions of personas, our experience tells us that, as we are heading towards integration of different channels, each persona combines both online and

Figure 24. Marketing persona template
Source: singlegrain.com

Background:

*Staff Accountant at Founder Accounting

*Completed his undergraduate degree at Penn State and his masters at Cornell University

*Has a serious girlfriend and two dogs (a Labrador retriever and a pug mix)

Demographics:

*Male

*Age 34

*Annual HH income: $125,000

*Lives in a townhouse-style condo in an urban area

Goals:

*Become a senior accountant within 3-5 years

*Achieve a salary of $80,000 so that he can purchase a single family home

*Network aggressively in order to build professional contacts

Tommy Technology

Hobbies & Interests:

*Running 5K races with his girlfriend

*Watching Game of Thrones

*Going out to brunch with other young couples

*Taking one nice vacation a year to established tourist destinations

Challenges:

*Wants to have a more modern website, but isn't the final decision-maker

*Struggles with being seen as the "young guy" in the office and being taken less seriously as a result

Common Objections:

*I love the idea of a new website, by my boss will never go for it! He doesn't see the value in new technology.

*I'd love to get started on a new website, but I don't think I can get buy-in from my boss. He never takes my ideas seriously.

Biggest Fears:

*Getting stuck in a job and not advancing up the corporate ladder as quickly as he'd like

*Economic recessions that mean he'll never be able to retire

*Life passing him by too quickly

offline behaviours. Today, it's the customer, not the channel (online or offline) that matters and the marketer needs to tailor their messages and approaches in order to create a seamless experience throughout the different touchpoints. The shifted consumer behaviour takes existing needs –the need of belonging to larger groups, the fundamental process of consumer behavior etc.- to a new context but it doesn't change our nature as humans. Therefore, what is mostly important for marketers is to understand how *people,* not consumers behave today, with the plethora of channels and alternatives and to design a journey and an offering of value both in monetary, rational and in participatory and emotional terms.

Answers

- The internet and the social media have created a new type of consumer, that is not passive recipient of sellers' messages, but a proactive consumer (prosumer) with the power to compare offering with just one click, to dismiss fraudulent offers, to demand transparency and access and to share their experiences and opinions openly. In this context, the power has been transferred from the seller to the buyer and it is the time where consumers take their revenge for the years of marketing monologues.

- When consumers actively participate in a brand community, they insert the community's traits into their own social identity, in a way making the brand a part of them. Over time, an ever stronger bond develops between the members, the community and the brand that leads, among others, to loyalty and co-creation. Sales promotions, coupons, offers and other extrinsic rewards might be very useful for short term results, but in the context of the brand building, it is the intrinsic benefits of belonging to a community that will make the difference.

- The way we shop has changed altogether, both in terms of behavior and operationally. Online and mobile shopping penetration is growing rapidly and by 2019 the internet users globally will be engaged in online shopping. Behaviorally-wise, consumers today are serial searchers, they are used to look for products and prices online, even while being at the store. The ease of access and the awareness that there is always a better deal, somewhere, have made them more price sensitive, but at the same time, they will not select a brand that is not transparent and moral.

- There are some basics on consumer behaviour, regardless if it is online or offline: culture, social norms, psychological factors and individual background and demographics are forming the way we behave and consume. When online, however, some new factors are added up: the brand and the way it is marketed, the firm's image and capabilities, the website design and how it addresses the users' needs and expectations, the characteristics of the product category, the overall consumers' attitude towards online shopping and the influence of the social media. All these have to be taken into consideration when crafting the online experience in order to engage and satisfy consumers online.

- Marketing personas are fictional characters that represent the goals, needs, demographics and behaviours of the different types of customers a company targets. Being very detailed and explicit, personas depict the different motives and factors that determine a purchase decision and help the marketer understand what's really important and how to address it. As an evolution of the target group, personas allow us to use the sophisticated segmentation methods provided online, for a matchmaking made in heaven (hopefully).

REFERENCES

B2CEurope.eu. (2015). *High delivery costs are the no.1 reason for abandoning online purchases*. Retrieved from http://www.b2ceurope.eu/de/news/high-delivery-costs-are-the-no-1-reason-for-abandoning-online-purchases/

Almquist, E., Senior, J., & Bloch, N. (2016). The Elements of value. *Harvard Business Review, 94*(9), 47–53.

Benmiled-Cherif, H., Kaufmann, H. R., & Manarioti, A. (2016). The influence of brand community on co-creation: A cross national study of the brand AXE in France and Tunisia. *World Review of Entrepreneurship, Management and Sustainable Development, 12*(2-3), 285–299.

Carroll, B. A., & Ahuvia, A. C. (2006). Some antecedents and outcomes of brand love. *Marketing Letters, 17*(2), 79–89. doi:10.1007/s11002-006-4219-2

Casaló, L. V., Flavián, C., & Guinalíu, M. (2008). Promoting consumers participation in virtual brand communities: A new paradigm in branding strategy. *Journal of Marketing Communications, 14*(1), 19–36. doi:10.1080/13527260701535236

Channeladvisor. (2011). *Online Shopping Survey*. Retrieved from http://go.channeladvisor.com/US-eBook-2011-Consumer-Survey.html?ls=PR&cid=701F00000002U0S

Christodoulides, G. (2008). Introduction. *Journal of Brand Management, 15*(4), 291–293. doi:10.1057/palgrave.bm.2550134

Cova, B., Pace, S., & Park, D. J. (2007). Global brand communities across borders: The Warhammer case. *International Marketing Review*, *24*(3), 313–329. doi:10.1108/02651330710755311

Deichman, A. (2010). *Wait, what? On Social Network Use and Attention.* Retrieved from steinhardt.nyu.edu/appsych/opus/issues/2010/fall/On_Social_Network_Use_and_Attention

Dessart, L., Veloutsou, C., & Morgan-Thomas, A. (2015). Consumer engagement in online brand communities: A social media perspective. *Journal of Product and Brand Management*, *24*(1), 28–42. doi:10.1108/JPBM-06-2014-0635

E-marketer. (2015). *US Adults Spend 5.5 Hours with Video Content Each Day*. Retrieved from http://www.emarketer.com/Article/US-Adults-Spend-55-Hours-with-Video-Content-Each-Day/1012362

eMarketer. (2013). *Key Digital trends, 2013*. Retrieved from http://www.slideshare.net/fullscreen/eMarketerInc/emarketer-webinar-key-digital-trends-for-2013

eMarketer. (2015). *Why Users put more stock in consumer reviews*. Retrieved from http://www.emarketer.com/Article/Web-Users-Put-More-Stock-Consumer-Reviews/1012929

Fournier, S., & Lee, L. (2009). Getting brand communities right. *Harvard Business Review*, *87*(4), 105–111. PMID:19736854

Gambetti, R. C., & Graffigna, G. (2015). Value co-creation between the inside and the outside of a company Insights from a brand community failure. *Marketing Theory*, *15*(2), 155–178. doi:10.1177/1470593114545004

Gartner. (2015). *How to build digital marketing segments*. Retrieved from http://www.gartner.com/smarterwithgartner/how-to-build-digital-marketing-segments/

Habibi, M. R., Laroche, M., & Richard, M. (2014). The roles of brand community and community engagement in building brand trust on social media. *Computers in Human Behavior*, *37*(0), 152–161. doi:10.1016/j.chb.2014.04.016

Hatch, M. J., & Schultz, M. (2010). Toward a theory of brand co-creation with implications for brand governance. *Journal of Brand Management*, *17*(8), 590–604. doi:10.1057/bm.2010.14

Ho-Dac, N. N., Carson, S. J., & Moore, W. I. (2013). The Effects of Positive and Negative Online Customer Reviews: Do Brand Strength and Category Maturity Matter? *Journal of Marketing, 77*(6), 37–53. doi:10.1509/jm.11.0011

Ind, N., Iglesias, O., & Schultz, M. (2013). Building brands together: Emergence and Outcomes of Co-Creation. *California Management Review, 55*(3), 5–26. doi:10.1525/cmr.2013.55.3.5

Invespcro. (2016). *Online consumer shopping habits and behaviour.* Retrieved from http://www.invespcro.com/blog/online-consumer-shopping-habits-behavior/

Kaufmann, H. R., Correia Loureiro, S. M., Basile, G., & Vrontis, D. (2012). The increasing dynamics between consumers, social groups, and brands. *Qualitative Market Research: An International Journal, 15*(4), 404–419. doi:10.1108/13522751211257088

Kaufmann, H. R., Loureiro, S. M. C., & Manarioti, A. (2016). Exploring behavioural branding, brand love and brand co-creation. *Journal of Product and Brand Management, 25*(6), 516–526. doi:10.1108/JPBM-06-2015-0919

Kaufmann, H. R., & Manarioti, A. (2016). *The Content Challenge: Engaging Consumers in a World of Me-Formation.* IMPACT.

Kissmetrics.com. (2015). *5 Ecommerce Stats That Will Make You Change Your Entire Marketing Approach.* Retrieved from https://blog.kissmetrics.com/5-ecommerce-stats/

Kotler, P., Wong, V., Saunders, J., & Armstrong, G. (2005). *Principles of Marketing.* Pearson.

Laudon, K. C., & Traver, C. G. (2011). *E-commerce 2011. Business, Technology, Society* (7th ed.). Pearson.

Laudon, K. C., & Traver, C. G. (2014), E-commerce 2014. Business, Technology, Society (10th ed.). Prentice Hall.

Marino, A. (2015, August). From Prosumers to Persumers: The Implementation of a Real Involving (Services) Marketing. Proceedings of the Toulon-Verona Conference Excellence in Services.

Merz, M., & Vargo, S. (2009). The evolving brand logic: A service-dominant logic perspective. *Journal of the Academy of Marketing Science, 37*(3), 328–344. doi:10.1007/s11747-009-0143-3

Nielsen. (2013). *The Digital Influence: How the internet affects new product purchase decisions*. Retrieved from http://www.nielsen.com/us/en/insights/news/2013/digital-influence-how-the-internet-affects-new-product-purchase-decisions.html

Nielsen. (2016). *The Where behind the wear: Americans are buying clothes in-store, online and on their phones*. Retrieved from http://www.nielsen.com/us/en/insights/news/2016/the-where-behind-the-wear-americans-buy-clothes-in-store-online-on-phones.html

Prahalad, C., & Ramaswamy, V. (2004). Co-creation experiences: The next practice in value creation. *Journal of Interactive Marketing*, *18*(3), 5–14. doi:10.1002/dir.20015

PriceWaterCoopers. (2016). *The Total Retail Report*. Retrieved from http://www.pwc.com/gx/en/industries/retail-consumer/global-total-retail.html

Reportbuyer. (2013). *Western and Central Europe B2C Ecommerce Report*. Retrieved from http://www.reportbuyer.com/consumer_goods_retail/e_commerce/western_europe_b2c_e_commerce_report.html

Schaefer, M. (2015). *The Content Code: Six essential strategies to ignite your content, your marketing and your business*. Library of Congress Cataloging-in-Publication Data.

Semenik, R. J., Allen, C. T., O'Guinn, T. C., & Kaufmann, H. R. (2012). *Advertising and Promotions: An Integrated Brand Approach*. South-Western Cengage Learning.

Shopify.com. (2013). *Why Online Retailers Are Losing 67.45% of Sales and What to Do About It*. Retrieved from https://www.shopify.com/blog/8484093-why-online-retailers-are-losing-67-45-of-sales-and-what-to-do-about-it

Singlegrain.com. (2014). *The Complete Guide to developing and using buyer personas*. Retrieved from https://www.singlegrain.com/buyer-personas-2/complete-guide-developing-using-buyer-personas/

Smith, P. R., & Chaffey, D. (2005). *E-Marketing excellence, the Heart of Business* (2nd ed.). Elsevier.

Statcounter.com. (2016). *Statcounter Global Stats*. Retrieved from http://gs.statcounter.com/#desktop-search_engine-ww-daily-20160401-20160431-bar

The Washington Post. (2015). *Why Louis Vuitton, Gucci and Prada are in trouble*. Retrieved from https://www.washingtonpost.com/business/economy/louis-vuitton-and-guccis-nightmares-come-true-wealthy-shoppers-dont-want-flashy-logos-anymore/2015/06/15/e521733c-fd97-11e4-833c-a2de05b6b2a4_story.html

Vargo, S. L., & Lusch, R. F. (2008). Service-dominant logic: Continuing the evolution. *Journal of the Academy of Marketing Science, 36*(1), 1–10. doi:10.1007/s11747-007-0069-6

Vernuccio, M., Pagani, M., Barbarossa, C., & Pastore, A. (2015). Antecedents of brand love in online network-based communities. A social identity perspective. *Journal of Product and Brand Management, 24*(7), 706–719. doi:10.1108/JPBM-12-2014-0772

Vivek, S. D., Beatty, S. E., Dalela, V., & Morgan, R. M. (2014). A generalized multidimensional scale for measuring customer engagement. *Journal of Marketing Theory and Practice, 22*(4), 401–420. doi:10.2753/MTP1069-6679220404

Chapter 4
Consumer Engagement in Social Media Platforms

ABSTRACT

If 'to be social' is the sum of people's online interaction intentions, that can be monitored by marketers but not coerced, how can we make best use of these powerful new media? The answer lies in understanding the internal, psychological needs that are fulfilled by the social media and how they are demonstrated and testified by liking, sharing and engaging in general with specific pieces of content, while rejecting others. In this environment, marketers are called to develop a "brand as a person" strategy, in order for their brands to mingle and interact with consumers beyond the traditional marketing communication framework. In this chapter, we explore and discuss the strategic use of the social media as a concept that needs to be thoroughly understood but seemingly hasn't been yet by a large majority of marketers.

Questions

- Why marketers can't afford to ignore the social media?
- How a brand can benefit from a social media marketing strategy?
- What are the psychological characteristics of social media users?
- How different 'sharer tribes' influence digital marketing strategy decisions?
- Why is brand-as-a-person better than brand-as-a-brand?

DOI: 10.4018/978-1-68318-012-8.ch004

INTRODUCTION

When both, scholars and practitioners are talking about social media, the word revolution comes up often. Yet, there might still be some readers that are skeptic about our space allocation dedicating a whole chapter on the social media marketing? So, let's talk numbers first:

According to the comprehensive research conducted and published by the 'We are Social' agency (www.wearesocial.com), more than 6 out of 10 people with access to the internet are accounted as active social media users, adding up to the overwhelming amount of 2.307 billion users. From a regional perspective, according to the same source, 59% of the total population of North America is active social media users, a percentage that changes to 50% for South America and 48% for West Europe and East Asia. In more detail:

To better understand the reasons for the penetration of the social media and how they have transformed the way we live, think and behave, Table 1 combines the aforementioned percentages, on the premise that all active

Figure 1. Social media penetration
Source: www.wearesocial.com

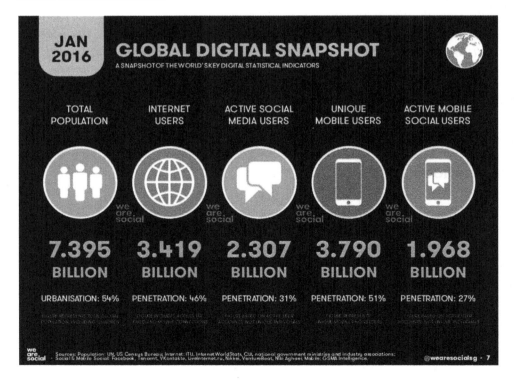

Figure 2. Social media use per region
Source: www.wearesocial.com

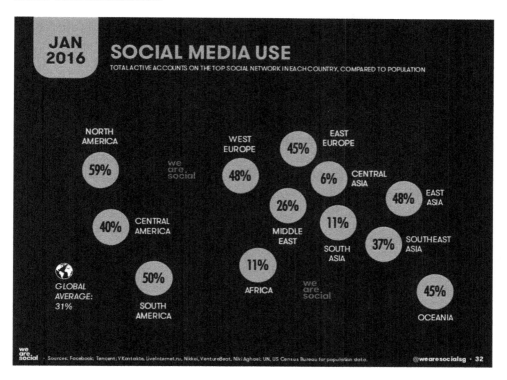

Table 1. Social media users as % of internet users

Region	Social media users/ Internet Users
Central America	91%
Southeast Asia	90%
East Asia	89%
North America	83%
East Europe	70%
South America	67%
Oceania	66%
West europe	58%
Middle East	49%
South Asia	41%
Africa	38%
Central Asia	15%

Source: Authors

social media users have internet access. The purpose of this meta-analysis is to showcase how dominant this new "habit" of maintaining a social media life has become and why we, as marketers must wholeheartedly and proactively embrace it: these numbers tell the story of a paradigm shift that mandates an in depth analysis and understanding of users' motives and needs when interacting in the social media arena.

Notwithstanding different definitions, social media are online networks where users generate and exchange content engaging in and maintaining an ongoing dialogue. More specific on the nexus between social media and corporate marketing, Dr. Fou of the Marketing Science Consulting Group, Inc. says: "Social media = people's conversations and actions online that can be mined by advertisers for insights but not coerced to pass along marketing messages. It's the new form of media that does not exist until it happens and that cannot be bought by advertisers to carry their messages" (www. heidicohen.com). Social media are ephemeral- the trendy Snapchat is the living proof for social media being ruled by users, not by marketers. In the traditional marketing context, marketers craft their tactics, for the following months or year, produce and broadcast them and then wait for the customers to respond. Here, in the social media world, things are diametrically different: Now, brands have to go where consumers go and tailor their messages and strategies on the spot, to accommodate social media users' behavior. In a way, this is another aspect of the "revenge of the customer" we discussed in Chapter 2, as now, users lead and the brands follow.

In the early days of the social media, Friendster and Myspace dominated the space, yet today their influence faded and they are another brick in the ephemeral wall. Today, when it comes to ranking existing social networking platforms, Facebook is salient in the landscape, since its introduction in 2004, while new services are launched continuously. Figure 5-3 illustrates the ranking of the different social media platforms as in April 2016; apart from the impressive numbers, what it is important for the marketer to notice is the variety of platforms, the different orientation of each and how they provide us with access to niche markets or very well defined audience groups, in terms of demographic and psychological categorizations. Note, that messaging apps like WhatsApp and Facebook Messenger are included in the list, since they are evolving to much more than mere texting replacement becoming an all in one service. For example, China's chat app, WeChat, number 5 in the ranking, apart from one to one and group messaging, features newsfeed sharing, and organizations/brands are following like Facebook, the money transferring services of Square and PayPal, in-store payment offers similar

Figure 3. Social media ranking per number of users
Source: www.statista.com

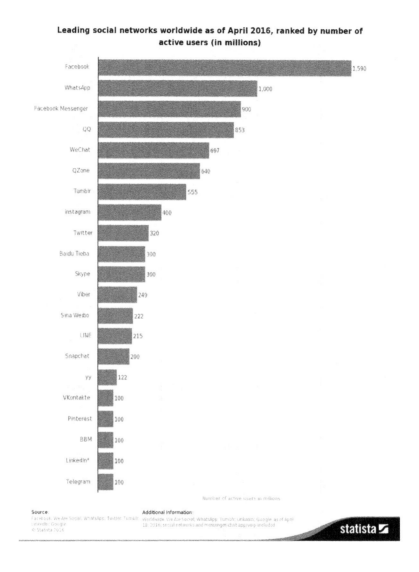

Leading social networks worldwide as of April 2016, ranked by number of active users (in millions)

to Apple Pay and Google Wallet, cab hailing abilities of Uber, food delivery ordering like Favor etc.

From a marketing perspective, social media are first and foremost a branding channel (eMarketer, 2013) where branded activities can be used to increase brand awareness and brand liking, promote customer engagement and loyalty, inspire consumer word-of-mouth communication about the brand, and potentially drive traffic to brand locations on and offline (Ashley & Tuten, 2015). Investment in social media and social network advertising is on the rise in terms of spending and proportion of advertising spending budgets (eMarketer 2013b, 2014). As this investment continues to grow, expectations of ever increasing sophistication and effectiveness of social media marketing are also on the rise. Practices that started out as largely intuitive and experimental, such as Facebook's page posting for example, have recently evolved in a combination of advertising and marketing art and science (Alhabash et al., 2015). According to the Social Marketing Industry Report (Stelzner, 2016), 90% of the marketers acknowledge the importance of social media marketing as a means to increase exposure and traffic and to build a loyal fan base. Interestingly, however, they state that it is complicated and difficult and they do not feel confident about their decisions and ROI.

Figure 4. Social media platforms used by marketers
Source: Social Media Marketing Industry Report (2016)

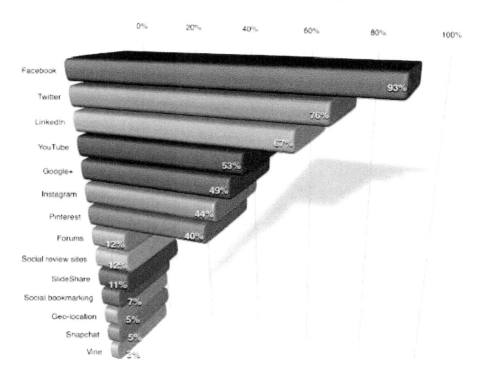

Here lays the initial premise of this book, that social media marketing is a *new* marketing paradigm, partly applying the same rules as traditional marketing but mostly introducing new terms and concepts that need to be studied by marketers from scratch. The aforementioned reservations and the executives' reluctance to adopt new channels (only 6% of the marketers reported that they are willing to) are illustrated in Figure 5-4, showing the very low penetration of new channels in the social media marketing mix and the ongoing domination of "traditional" online channels like Facebook, Twitter and LinkedIn.

Social media are here to stay. Their rise and pervasiveness show that they answer a pre-existing psychological need, one that makes people change their priorities and habits, in order to create and share their personal moments and opinions online. Getting to understand this fundamental need behind social media use is the very key to crafting effective and successful social media marketing plans. Apparently, given a number of new channels and the fundamental differences between the social media and traditional media, a new marketing approach is called for, backed up with, so far scattered, theoretical and practical knowledge to provide the marketers with the needed confidence to get out of their comfort zones and adopt novel perspectives, tools, and techniques.

THE PSYCHOLOGY OF LIKE AND SHARE

As mentioned already, marketers acknowledge the importance of a well-crafted social media marketing strategy, as social media are amongst the top marketing tools employed despite still regarded as challenging and difficult (Stelzner, 2016; Wasp Barcode Technologies, 2016). This is the product of a very pragmatic observation: Social media impact and change the behavior of the customers, both online and offline. In their own words, consumers say that social media play almost as big a role in purchasing decisions as television does (www.adage.com).

At this point, let's ask us: How can a brand benefit from a social media marketing strategy? For starters, posts and updates on brand social media profiles directly impact website traffic and search engine rankings (Stelzner, 2016); in turn, in the context of an integrated marketing strategy where online channels are used to generate offline results, this SEO implication indirectly impacts the sales performance and other critical brand measures (See chapter 2 for more information about Search Engine Optimization).

Figure 5.

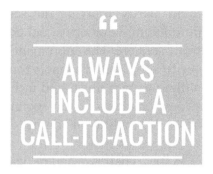

From a simplistic point of view, when a brand post appears on a user's Facebook timeline, it is an immediate addition to the awareness scores of the brand. This is the starting point for any kind of customer-brand relationship and a reminder as well. However, what we intend is to motivate and trigger customer behavior and to attract it to our owned media, i.e. our website of a specific landing page. Obviously, the chances for a customer to click on the link pointing to the brand website or any specific landing page are higher than without the post appearance. But, here applies a fundamental rule of social media marketing that makes things easier and more effective: In order to convert social Media reach to brand related activity, a Call-To-Action prompt must be included in all posts and updates. Regardless if it is a website link, a "Shop Now" or a "Contact Us" button, the marketer should design a clickstream path from the social network to brand owned channels, in order to, at least, measure the impact of their tactics and to identify the ones that engage consumers in the most valuable manner. Website traffic and "vanity metrics" (friends, followers, "likes") are the most common metrics marketers use to measure the business impact of social media, but only 14% manage to tie social media to sales levels (The CMO survey, 2015). This distance between social media marketing and sales performance starts a vicious circle created by a lack of integration resulting in very commonly observed failures in marketing strategies today.

In spite of inadequacy of used marketing metrics to capture to impact to sales, there are solid findings that there is one metric that cannot be overseen. According to Google's report (2014), people who engage with a brand on social media daily are likely to make twice as many purchases from that brand than someone who engages only monthly. In addition, a Forrester Research (2013) study showed that individuals who have engaged with brands online are more likely to complete actual purchases than those who did not have online engagement. In their research on how social media clicks impact actual behavior, Alhabash and colleagues concluded that positive evaluation of the messages of a brand broadcasts on the social media channels moves customers closer to perform the prompted behavior offline (Alhabash et al., 2015). This means that liking a post about a new product augments the possibility of actually buying the product. The researchers' focus was on the evaluation of the message itself, which starts the conversation on the importance of content management: what we publish online, when and how- a discussion that will be elaborated in Chapter 6. Ho-Dac et al., (2012) found that online customer reviews also affect sales, a phenomenon that is evident in in the case of TripAdvisor and its impact on hotel bookings. As already discussed in Chapter 3, consumer behavior is influenced more by reviews when referring to weaker brands but the more and better the reviews, the higher the sales and ultimately, the higher the brand strength and, in a way, the immunity against bad reviews (Ho-Dac et al., 2012).

This latter finding raises a question: Why are we, as social media users, willing to change our opinion and behavior about a product or brand based on a review made by someone we even don't know or are never going to meet? The answer can be found in the concept of online brand communities (you can find the theoretical background in Chapter 3), those groups of consumers developed around a brand that are affiliated by their common interest in it. Online brand communities behave in the same manner as offline brand communities (Dessart et al.., 2015). Members have a great tendency to go beyond their personal character identity (i.e. identity related to a person's individual sense of self) and to develop a social identity, that is, an individual's self-concept that derives from the knowledge of being part of a social group (Facebook brand fans) or participating in the community of reviewers in TripAdvisor. Adding to this intrinsic satisfaction, the fact that consumers are cautious towards marketing messages and tend to easier accept peer reviews than corporate product statements, explains why we are prone to trust a stranger that belongs to the same community with us more than the official brand voice or, sometimes, our instincts. Of course, this understanding of the underlying social media user needs, guides the marketer to craft a strategy to intrigue and manage reviewing in particular, as a means to create Word of Mouth for the benefit of the brand. Realizing, that commenting and posting a review is an act of co-creation in the context of the community, demonstrates in a very straightforward manner, why brand representatives are strongly encouraged to reply to the comments and reviews and actively participate in the dialogue, rather than remaining silent observers.

Apart from commenting and reviewing, the social media as the locus of the online brand communities can be a great source of innovation and value co-creation, especially when brand representatives become honest and equal members of the team. Brands have rather little authority on their communities and this is the major risk and concern that bothers marketers: once consumers start sharing experiences and opinions, there is no way to stop or control them. Those who tried have succeeded only in making the essence of the community obsolete. The more successful communities are usually run by enthusiasts and customers of the brands and products. This is confirmed by a publication in the Wall Street Journal (Dholakia and Vianello, 2009): in their efforts to set up brand communities that will remain under their command, companies are missing out on a marketing tool with huge potential, particularly in this weak economy. A well-designed brand community can be used to conduct market research with very quick turn-around; generate and test ideas for product innovations; deliver prompt and high-quality service to customers having a problem; strengthen the attachments that existing customers feel toward the brand; and increase good publicity through word-of-mouth. The only thing marketers have to take to heart is to allow the fans to express themselves without censoring or trapping them inside strict rules, monitor the conversation and maintain a positive, brand enhancing attitude, be open and receptive and make community members feel heard and important.

Let's take the example of Beauty Talk- Sephora Community and how it integrates with the brand's social media messages:

This is a community dedicated to beauty, nested in the website of Sephora, allowing consumers to ask beauty related questions and advice, discuss products and share experiences and tips. The representatives of Sephora are present, replying to threads and answering questions, without any effort to hard sell or spoil the sharing experience with marketing agendas. As a result, this conversation drastically increases the website traffic whilst building authority for the brand in the online beauty discussion. At the same time, on their Facebook Page, Sephora brand representatives maintain the same friendly tone of voice and redirect consumers to the community, converting the social media engagement first to website traffic and then to (potential) loyalty through participation in the community. From the consumer's point of view, being a part of a larger group, enjoying the feeling of sharing and belonging is a fundamental psychological need that finds actualization in social networking altogether.

Figure 6.

There is extensive research on why and how we have become so engaged in social media. Pew Research recently reported that 90% of young adults (18-29 years old) are active social media users (Pew Research Center, 2015) and provided the personality traits determining this behavior. The research discovered that social media are mostly used by extrovert people, which are open to new experiences but having a higher emotional instability (Correa et al., 2010). This is interesting in many ways:

- In the past, similar research studies have found extraversion to be negatively related to the use of social services such as chat rooms (e.g., Hamburger & Ben-Artzi, 2000). The reason is seen in that social interactions through these online applications differed from offline interactions due to the lesser importance attributed to physical appearance and physical proximity and to the comfort assured by anonymity. As a result, introverted people, as well as those who experience social anxiety and loneliness, tended to use the Web to assuage their real-world isolation in these early studies of Internet use (Amichai-Hamburger & Ben-Artzi, 2003; Bargh et al., 2002). However, today, this relationship between extroversion and social media has turned to positive: more extrovert people use the social media. The explanation provided is, that today we don't use the social media to

Figure 7.

❝

***Social media are
mostly used by
extrovert people, that
are open to new
experiences, but
have higher
emotional instability.***

hide our identities, on the contrary: we share and promote ourselves, we build a new identity through the social media. (Correa et al., 2010).

- Openness to new experiences as a trait of the avid social media users is related to the adjustability of social media users to the fast-paced changes occurring in the technological level but also to the new platforms launched regularly, new services etc. This implies that people who find it difficult to accept the new, be it an experience or a software environment, cannot keep up with the speed of the social media.

- The emotional instability as a predictor of social media use is explained by higher levels of neuroticism, negative affectivity and anxiety (Correa et al., 2010; Hamburger & Ben-Artzi, 2000). Given that emotional instability is related to loneliness and a difficulty in engaging in face-to-face interactions, it makes sense why when under this psychological stage, we seek comfort in the virtual social media world. If we accept that, when feeling content and sociable, people tend to prefer the "real" social life rather than the virtual one and that they hang out on Facebook, Instagram and the rest of the social platforms while being bored or disappointed, this can be a beacon to the marketer about the purpose of content published: Social media users want to be entertained and to feel important and significant. By the same token, use and gratifications theory suggests social media participants are likely to desire entertainment and informativeness, but perhaps entertainment is a stronger motivator of engagement with top brands than informativeness (Ashley & Tuten, 2015). These insights will be very useful and effective when later applied to the content management decisions as they suggest an approach to content creation that goes far beyond of merely sharing brand and sales messages.

Recent research points to the use of social media with the aim to build and promote our self-identity. Amongst our fundamental needs as humans is the one to promote ourselves, support our beliefs and share our ideas (Zhu & Chen, 2015). This goal has found an avenue in the limitless possibilities of the internet and the social media, creating a stream of "me-formation", to take the term proposed by Rutgers University a step further (Naaman et al., 2010). According to this research, about half the content posted online is about "me", sharing of personal information, moments and perceptions through status updates, tweets, and photographs, reflecting a modern way to express our identity-related need to talk about ourselves. There even is a biological explanation to this: a recent research discovered a strong connection between Facebook and the brain's reward center, called the nucleus accumbens. This area processes rewarding feelings about things like food, sex, money and social acceptance. This means that when we get positive feedback on Facebook, the feeling lights up this part of our brain. The greater the intensity of our Facebook use, the greater the reward (Meshi et al., 2013).

Given the way the social media function, the values or activities we engage in (in terms of like, comment, share for Facebook and the equivalents for the other platforms) become a part of our identity. This holds the answer on how we select what to engage in in the social media world. Research findings show that there is a significant difference between the psychologies of liking a piece of content and sharing it/ re-tweet it/ repost it etc. While liking is a typical, low-involvement sign of approval, sharing means to endorse and adopt the content.

People who share content are motivated by personal, intimate needs, like expressing themselves, identify with something, and support whatever matches their existing or desired identity, while hoping they will be rewarded by their network for the share. Each share is a message to the user's network of friends and acquaintances and to the entire community, a confession about personal beliefs and values. What we choose to share and even what we choose not to, mirrors our identity (Schaefer, 2015). From a cognitive vantage point,

Figure 8.

❝ *A world of meformation* ❝

clicking on the Like button is an easier and less involved behavior compared to sharing and commenting on persuasive messages (Alhabash et al., 2015).

According to an extensive research of the Customer Insights Group for the New York Times (2011), six different segments of sharers exist, all bonded by a common behavioral denominator: sharing is a personal action of relationship building, either through making available to our network what we think will be entertaining of by defining ourselves to others.

- **The Altruists:** Sharing is an act of thoughtfulness; they want to be helpful to their network and to stay connected with their medium of preference being the email.
- **The Careerists:** They share in order to make a statement about their professional stance; this is why they mostly use LinkedIn. Since they use social media sharing to build an identity, they carefully select what they share and evaluate the content in terms of how valuable it will be for their image and their network.
- **The Hipsters:** They share to define themselves and they believe that the means is the message, therefore, they can be found on the newest platforms. Their purpose is not to share information, in terms of usefulness but to build their personal identity through what they choose to share.
- **The Boomerangs:** This is the provocative type of sharer that mostly uses Twitter and Facebook to build an identity of being controversial and a "Firestarter." They seek reaction and validation through sharing and they don't stop until they get it.
- **The Connectors:** They share to bring people together, they are the users that share events and tag their friends on Facebook posts or share via email. They are thoughtful as the altruists but their purpose is not to be useful but to make plans and be sociable.
- **The Selectives:** They are very careful when sharing and they use email or specific lists, in order to select relevant recipients. They tend to be resourceful, while sharing content is a thoughtful act performed to inform and connect.

Underpinning all the sharing activities, of course, is a prerequisite, which is the content itself. Regardless of the psychology and purpose of sharing, given that what we share is always a signal about ourselves, our identity, our aesthetics and sense of humor, only good, high quality content will stand a chance. On the other hand, for the marketer these 6 types can be included in

Figure 9. Types of sharers
Source: www.statpro.com

the persona building, as each group responds to different content, is found on different media and has different needs. A brand manager can use this segmentation in two ways in order to maximize sharing and, therefore, the impact of corporate social media marketing:

- Select one of the sharers' types that best matches the overall targeting of the brand and develop content and campaigns to satisfy the specific values and needs behind their sharing habits. For example, a brand that is positioned as rebellious and provocative might find it useful to target the Boomerangs. By all means, it can do so only by creating equally provocative material and by motivating users to react, through intrinsic and extrinsic rewards. Simultaneously, implementing successfully a tactic like this will directly address intimate user needs and trigger the formation of a compact online community built around the brand.

- Target all the aforementioned types, in different platforms and with different messages. For a brand, let's say at the beginning of its online life cycle (or at its launch phase in general), gaining awareness of different audiences is crucial. Obviously, the social media, like anything else in marketing, don't comply with the "one size fits all" mentality; therefore, the brand managers should develop a detailed strategy with differentiated content types for each sharer type. Although there is the risk for the brand to become too many things and ultimately confuse recipients, but when the brand values, image, and tone of voice are consistent and congruent with those of the audience, this differentiated tactic can really pay off.

SOCIAL MEDIA AND THE BRAND AS A PERSON

If the social media are a part of an integrated marketing strategy, and this should be the path to follow, h the ultimate outcome is a strong consumer brand relationship that will lead to sustained loyalty. All our efforts as marketers end up to this: to make customers loyal supporters, resistant to the marketing efforts of the competitors, willing to adopt brand extensions and to pay a price premium as they are focused on the overall value of the brand experience and not merely the price (provide source). The 'brand experience' conducive for achieving loyalty is formed through all kinds of interactions between consumers and the brand and is the sum of sensory, affective, intellectual, behavioral and social inputs (Brakus et al., 2009). From this perspective, being part of a brand community, online or offline and enjoying the benefits of participation is a factor for positive evaluation of the brand and engagement in it. As mentioned already, the social media profiles as the locus for community building can serve this purpose in an excellent manner and evolve to a strong competitive advantage.

Following an interesting approach to the evolution of the relationship between the brand and the customer, it is proposed that everything starts as an object-centred engagement; it then becomes a self-centred engagement and, finally, evolves to social engagement (Schmitt, 2012). Those 'layers' reflect an understanding that different needs, motives, and goals result in different psychological levels of engagement. In the first layer, the consumer-brand relationship is a functionally driven engagement, focused on the utilitarian benefits of the brand and driven by traditional marketing practices to induce awareness and to present the functional characteristics of the product/ service. In the second layer, the brand is related to the identity of the consumer, while, on the third level, the brand provides a sense of community. From a similar perceptive, but incorporating the fledging concept of co-creation, another study, led by one author (Kaufmann et al., 2012) of this book illustrates the different roles of the consumer in the relationship with the brand, as follows:

- At the initial stage, the consumer shows a primal attraction to a specific brand and engages in gathering information about it, acting as a browser- a loose relationship similar to the object-centred layer described earlier.
- As congruence between the consumer's values and those of the brand is discovered and the latter evolves to a self-identification medium, the consumer becomes a mingler, a member of a community formed around the brand from people sharing the same values and ideas.
- At the final stage, termed by the authors as "resonance" the consumer becomes an active member of the community, feeling the emotional obligation and commitment towards the group, participating in the creation of the brand and its value. At this point, a consumer brand relationship is a social act, a reward itself reflecting the emerging need of belonging.

To attract the attention of the customers and initiate an object-centred engagement, traditional marketing practices have proven to be very effective. However, as the relationship becomes more self-related, it's the personality of the brand, the human characteristics attached to it (Aaker, 1997; Aggarwal and McGill, 2012) and the emotions developed through experience that defines the nature of engagement. In the final stages of the aforementioned models- social engagement and resonance- the role of the consumer is shifting from that of a passive user to that of a co-creator and active participant in the value

Figure 10. Three stages of engagement
Source: authors

generating process, and the brands are becoming social symbols that signal a coherent group in which brands themselves should actively participate.

Interestingly, social media marketing can moderate the transition from the first stage of utilitarian relationship to a more emotional state as, according to research, increasing consumers' knowledge about a brand (through social media) also increases the emotional attachment to it, regardless if the content of the brand's social communications was functional or emotional in nature (Ashley & Tuten, 2015). From this angle, when social media updates appear on the timeline of users, the latter eventually find themselves not only acquainted with the brand but at the beginning of an emotional relationship, too, given that the content is appealing and self- expressive, of course. Simply put, if consumers systematically like content created and published by a brand, at the end, they find themselves feeling positively towards the brand. Remember what we said earlier, about how daily engagement with a brand impacts on purchase possibilities (Google, 2014). Since we have discussed how people like and/or share content, and the psychological motivation behind it, we understand why brand content needs to be meaningful, not merely promotional, in order to really express oneself and to lead them to demonstrate this self-expression by engaging with the content. This idea of self-expressiveness is ubiquitous in the branding literature following the identity theory that suggests that brand commitment connects an individual to a stable set of self-meanings, which produces consistent lines of activities, such as purchase behavior. Self-expansion theory suggests that consumers communicate with and about brands due to overlapping identities and parasocial relationships with the brands (Ashley & Tuten, 2015). In other words, social media is a field of self-expression and consumers strategically choose those brands

Figure 11.
Source www.piquant.com.sg

IF YOUR BRAND
WAS A PERSON
WOULD YOU BE
FRIENDS?

they will discuss in online communications to construct positive self-images (Schau & Gilly, 2003).

Between the lines, one more condition comes up: for an emotional relationship between the consumer and the brand to occur, the brand must be somehow anthropomorphized and act in the role of brand-as-a-person; and the social media is a great way to obtain this. As observed, brands that used to be perceived as inanimate are becoming humanized through intimate conversations with consumers in the realm of social media (Chen et al., 2015). Indeed, marketing researchers in the field of brand personality, the human characteristics attached to a brand (Aaker, 1997), that make brands act like people, have indicated that consumers are likely to perceive brands to be humanlike social agents with whom they may form relationships. As such, marketers have sought to capitalize on the brand-as-person metaphor by taking advantage of the mechanism by which consumers anthropomorphize brands and interact with them in ways similar to interpersonal communication (Aggarwal and McGill, 2007). In the context of the social media, where users interact with brands in the same manner as they do with their friends, the personification effect is very high, again, with the support of the right content that is not restricted to marketing messages but it matches the recipients' interests and triggers engagement. In fact, engagement has been defined as "the cognitive and affective commitment to an active relationship with the brand as personified by the web site or other computer mediated entities designed to communicate brand value" (Mollen & Wilson, 2010, p. 5). If we look deeper into the mechanisms of anthropomorphism and its extension to brands, Epley et al. (2008) offer a triple faceted explanation:

- First of all, everything we know as humans, including that about the self and others, is somehow taught by or in relation with human beings and the conclusions people derive from ample phenomenological experiences by being humans and observing others. Learning is bonded to humans. Therefore, every time we learn something, as a result of a message sent by a brand, the brand feels like more human-like, as personification messages anchor anthropomorphic inferences about inanimate brands.

- Second, being social and participating in likeminded groups and communities is propelled by people's fundamental need for companionship. Driven by sociality motivation, consumers tend to anthropomorphize inanimate brands and consider them to be sources of social relationships that can fulfill their need for companionship.

- Third, *effectance* motivation refers to people's inclination to perform effective interactions with their surroundings as a means to promote stability. Anthropomorphizing inanimate brands is the only way for a consumer-brand relationship to make sense, in terms of effective relationship management. As such, the interactive platform of social media seems to be a good fit for prompting consumers' tendency to anthropomorphize the nonhuman.

Practically put, let's say you work for a bank and you decide to build a content strategy focused on educating your audiences on subjects related to finance and risk management. You produce a lot of content, you upload it to a dedicated website/ mini site and you deploy a social media marketing plan in order to communicate it to your targeted audiences. Probably some people will actually engage with your content and start engaging with your social media posts and visit your website whenever they are looking for information or answers referring finance or risk management. Having made your website their reference point for this particular subject in a subconscious level, they will start attaching human characteristics to your brand, in order to rationalize what they experience. This will happen as the result of our rebuff to accept that something with no soul or real existence can teach us things and we can actually trust or affectively commit to it- therefore we tend to personify brands. What kind of characteristics they will select to attach, depends on your marketing strategy, the brand image, the tone of voice and general posture the brand maintains throughout the different contact points and of course the archetypes we all have pre-programmed in our minds. The clearer and more coherent the personality, the easier we will relate to it. Therefore, perhaps we should start considering the social media and digital marketing at large, as a one-of-a-kind opportunity to make our brands be perceived as persons worth "hanging out", be "friends" with and ultimately, be loyal to.

Social media as platforms for collaboration, co-creation, and vivid dialogue allow brand managers to build their brands in an experiential and direct way, with the participation of the end users. This paradigm shift has changed the rules of the game, as brands are now initiators but not controllers; they follow the lead of their customers, not the other way round, they are exposed to public criticism and not safe behind closed doors. Although already implied several times in our book so far, this thought is worth another moment: while in the traditional marketing context we tout our messages (by placing them on a magazine or the TV) and we wait for our customers to come, the digital world works the other way round: we closely monitor where our audiences can be found (websites, social media platforms etc) and what they prefer to read and do, we form our marketing plan and we go where they are. This is why we insist so much about the importance of the social media in modern marketing- because if you are trying to go out and find your customers, this is where they will probably be. Being an empathizer (as discussed in chapter one) but also a metrics master, will allow the digital marketer to decode their behaviour and invent new ways to engage with them. And while this analysis and planning takes place in the back end of social media marketing, it's in the front end where the stakes are: there, post by post, comment by comment, tweet by tweet, marketers must infuse like in their brand as if they were a person that people would actually like to be friends with. So, next time you decide to oversee a review or publish a post solely about your brand offerings, think of the following: If you met a person acting like your brand does, would you bother to make them your friends?

WHEN IT COMES TO SOCIAL MEDIA MARKETING, DO IT LIKE A GIRL: CASE STUDY

In 2014, the feminine brand 'Always' launched its iconic #LikeAGirl video campaign, which criticized the social norms which limit the confidence of women. If you've watched it, you'll probably agree that this ad feels like a documentary or an activist video, which makes it incredibly easy to forget that it is indeed just an ad trying to promote a specific product. Yet, the formula worked so well across social media platforms that the brand launched the

Figure 12. Always #LikeAGirl

second installment, under the ambitious title "Unstoppable" but with the same premise and winning hashtag. Once again, always hit it out of the park: in September 2015 alone, #LikeAGirl appeared over 17,200 times on social media, with 180,000 engagements on a global scale (www.talkwalker.com). Always #LikeAGirl generated considerable global awareness and changed the way people think about the phrase 'like a girl', achieving more than 85m global views on YouTube from 150+ countries.

The objective of the campaign was to familiarize young consumers with P&G 's brand positioning to empower girls since adolescence. Based on research findings the creative team built a campaign that was also a social experiment, around the negatively charged phrase "Like a Girl", in order to show that doing things "Like a girl" can be synonymous to doing amazing things. The use of this very straightforward hashtag allowed the users to engage in the conversation globally, around the multiple platforms. According to D&AD, that participated in the campaign design and execution: "prior to watching the film, just 19% of 16-24s had a positive association toward 'like a girl'. After watching, however, 76% said they no longer saw the phrase negatively. Furthermore, two out of three men who watched it said they'd now think twice before using the 'like a girl' as an insult. Always' brand equity showed a strong double digit percentage increase during the course of the campaign while most of its competitors had to cope with slight declines" (www.dandad.com). Six months on, Always ran a 60-second spot highlighting the campaign during the 2015 Super Bowl. Two months later, it released a follow-up video showing how the meaning of the phrase is already changing to mark International Women's Day.

- **What Makes This Campaign a Milestone in Social Media Marketing**: The combination of consumer insights, creativity, and technical knowledge and the strategic integration of the key messages throughout different online and traditional platforms. The marketing team addressed a very pragmatic need, to feel confident, in an inspired execution that made girls around the world feel empowered and vindicated. The video itself (https://www.youtube.com/watch?v=XjJQBjWYDTs) leverages the anticipated emotional responses until they reach a high level of gratification. The use of this one hashtag, the collaboration of different channels and the integration of the campaign with traditional media (i.e. the 60 seconds spot during the 2015 Super Bowl) worked in tandem to produce an award-winning campaign with real and undeniable impact on the brand.

- **Lessons We Learn From This Campaign**: "Always" has moved beyond the narrow boundaries of the product category and has built a campaign that left out the functional characteristics of the product itself but raised the bar, aiming to create value through emotional and "life-changing" elements (Chapter 3). By crafting an emotionally charged brand message, they managed to coil the targeted audiences, to invite them to join a like-minded community and to share a message that was self-expressive to many. Women around the world embraced the message and used the hashtag because they agreed with it and with the purpose of this campaign; their joined effort resulted to a change of perception about the "Like a girl" characterization, and this is a co-created achievement that the brand and its community can be proud of. Note that, despite the focus of the entire project and its objective to be relatable, the brand values where present throughout the campaign, coherently demonstrated in the different platforms. Contrary to the Chino San Pellegrino case we discussed in chapter 3, here we have an example of aligned internal and external messages broadcasted in a clear and coherent manner that brought together a community of targeted consumers with strengthening the brand equity.

Answers

- Apart from the thorough penetration of the social media in a way that changed our ways and behaviors, they are compelling marketing channels. Marketers are presented with the opportunity to build a reputation and coil brand fans around a community that will become the source of competitive advantage. The variety of social media platforms offers unique alternatives of targeting, even in very well determined niche markets, in an unprecedented way that can make today's marketing effective on much more levels than before.

- Social media marketing raises brand awareness and liking and subtly creates an emotional connection, as consumers are systematically exposed to branded content. By leading social media users to the website or landing pages, the brand enjoys indirect benefits, including more traffic, hence, better ranking in the search engines etc. Additionally, there is compelling evidence that social media engagement impacts directly on sales performance, as users engaging regularly with a brand will more likely proceed to an online or offline transaction than those who don't. From a relational viewpoint, social media activity allows users to build and manifest their identity and provides them with intrinsic, participatory benefits as they develop a feeling of belonging to larger groups of like-minded users (pages & communities).

- Social media penetration is overwhelming and almost universal in the age group of 18-29, but there are some psychological characteristics that define our "virtual" behavior. Researchers have found that, contrary to the past when internet was the safe place for the introverts, avid social media users today tend to be extroverts and open to new ideas and experiences. The use of the social media for entertainment rather than informativeness, a preference that is backed up with findings showing that social media use is positively related to emotional instability; this means that when we feel down we are seeking comfort on Facebook, Twitter etc. Therefore, sharing, participating and having fun are the key drivers of engagement online, a useful triplet for the digital marketer.

- The typology of 6 sharer tribes (altruists, careerists, hipsters, boomerangs, connectors, selectives) adds a useful segmentation method to online and social media marketing. Depending on the life cycle stage and the marketing objectives, digital tactics can be focused on a single tribe and target it with tailor-made content to accommodate their needs and maximize engagement. Or, they can be crafted for multiple tribes, going for higher reach, as long as messages throughout the platforms maintain the same values and tone of voice.

- In their effort to rationalize their emotional connection to a brand, people tend to humanize and attach human characteristics to them, and when they succeed, they easily identify themselves with these brands. Engaging in an actual dialogue through the social media, learning and exchanging knowledge and participating in a community where the brand -through the voice of its representatives- acts like a person, is an excellent way to anthropomorphize the inanimate brand and initiate strong emotional bonds that couldn't be developed with impersonal corporate and names.

REFERENCES

Aaker, J. L. (1997). Dimensions of brand personality. *JMR, Journal of Marketing Research*, *34*(3), 347–356. doi:10.2307/3151897

Adage.com. (2015). *What the changing role of social media means for brands.* Retrieved from http://adage.com/article/digitalnext/tv-s-influence-consumer-behavior-decreases/297501/

Aggarwal, P., & McGill, A. L. (2012). When Brands Seem Human, Do Humans Act Like Brands? Automatic Behavioral Priming Effects of Brand Anthropomorphism. *The Journal of Consumer Research*, *39*(2), 307–323. doi:10.1086/662614

Alhabash, S., McAlister, A. R., Lou, C., & Hagerstrom, A. (2015). From Clicks to Behaviors: The Mediating Effect of Intentions to Like, Share, and Comment on the Relationship Between Message Evaluations and Offline Behavioral Intentions. *Journal of Interactive Advertising*, *15*(2), 82–96. doi:10.1080/15252019.2015.1071677

Amichai-Hamburger, Y., & Ben-Artzi, E. (2003). Loneliness and Internet use. *Computers in Human Behavior*, *19*(1), 71–80. doi:10.1016/S0747-5632(02)00014-6

Ashley, C., & Tuten, T. (2015). Creative strategies in social media marketing: An exploratory study of branded social content and consumer engagement. *Psychology and Marketing, 32*(1), 15–27. doi:10.1002/mar.20761

Bargh, J. A., McKenna, K. Y., & Fitzsimons, G. M. (2002). Can you see the real me? Activation and expression of the true self on the Internet. *The Journal of Social Issues, 58*(1), 33–48. doi:10.1111/1540-4560.00247

Brakus, J. J., Schmitt, B. H., & Zarantonello, L. (2009). Brand experience: What is it? How is it measured? Does it affect loyalty? *Journal of Marketing, 73*(3), 52–68. doi:10.1509/jmkg.73.3.52

Chen, K., Lin, J., Choi, J. H., & Hahm, J. M. (2015). Would You Be My Friend? An Examination of Global Marketers Brand Personification Strategies in Social Media. *Journal of Interactive Advertising, 15*(2), 97–110. doi:10.1080/15252019.2015.1079508

CmoSurvey.com. (2015). *The CMO Survey: Highlights and Insights.* Retrieved from https://cmosurvey.org/wp-content/uploads/sites/11/2015/09/The_CMO_Survey-Highlights_and_Insights-Aug-2015.pdf

Correa, T., Hinsley, A.W., & De Zuniga, H. G. (2010). Who interacts on the Web?: The intersection of users personality and social media use. *Computers in Human Behavior, 26*(2), 247–253. doi:10.1016/j.chb.2009.09.003

Dandad.org. (2015). *Case Study: Always #LikeAGirl.* Retrieved from http://www.dandad.org/en/d-ad-leo-burnett-holler-always-likeagirl-campaign-case-study/

Dessart, L., Veloutsou, C., & Morgan-Thomas, A. (2015). Consumer engagement in online brand communities: A social media perspective. *Journal of Product and Brand Management, 24*(1), 28–42. doi:10.1108/JPBM-06-2014-0635

Dholakia, U. M., & Vianello, S. (2009). *The Fans Know Best.* Retrieved from http://www.wsj.com/articles/SB10001424052970204482304574222062946162306

eMarketer.com. (2013a). *Advertisers boost social ad budgets in 2013.* Retrieved from http://www.emarketer.com/Article/Advertisers-Boost-Social-Ad-Budgets- 2013/1009688 eMarketer.com. (2013b). *B2Cs, B2Bs See Digital, Social Ad Spend Rising, as Traditional Stalls*. Retrieved from http://www.emarketer.com/Article/ B2Cs-B2Bs-See-Digital-Social-Ad-Spend-Rising-Traditional-Stalls/1010270

eMarketer.com. (2014). *Social Ad Spending per User Remains Highest in North America*. Retrieved from http://www.emarketer.com/Article/Social-Ad-Spending-per-User-Remains-Highest-North-America/1010505

Epley, N., Waytz, A., Akalis, S., & Cacioppo, J. T. (2008). When we need a human: Motivational determinants of anthropomorphism. *Social Cognition*, *26*(2), 143–155. doi:10.1521/soco.2008.26.2.143

Forrester Research. (2013). *Engaged Social Followers Are Your Best Customers*. Retrieved from http://go.wf-social.com/rs/wildfire/images/ REPORT_Forrester_Best_Customers.pdf

Googleapis.com. (2014). *Brand Engagement in the participation age*. Retrieved from https://think.storage.googleapis.com/docs/brand-engagement-in-participation-age_research-studies.pdf

Hamburger, Y. A., & Ben-Artzi, E. (2000). The relationship between extraversion and neuroticism and the different uses of the Internet. *Computers in Human Behavior*, *16*(4), 441–449. doi:10.1016/S0747-5632(00)00017-0

Heidicohen.com. (2011). *Social Media definitions*. Retrieved from www. heidicohen.com/social-media-definition

Ho-Dac, N. N., Carson, S. J., & Moore, W. I. (2013). The Effects of Positive and Negative Online Customer Reviews: Do Brand Strength and Category Maturity Matter? *Journal of Marketing*, *77*(November), 37–53. doi:10.1509/ jm.11.0011

Kaufmann, H. (2012). The increasing dynamics between consumers, social groups and brands. *Qualitative Market Research: An International Journal*, *15*(4), 404–419. doi:10.1108/13522751211257088

Meshi, D., Morawetz, C., & Heekeren, H. R. (2013). Nucleus accumbens response to gains in reputation for the self relative to gains for others predicts social media use. *Frontiers in Human Neuroscience*, *7*, 439. doi:10.3389/ fnhum.2013.00439 PMID:24009567

Mollen, A., & Wilson, H. (2010). Engagement, telepresence and interactivity in online consumer experience: Reconciling scholastic and managerial perspectives. *Journal of Business Research*, *63*(9), 919–925. doi:10.1016/j. jbusres.2009.05.014

Naaman, M., Boase, J., & Lai, C. H. (2010, February). Is it really about me? message content in social awareness streams. *Proceedings of the 2010 ACM conference on Computer supported cooperative work*, 189-192. doi:10.1145/1718918.1718953

Pew Research Center. (2015). *Social Media Usage: 2005-2015*. Retrieved from http://www.pewinternet.org/2015/10/08/social-networking-usage-2005-2015/

Piquant.com.sg. (2014). *How brand personality outshines brand attributes*. Retrieved from http://www.piquant.com.sg/brand-personality-outshines-strong-attributes/

Schaefer, M. (2015). *The Content Code: Six essential strategies to ignite your content, your marketing and your business*. Library of Congress Cataloging-in-Publication Data.

Schau, H., & Gilly, M. (2003). We are what we post? Self presentation in personal web space. *The Journal of Consumer Research*, *30*(3), 385–404. doi:10.1086/378616

Schmitt, B. (2012). The consumer psychology of brands. *Journal of Consumer Psychology*, *22*(1), 7–17. doi:10.1016/j.jcps.2011.09.005

Statista.com. (2014). *Global Social Networks Ranked by Number of uses*. Retrieved from http://www.statista.com/statistics/272014/global-social-networks-ranked-by-number-of-users/

StatPro. (2013). *The psychology of sharing* [Infographic]. Retrieved from http://www.statpro.com/blog/psychology-of-sharing-infographic/

Stelzner, M. (2016). *Social Media Marketing Industry Report*. Retrieved from http://www.socialmediaexaminer.com/report/

Talkwalker.com. (2015). *5 great social media campaigns to inspire your 2016 Marketing Strategy*. Retrieved from http://blog.talkwalker.com/en/5-social-media-campaigns-inspiration-2016-strategy-social-media-analytics/

The New York Times. (2011). *The Psychology of Sharing: Why do people share online*. Retrieved from http://nytmarketing.whsites.net/mediakit/pos/

Waspbarcode.com. (2015). *State of Small Business Report*. Retrieved from http://www.waspbarcode.com/small-business-report?utm_source=Webbiquity.com&utm_medium=social

Zhu, Y., & Chen, H. (2015). Social media and human need satisfaction: Implications for social media marketing. *Business Horizons, 58*(3), 335–345. doi:10.1016/j.bushor.2015.01.006

Chapter 5

Content is King:
The Role of Content Management in Online Marketing

ABSTRACT

This chapter is dedicated to the fledging issue of content, in terms of the different types of media and information posted on the social media and relevant platforms to broadcast the brand messages and to engage the consumers. This specific theme of content strategy is one of the major novelties introduced in digital marketing, as not only there is no equivalent in the traditional context but the digital marketer needs to adopt a new mindset and break some well-established boundaries. Besides the different content development approaches, we also discuss the different ways to attract and build an audience, applying techniques, both for organic and paid growth, as an engaged audience can be a valuable source of competitive advantage for the brands and the companies.

Questions

1. Why does not always the strongest survive in the internet?
2. How can the content become as important as the product/ service?
3. How does the marketing mix change when applied online?
4. What has leadership to do with content?

DOI: 10.4018/978-1-68318-012-8.ch005

INTRODUCTION

In the previous chapters of this book, there is a lot of discussion about the content, the related strategies and why they are so important. Even only one minute in the social media will make the problem very visible: too many posts (tweets, pins, photos etc.) - too little time. With our attention span reduced to 8 seconds, according to a recent Microsoft research (Watson, 2015) and our augmented ability to do multiple things at a time without really focusing on any (Deichman, 2010), it has become a real challenge for marketers to attract and keep the users' eyes on their content. The new reality today has exposed us to a plethora of articles written about any given subject, and we face the enormous, unstoppable production of content, surmounting the demand. New standards emerge for marketers but also for content consumers. This is not a hype nor a newly emerging trend: As humans, we have the fundamental need to promote ourselves, support our beliefs and share our ideas (Zhu & Chen, 2015), and when we get the feedback we are expecting, for our brains this is a rewarding equivalent to sex, money and social acceptance (Meshi et al., 2013). With over one million selfies taken per day, we are clearly living in the era of "me-formation", where literally our favorite subject of talking and sharing is ourselves. Remember the Rutgers University research in Chapter 5, about the streams of "me-formation" flooding the Internet (Naaman et al., 2010). The marketer really has to deal with the following challenge: the digital environment is too noisy, too cluttered, and the bar rises to the level of producing and sharing content that, when compared with "me" content, posted by friends and relatives, it will win the contest and grab the user's attention. How can we do this?

In an attempt to compare traditional and digital marketing, we often talk about a shift in focus: beyond the Service Dominant Logic to a new era of Co-Creation Dominant logic (Kaufmann & Manarioti, 2016). Traditional marketing is mostly about the products/ services and the brand, and, even when it is customer-focused and behavioral, the presence of the company is intense throughout the communication. For example, there is probably zero possibility to watch a TV commercial where the product will be absent or the brand logo will not be presented. Traditional marketers are used to talking about their products; one could say they are addicted to it, as the business pendant to me-formation, except that the discussion is not focused on a person but on the brand. Relating this mindset to the online context means that the brands will produce and share content that will promote and advertise their product/ services, stores, and offers. In addition, brand managers will prominently place this content in front of the users, pushing the information to them scheduling a TV commercial or a print ad. This is a successfully tested practice with only one shortcoming: the content will be ignored, because online plays by other rules than offline. In the online marketing context, it is not the strongest but the most interesting and relevant one that survives; the focus is on what is useful for the readers, what matches their interests, what type of content they want to consume. As discussed in Chapter 5, digital marketers go where consumers are (Ashley & Tuten, 2015) and tailor their means and messages to fit in the small area where the brand's purpose and the interest and the need of the user converge. This is why puppies, kittens, and funny gifs are prominently featured on brand pages, and it's this new mindset that constitutes the major shift that is the cornerstone of content creation in modern marketing.

CONTENT AS A PRODUCT

In the digital marketing vocabulary, content is anything posted on websites and social media- from blog posts to status updates and from selfies to the bucket challenge video series. Everyone is a potential content creator, including people, NGOs, celebrities, brands, and, judging from Instagram, even pets. Back at the outset of the internet, the best regarded content was usually the most visible- a kind of digital fairness and justice due to the relevant scarcity of supply. But, due to the immense production of content today, getting a share of voice online is neither easy nor straightforward, although strokes of luck will still occur if your product catches the eye of Kanye West, for example. In most cases, however, success is the result of hard and smart marketing effort: research, planning and consistent execution, on a daily or even hourly basis. The task is to identify what the targeted audiences are interested in, to produce original and interesting content. This content should balance between showcasing the brand voice and values, but avoid screaming "buy my product now", and be interesting and relatable to the targeted audiences. Then, this content need to be disseminated through the different platforms in order to end up to the proper timelines. A helpful guideline here is the 70-20-10 rule (SmartInsights.com, 2016):

Figure 1. General Electric Instagram feed from June 2016
Source: Instagram.com

- 70% of the content created by a brand should target brand reputation, therefore be compatible with the users' preferences and shareable. This is why brands like Kraft (kraftrecipes.com) invest in recipe related blogs, Philadelphia Cheese Facebook page is full of ideas for creative cooking, Maybelline excels in producing makeup tutorials, while GE's & Nasa 's Instagram feeds are full of eye-catching images and quotes. All the above achieve very high engagement levels through creating content that it is interesting and easy to share, related to the brand but not trying to hard sell.

- 20% of the content created should be more premier content, and more costly, designed to attract new audiences, like viral videos or infographics- like the Unique Connection Mother's Day Video for Pandora Jewels or the Two Bellmen Movie for Marriott Hotels. Both projects were very innovative and well executed, they gained the attention and engagement of the audience and obviously absorbed a large share of money, time and effort.

- 10% of the content should be promotional, technical or more "risky". Mostly functional content to inform about offers, product extensions, characteristics etc. Although it is too brand focused to become viral, the users that are engaged in the rest of the brand content, probably are willing to accept this kind of messages, when broadcasted rarely and in a non-intrusive manner.

Figure 2. An illustration of the 70-20-10 rule

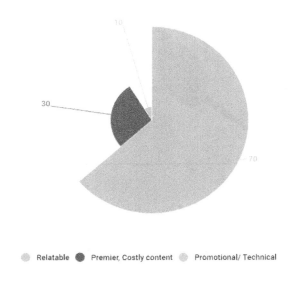

Figure 3. An illustration of the 80-20 rule

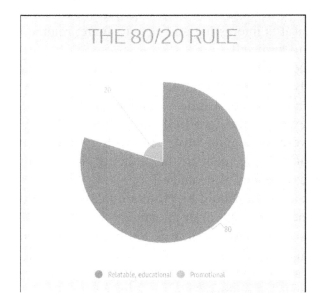

A close proximate to the 70-20-10 rule is the 80/20 rule, inspired by the popular Pareto concept. The 80/20 rule (Pulizzi, 2010) suggests that the 80% of the content we create and share should be interesting for our audience, educational, relatable, in other words focused on what our audiences what to read about. Then, the remaining 20% can be promotional, talking about products, offers, sales etc.

Finally, there is the rule of thirds, proposing that our content should be trisected as follows (www.relevance.com, 2014):

- One third of what we publish should be about our business (an equivalent of the 20% promotional content of the Pareto rule).
- One third should be educational and interesting, related to the industry and valuable for your audience.
- Then, the final third should aim to present a more human aspect of the brand, with direct conversation with consumers, photos of the teams, sharing personal thoughts etc.

Figure 4. Rule of thirds
Source: www.relevance.com

1/3 is about your BUSINESS	1/3 is about INDUSTRY TOPICS & TRENDS	1/3 is about YOU
Example 1: Company blog posts.	Example 1: Blog posts from industry experts.	Example 1: Respond to a tweet you found useful or interesting.
Example 2: Company webinars, seminars and networking events.	Example 2: Share a helpful ebook with your own insights and thoughts.	Example 2: Talk about a big event going on in your city.
Example 3: Sharing information about new products & services.	Example 3: A helpful presentation from Slideshare or a TED talk.	Example 3: Ask questions to your network.

Although different in the percentage distribution, all three rules have a commonplace: Brands should not talk too much about themselves and their achievements, otherwise they will alienate audiences. Contrary, they should get "put their pride aside and share other businesses' content" (Hootsuite, 2014) and include content curation in their strategies. Content curation is the "act of discovering, gathering, and presenting digital content that surrounds specific subject matter" (Mullan, 2011) and it differs from content creation as it refers to re-use existing content rather than generating new. By sharing or reposting interesting articles, inspirational quotes, innovative thoughts etc from sources that are related to the brand's industry, we comply with the content rules (all of them), we save time and we present an extrovert and social personality for our brand. As we previously discussed about the idea of a brand as a person, publishing only about products and offerings is like those people that only talk about themselves- and that we mostly tend to avoid, aren't we?

Although there is a lot of research and case studies to back up this content analogies, but according to a 2015 research most brands are still preferring functional content rather than experiential and emotional one, and they are heavily relying on discounts in order to trigger engagement (Ashley & Tuten, 2015). However, in the same way sales promotions may stimulate preference but jeopardize loyalty, as they motivate price sensitive behaviours, tactics like coupons, discounts, and other extrinsic rewards will not produce valuable long-term engagement. This is the first part of the answer to those who might wonder why don't we just skip the part of content that is not about us and publish only what is really useful- and sales-related- for the brand. The second part is more technical but very critical: it is because of the way the internet works, the search engines and the social media algorithms. Google, Facebook and all social media platforms select their organic (meaning not paid) results based on some signals of relevance and significance. As already discussed in Chapter 2, the reputation and authority of the source and the structure and keywords of the content are very determinant for the search engine optimization and page ranking. Facebook, and the other platforms are monitoring users' behavior to find preference signals: when a user interacts with a page and a specific type of media, the algorithm selects content compatible with these terms to present on the user timeline organically. So, if we build a strategy founded on our brand positioning but elaborated outside the narrow limits of product communication by producing videos, infographics, blog posts, images, podcasts etc. that are really relevant to our audiences, latter will probably reward us with their like, share, retweet, repost etc. Their behavior will be recorded by the social media algorithms as a sign of approval and our following posts will have higher chances to get organic reach. Simply put, we try to give our audiences reasons to systematically engage with our content, in order to boost our organic reach along with the benefits mentioned in the previous chapter (awareness, familiarity that leads to preference, sales boost).

A very important parameter for organic reach is also frequency, as sporadic posting is not appreciated, since it cannot support the premise of authority. Moreover, like poor copywrite is no good for SEO, a partly inactive social media account is no good for organic reach. There is a lot of research on the optimal posting, and the numbers change constantly, but as for now we can rely on an approximation like the one shown below:

Therefore, to build authority and reputation and to trigger engagement, a brand has to maintain a consistent online presence by producing frequently large volumes of fresh and relevant content. In this aspect, the 70% proportion of the content that will be easy to like and share is the passport to brand reputation and audience population, to start with. The brands are encouraged to speak in an integrated voice throughout the communication, but the content itself is user-driven or even user generated. While building an online reputation in an affordable and effective manner, brand managers can invest in more costly media, like developing games, writing E-books, conducting extensive surveys, producing videos and animations, building microsites or brand content tools etc. This will build brand authority and communicate the brand essence. This material is definitely more brand focused but it is *relevant to* targeted audiences' preferences. For example, the WESTIN hotels developed an Out of the office message generator (westinooogenerator.com) to compose ready to share out of the office messages. The concept is brand related and promoting, the website is fun and easy to use and the users have many reasons to engage with the service. The remaining 10% of the content that is informational and promotional will benefit from the organic reach obtained by the 90% strategy, so even if it is not the first choice of the target audience for their timeline, they will probably accept it and allow it- at least they will not hide it and unfollow the page.

Following the insights provided to us by Persado (persado.com), the developer of a cognitive content platform, "that generates language that inspires action", our reactions variate depending on the language and specific words we are using in our content- headers, Call-to-actions etc. – and their emotional and motivational cues. In one of their case studies, for a large US organization aiming to raise awareness through a Facebook photo contest, a change in phrasing resulted in 213% raise in photo submissions and a 74.8%

Figure 5. Infographic: optimal social media posting frequency

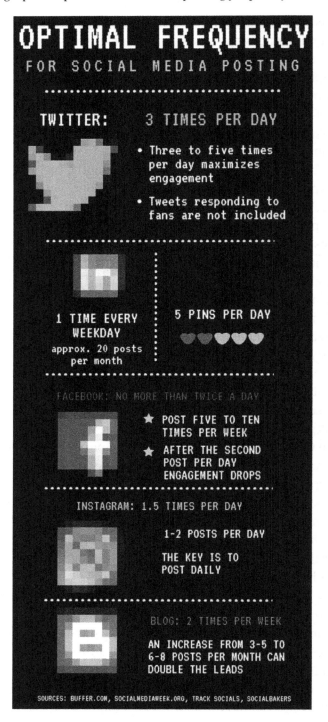

decrease in the cost per click. For the process, the Company provided Persado with one original Facebook ad message to optimize and four images to test in the process. With that, Persado machine-generated 16 message variations to run a one-week test on a subset of Company's Facebook audience. After deploying the variations, Persado analyzed campaign results to amalgamate those 16 messages into the single best message. The Company broadcast the amalgamated message to the remainder of their target audience. Naturally, we asked for extra details on how it works- and we are thankful for the interview provided at the end of the chapter- and here is what we've found out about how cognitive content creation works: After learning the precise words and phrases to inspire action for the Company's audience, Persado's cognitive content generator concluded the most powerful customer triggers:

- The top three performing variants featured the same image with different text, demonstrating the power of choosing the right images can yield.
- The headline provided by the company was: "Enter for a chance to win". Yet, the proposed "Click here to take a look" is directional and more functional/CTA-like in nature, and is effective because it piques curiosity.
- This message "Announcing a photo contest" was selected over the "Help us celebrate with a photo contest". Language that falls under the Fascination emotional category ("Announcing"), paired with an explicit mention of what is being advertised ("Homepage PhotoContest") proved to be the best compelling message.

TO BUILD AN AUDIENCE

While the internet and social media users produce "me-formational" content, brand content cannot be self-referential, rather it has to be relevant and interesting enough to make users identify with it and give it a vote of confidence by liking/ sharing it etc. But in an over-crowded, saturated online environment, the question arises as to what content is good and relevant enough to make it to the timeline? The answer is out there, in the mind of the existing and potential consumers, in the preferences, habits, needs and fears of our personas. Whilst in traditional marketing, first we segment and target, in digital marketing, first, we build our personas, in terms of content they consume, types of media they prefer, social media behaviour etc. and themes

Figure 6. Creating relevant content
Source: http://contentmarketinginstitute.com/

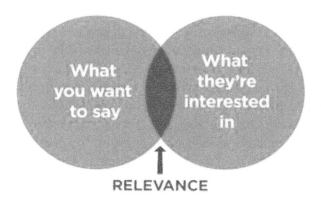

they engage in. As figure 3 illustrates, understanding what consumers are interested in and where it converges with the brand messages, is the starting point for crafting a relevant content strategy.

In his book, Content Inc., Joe Pulizzi, whose own personal experience has made him the evangelist of audience building, supports that "the absolute best way to start a business today is not by launching a product, but by creating a system to attract and build an audience. Once a loyal audience is built, one that loves you and the information you send, you can most likely, sell your audience anything you want" (Pulizzi, 2015 p.18). In other words, building a loyal audience can be the source of a very strong competitive advantage while their loyalty will make them receptive to new ideas, new products etc. The audience here is a close proximate to the community and, again, as extensively discussed in Chapter 3, the center of the conversation is co-creation and how we trigger it. Both, in communities and in audiences, the objective is to generate a vivid conversation; therefore, honesty and trust are key points for success. Of course, building an audience in such a noisy environment is not an easy task as it is very common for good content to pass unnoticed. A good tactic to help the content "ignite" is to identify and focus on your "Alpha Audience", those members that tend to be more active and also have an influencing power to others (Schaefer, 2015). Crafting strategies to approach and motivate will create a multiplying factor of reputation, as those influencers will become the brand advocates and will initiate a circle of word of web. Furthermore, as explained in Chapter 4, when the content will become self-expressive, when members of the community will use it in order to communicate their own identity to others, then the brand becomes a social construct, a bearer of meaning for a community of loyal fans and ultimately brand users. Thus, what Pulizzi has been advocating for is that, if marketers manage to produce content that is so interesting and engaging for a group of people, they will, in turn, respond and follow the brand, get to know it and develop emotions for and ties with it, even if they have never used it in their lives, and that is a good premise to convert them to consumers. From this perspective, the content IS the product, the starting point, and all the rest will follow.

Types of Content

So far, we have already established why we need high quality and frequent content relevant to the target audiences' interests spread around the internet, through the social media, the search engines or other websites. Now, we will look at the different types of content that marketers can use and select from. Note, that each type is more appropriate for one objective or another and that the various types are better when used combined.

Photos/Illustrations

Images are so powerful that some social media, like Instagram, Snapchat and Pinterest are mainly built around them. Images are quickly processed and easily understood, both on a cognitive and emotional level, while they are eye-catching and, mainly, sharable. Images can be used in texts and websites to make the reading more pleasant, or posted separately in the social media. Although images usually are part of the 70% of the content structure, when marked with the brand logo and conforming to a specific style for the visual content, each of them contributes to build the brand identity. Since images and illustrations are the backbones of content sharing and despite the handy tools like Canva and Pablo, it might be recommendable to work with a professional graphic designer, who will make the best out of your photos, produce really relevant content and unleash the potential of your brand.

Blog Posts

In content-intense time, blogs are essentials to any marketer as an easy and effective avenue for knowledge expression and opinion sharing. Building a blog is not very demanding, in terms of technical requirements, but maintaining a blog needs discipline and effort. As discussed earlier, a minimum of two high quality, interesting posts per week is required for being considered 'in the game'. However, having a blog allows the marketers to:

- Create content that is interesting for their audience, from how-tos and tutorials to generic posts on subjects that are loosely related to the brand and capturing for the readers;
- Obtain authority on specific keywords by building blog posts around them and by using these posts as landing pages;
- Set the brand tone of voice and share the brand's opinions and values and so many more uses.

It is not an exaggeration to say that, especially but not exclusively for the B2B sector, blogs are a must.

Videos

It is every digital marketer's dream that one of their brand videos becomes viral and conquers YouTube and the Internet at large, but mostly it remains wishful thinking. Brand videos have to be entertaining, but also relatable and expressive, if they are to be shared and to have a chance in virality. This type of content is very articulate and helpful in storytelling, while quite demanding in skills and resources, but internet users like videos, and they show their preference for them on any given occasion. Brands like GoPro and Red Bull have built their entire marketing strategy around videos, but even smaller brands can benefit even from minimum use, like adding a "meet our team" footage on their "About us" webpage.

Newsletters

It is a widespread tactic among marketers and a good option to create and share content, as long as the recipients' lists are built legitimately, with the consensus of the users to avoid being flagged as spam. Newsletters can reinforce the sense of community, especially when offering exclusive benefits to members, can bring traffic and engagement to the websites and keep the brand in the mind of the customers in a valuable and meaningful way. What matters about the structure of the newsletter is not different than for other content: Headlines, subject lines, and articles must be interesting for the recipients; otherwise, they will refrain from opening it or receiving it altogether. The newsletter is not, however, an independent piece of content; it is the pathway to the website and other owned channels. From this perspective, the objective of the newsletter is to generate traffic for the website as it obtains high open and click rates and click rates gained through interesting articles, eye catching images, and useful tools that are all accompanied by a link towards the original source.

Case Studies/White Papers/E-Books

Quite demanding in terms of time and effort, case studies, white papers, and e-books are very appropriate for the 20% tier of the content strategy. Designed to educate rather than sell and with low chances to become viral, these three types of content are more sophisticated, yet very useful for niche market penetration. By sharing knowledge, elaborating on complex concepts or explaining technical characteristics and processes, brands communicate their in-depth knowledge and build authority in specific strategic areas. Particularly for the e-books, they can be used as additional sources of income if the brand managers decide to sell them rather than to give them away as promotional content.

Presentations, Podcasts, and Webinars

The other side of the same coin relating to knowledge sharing, presentations, podcasts, and webinars are a more vivid and direct way to explain and educate consumers. Additionally to the benefits mentioned for the previous triplet, these content types provide marketers with access to new platforms, like Slide share for presentations, iTunes, and Sound Cloud for Podcasts, Udemy for webinars etc.

Infographics

They are considered to be highly sharable as the combination of image and data makes even complex concepts seem understandable. Benefiting from the power of the image but enhanced by the significance of the numbers, infographics provide the marketers with a creative, memorable way to access niche audiences and trigger conversations.

Q&A

The latest updates on the popular social media platforms signal the beginning of the life social events era, and Q&A can be an interesting concept to explore. Either in terms of discussion through comments, hashtags or tweets or with life oral responses by brand representatives, Q & A events are a great way to actively engage with the consumers, to humanize the brand while building a reputation for being direct and supportive.

Mobile Apps and Branded Tools

Both, apps and branded tools are designed to be helpful to the users and to support them in performing specific tasks. From templates to calculators, from maps to guides, from logo to out of the office generators, these tools can be very useful material for exposure to new audiences but also engagement with existing ones. As downloading a mobile app or signing in to download a template is 'an opt' in for engagement, marketers have the opportunity to directly interact with their audience and start a conversation with them.

Microsites

According to Hubspot, "a microsite is an individual web page or small cluster of web pages that act as a separate entity for a brand. A microsite typically lives on its own domain, but some exist as a subdomain" (Hubspot.com, 2016). Microsites are used to communicate a brand's focus on a specific area or to create and engage a likeminded community, like in the case of www. kraftrecipes.com or the www.fu2016.com for The House of Cards.

While crafting their content strategy, the digital marketer first decides on the objectives, and then will translate them into themes. Depending on the audiences and the themes themselves different types of content will be used for every occasion, and then their dissemination will be scheduled and put in paper. At this point, let us introduce the notion of "re-purposing", meaning transforming the content into different types in order to address different audiences or gain access to other platforms and social media. For example, an article posted on a blog can be re-purposed as an infographic, as a presentation, and as a podcast; a webinar can be reused as an e-book, a presentation, and a podcast etc. This is not only a smart way to maximize the impact of each piece of content, but it also creates a multiplier for the content creator by making each piece to three.

ABOUT THE HASHTAGS

Closely related to content, the hashtags are a great way to initiate or join a conversation across platforms and allow the brand to access new audiences or to interact with existing ones. Instagram is based on the hashtags with the recommended number for each post to be at least 11; Facebook still struggles to actively put them into use but their effect is questionable: more than 3 per post have a negative impact on reach and engagement. And Twitter launched the visual hashtags taking technology and implementation a step further; so obviously, hashtags are here to stay. What is interesting, however, is that marketers are not yet familiar with their strategic use, and it is quite common to witness hashtag misuses or failures.

First of all, for a hashtag to be successful and to become viral, it has to be simple and to make sense, as in the #LikeAGirl case we mentioned in Chapter 5. Brand related hashtags are very useful as they become a kind of signature for the brand, a word or phrase that connects brand fans around the globe and the Internet, like the #ShareACoke for Coca-Cola, the #JustDoIt or Nike or the #PutACanOnIt Red Bull Campaign. It is also common for the brands to initiate campaigns or contests to trigger the use of the hashtag until it becomes popular enough.

Another very interesting use of hashtags is when brands follow trending topics and join the conversation with their brand voice but like a person would

Figure 7.

do. Apart from making the brands look very much like humans, this kind of interaction opens the doors to new audiences of people that follow the trend, not the brand. A great example is how Denny's Diner (@DennysDiner) joined the #Collegein5words trending topic with the hashtag of the photo below:

As seen by the like and retweet numbers, this gesture was much appreciated, and it fostered the brand's reputation and its humorous brand voice.

Brands can also either launch or participate in chat hashtags like the Super Bowl game hashtags #SB51, #SB52 etc. Users attend and join the conversation by typing the hashtag, and so can brands do, gaining the same benefits as in the trendy hashtags case. Finally, content related, generic hashtags can be used by brands for searchability and optimization purposes but also to highlight brand values. Some examples are the #Eggseverywhere posts by Cadbury (@cardbudyuk), the #pride or #summer post by Tesla (@Teslamotors) or how Spotify uses the artists' hashtags to be listed in their results as well.

For brands that aim to build and sustain communities, hashtags are very powerful and straightforward tools. However, since they have no equivalent in the traditional marketing universe, marketers must spend some time and effort to understand their use, their value, and their strategic usefulness.

TRADITIONAL: DIGITAL MARKETING INTEGRATION AND THE ONLINE MARKETING MIX

At this point, we have already covered some critical subjects on digital marketing that are mandatory to be understood before starting the e-marketing mix conversation. As the context, the media and mostly the customer behavior are different, the traditional approach not only is insufficient but it will probably be unsuccessful as well. As repeatedly mentioned, digital marketing demands a shift in the marketer's mind. Having said that, we will borrow from the classic marketing literature the popular scheme of the 4Ps in order to structure its equivalent to the digital terms and practices: first the e-product, then the e-price, following the e-place and ultimately the e-promotion.

First of all, what is really the product on the internet? How can we compensate for the feeling that customers normally have when they enter into a shop where they can actually touch or smell a product? Can we deliver the same benefits online? And will it be enough to turn them into loyal customers, which is the constant pursuit of any marketer?

Figure 8. Elements of the e-product

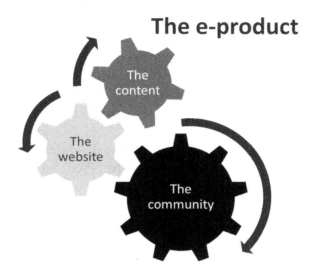

The online product is not one thing, it is the sum of many: first comes the web design, as discussed in Chapter 2. It is the equivalent of the store and the closer it is to the users' needs and expectations the better the user experience. This is followed by the content, as we are currently discussing it, the production and dissemination of online material that express the brand values in a relatable way that will attract and engage the targeted audiences around a brand community. Last, but definitely not least, the brand community is an integral part of the online product to be considered, as it is the locus of co-creation and participation for the brand and its members. Therefore, when we are talking about what we "sell" online, we must address all three aspects of tactics and campaigns as parts of a digital marketing strategy, otherwise, we will be kept behind by our traditional marketing mindsets.

When it comes to the e-price, one can say that it really challenges traditional selling approaches. Now, just with a click, users can find and compare prices, e.g. www.trivago.com and get the best deal. For the company, this is a pressing factor as they are called either to re-structure their costs in order to offer competitive pricing, i.e. by investing in technology or to augment the value by adding other benefits, like emotional, experiential or participatory ones. Neither online nor offline the focus on the price is a good recipe for building loyalty, and particularly on the internet, where price comparison is easier than ever, branding and community building have become more critical building blocks of the success.

Another common activity in terms of e-pricing are online auctions where the consumers determine the price as exemplified by EBay. The concept of price discrimination is similar and it refers "to selling products to different people and groups based on their willingness to pay" (Laudon and Trevor, 2011, p.441). The internet provides the marketer with the tools and insights to identify these groups and address them accordingly while the consumers are behaving as co-creators, able to co- determine the price they want to pay for the product.

As a result of the unhindered access to a vast volume of free information and knowledge, brands occasionally adopt the "Free and Freemium" pricing strategy, as a promotional tactic, as a part of the content strategy or as a bait in order to persuade users to buy long-term memberships. "This freemium pricing model is a cross-subsidy online marketing strategy where users are offered a basic service for free, but must pay for premium or add-on service. The people who pay for the premium services hopefully will pay for all the free riders on the service. Skype uses a freemium model: millions of users can call other Skype users on the Internet for free, but there is a charge for calling a landline or cell phone" (op.cit., p.443). Policies like the free trial or anytime cancellation have proven to be very successful as they make it easy for the consumers to try, with no strings attached; while the companies transfer the power to them, they are able to stay or leave whenever they want. This transfer of power is very compatible with the balance on the internet, as the user is the captain in all relationships; brands respond and follow their leads.

Usually, after the free and freemiums come the versioning, consisting of "creating multiple versions of the product/ service and selling essentially the same product to different market segments at different prices" (op.cit., p.443). For example, Dropbox offers a free version and different levels of service in different prices to select from.

When it comes to place, very few things can compare to traditional marketing, as there is no specific place on the internet. In fact, the closest meaning to the online location is the domain name, where the links are placed on other websites and show how easily discoverable they are, which brings us back to the search engine optimization discussion. On the other hand, this opportunity to sell without borders and address a global market, even if a company is based in a rural garage, raises new challenges referring to the supply chain structure, the delivery speed, and costs. Nowadays, consumers can buy directly from manufacturers avoiding retailers or other intermediaries or be indifferent to manufacturers' marketing efforts, as an expression of their loyalty to popular e-shops like amazon.com. As the customers value convenience, costs in terms of time and money that occur due to physical place constraints can alter the buying decision. This is why the marketer is called to thoroughly study alternatives and calculate different delivery cost scenarios in order to determine the locations that can be targeted without diluting the initial price strategy. Needless to say that consumers care about the total price taken from their wallet during checkout. Since, if you made a great deal with your supplier and you offer a specific category at 25% discount, but, due to shipping costs the final price is higher than that of your competitor, you didn't actually succeed. Note, that the first reason for abandoning online purchases is high shipping costs, according to multiple recent researches (Shopify.com, 2013; Kissmetrics.com, 2015; B2CEurope.com, 2015)

Finally, when it comes to e- promotions, marketers have a variety of methods to choose from, including paid advertising, affiliate marketing, and of course content distribution through the social media, that is already discussed.

Paid Advertising: Pay Per Click

The internet and social media are heavily based on 'free' promotion, meaning organic reach we obtain through search engine optimization, good content, and networking; however, a brand can always find its way to visibility through advertising. Remember that, from a marketing point of view, the unsurmountable benefit of the internet is the detailed tracking of the users' behavior, therefore, modern advertising schemes are result based, and the advertiser pays every time their ad is clicked. Systems like the Google Adwords, Bing Advertising, Facebook, Instagram etc. operate on a Pay-Per-Click (PPC) basis.

For a PPC campaign to be successful, there are some critical steps to be considered, throughout the planning and execution phases, according to a great body of practitioners (eg: Boyd, 2016; Holden, 2010; Wainwright, 2012; Patel, 2016):

- **The Objective:** As always, we start by making clear what we want to achieve with the specific campaign. Is it website traffic or sales growth? Is it engagement or new customers' acquisition?
- **The Audience & The Media:** Having defined the objective, we can now identify the target audiences. The Internet allows to implement very broad target strategies- like global targeting- to very specific ones, like a list of emails or people who have recently visited our website. For example, if we are looking to grow our audience by broadly attracting

people interested in Architecture, we could work well with AdWords Campaigns, built around the relevant keywords; or, if we are looking to motivate our existing audience to engage, we could use Facebook Pixels to target people that recently visited our website. When working with AdWords and other keyword-based advertising schemes, selecting the appropriate keywords is the cornerstone to campaign success. Although each strategy is idiosyncratic and completely in conjunction with specific objectives and targets, there are some general rules of thumb applicable to most situations:

- **Use Tools, Observation, and Insights:** To understand how the targeted users are thinking. Remember the example we used in Chapter 2 for the promotion of a new service for online transactions based on an innovative process that you have built. As we said, chances are that people are not aware of your innovation, therefore they will not look it up using the exact terms you do. To select the right keywords, you have to ask yourself: what would they look for that is related to my service; and if my company appears as a suggestion, would it be relevant to them? For example, keywords like online transaction costs, online transactions, e-wallets etc. might prove very effective. Again, what is important here is to understand that while selecting keywords you are trying to enter your users' minds, so sticking to your brand vocabulary is not effective.

- **Take Action to Avoid Attracting Irrelevant Traffic That Will Cost You Money:** Using PPC advertising to obtain general, untargeted exposure is like buying a Harley Davidson motorbike to hang your clothes on. The philosophy behind the entire system invites marketers to be very specific to what they want to say to whom; charges occur only the goal is reached. Being too broad and implicit, apart from wasting an opportunity, will also cost money, as you will attract and be charged for irrelevant traffic that will bounce. We suggest to avoid using the "broad match" option and apply the use of negative keywords, to filter the quality of clicks the advertisement gets.

- **Use Specific Landing Pages:** When we optimize the content of our website, we match every web page with a keyword, as described in Chapter 2. So when we set up our campaign for this specific keyword, it is only fair that the landing page will be the optimized page not the home page, right? This is the idea behind landing pages that allow us to measure the effectiveness of the ad, but also the quality of the webpage content and the user behavior. Again, sending all the ads to our homepage is like taking for granted that users will take the time to navigate to our website in order to find the information they are looking for but we failed to provide in the first place. For all the reasons we have already explained, this behavior cannot be taken for granted.

- **Test, Monitor, and Optimize:** PPC campaigns are evaluated solely by the reaction of the audience, so the marketer has no chance to understand how the campaign went without closely monitoring the user journey. It is highly recommended to set up experiments and run different versions of ad text, images etc. to see which one performs best. Understanding this will allow the marketer to see through users' behavior, to make changes and optimize the campaign for maximum ROI. Keep in mind that the internet is live and very responsive, contrary to traditional media: while after sending a print ad for printing, there is nothing that can be changed, on the Internet everything changes, in a fast and… stormy way.

- **The Monitoring:** Either on keyword-based campaigns or on any other format- like Facebook boost or page promotions, Twitter Ads, Tumblr Ads etc.- monitoring the performance of the campaign and interfering to make it more effective is crucial. From setting up different versions of the same campaign, to running multiple campaigns at the same time, the ease of use of the new tools and the relatively low cost of media buying is an opportunity for the marketers to experiment more, be more creative and ultimately to get better results.

Paid Advertising: Banners

Banner/ Display advertising heavily relies on creative banner design, contrary to text ads promoted by search networks. Placing a banner on a website is, again, a result of specific targeting, but the marketers can address one of the large global advertising networks for better and more effective placement. The problem with display advertising is, that in the past it has been misused. Websites used to be too cluttered and, today, users literally don't see the ads or apply ad blockers when marketers become more intrusive. Additionally, since users access the Internet from their mobiles, banners have to be responsive which is a challenge for designers. In a nutshell, although a great tool for exposure and traffic generation, banner advertising will rarely produce adequate results when not combined with other digital promotional tools.

Affiliate Marketing

Affiliate Marketing has been challenged lately, specifically after the Google Penguin Update in 2012, where link spamming was not only discouraged but in fact punished. In its core, affiliate marketing is paying a commission to other websites to promote your products, and it has been extensively used and, naturally, misused. Since the radical change in the landscape and the domination of mobiles in the internet access, affiliate marketers have become less aggressive: they replace intrusive banners with subtle text links and focused more on the relevance and quality of linking. Although the initial reaction to Google's update was to declare affiliate marketing dead, the truth is that the practice has shifted to a more essential, meaningful level and it is still very much alive. Search engines are stricter now on judging the naturalness of linking, but being referred by other websites, that are important and relevant, will always be a vote of confidence and, therefore, important both for SEO purposes and for website traffic as well.

Figure 9. Online and offline marketing integration
Source: http://www.smartinsights.com/

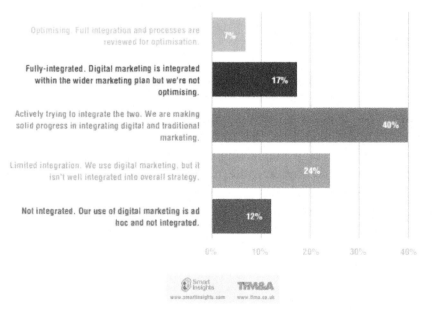

Overall, the e-marketing mix is fairly different from traditional thinking, and it requires new skills and mindsets. Arguably, it is not competitive to well established practices, it is complementary to them, therefore, a call for integration under a holistic, synergizing marketing strategy is in place. However, the survey results by SmartInsights.com (2016) as presented below are alarming as they reveal a hard truth about how close we are to integrate traditional and online marketing practices: Only 24% of the participating companies claim to really integrate, while the majority reports that they actively are trying to, but the main barrier to integration is a lack of communication among the responsible teams and the lack of a common strategy.

Based on a study published by Straker, Wringley, and Rosemann (2015) the main reasons behind this fail to integrate online with traditional channels are:

- The lack of skills, knowledge and understanding by digital marketing practitioners, especially since the needed skills are multiple and very demanding, as discussed in chapter 1.
- Wrong use of the digital channels, for example applying the traditional marketing rationale to digital channels and instead of trying to find audiences where they are, sit and wait for them to come.
- No strategic plan that integrates all channels under one strategy and utilizes them in a synergistic way to reach strategic objectives.
- Irrelevant and not value & identity focused messages: either too focused on brand promotions or unable to maintain a coherent linkage between the brand values and the content published
- Vertical rather Horizontal Organization that leads to traditional and digital marketing being handled by different teams, usually separated and with no communication or common objectives.
- Lack of research and theory. Although many concepts remain the same as in the traditional marketing literature, the environment is so different that new models and theories need to be formed, or at least existing ones need to be updated.

As an effort to fill the aforementioned gaps, one of the author of the book, prof. Hans Ruediger Kaufmann has proposed an approach to an integrated channel strategy, consisting of 4 different stages:

- First, setting the corporate and marketing objectives, as a whole, not separated in traditional and digital marketing ones. Obviously, the KPIs will be different for each angle, but the introduction of an integrated mentality does make the difference.

- Then matching the identities of the employees, the brand and the customers. Remember that our goal is to great active, loyal communities of like-minded followers that perceive the brand and a way to express and communicate their existing or perceived identities. As highlighted in several parts in this book, the role of employees is crucial, as, when their behaviour is aligned to the brand values, they anthropomorphize the brand and they motivate the community. Note that, this is the essence of the Co-Creation Logic that we have discussed earlier, initiating the strategy by how identities will be expressed inside the brand context.

- The following step refers to traditional and online segmentation, using buyer's personas that incorporate traditional demographic, psychological and behavioral characteristics but also add the elements of their digital behaviour. Remember that, from an integrated marketing point of view, we do not separate digital and offline behaviours, since their common denominator is the people we target and their internal goals, needs and motives.

- Finally, we target and position based on identity congruence, consistently throughout the channels. At this final strategic point, we design and deploy tactical plans to disseminate our messages in a way that is adapted to the different nature of each platform but remains consistent with the brand values and self-expressive to the targeted audiences.

Figure 10. Covering the most salient gap: an integrated channel strategy by Prof. H.R. Kaufmann

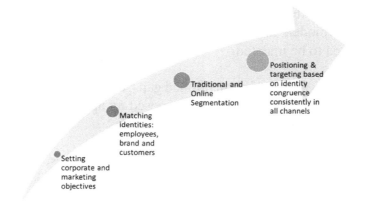

From this perspective, it is very clear why being a strategic integrator is a focal skill of the digital marketer, as integration goes beyond marketing and becomes a leadership challenge, an issue of company culture, structure, and inter-departmental communication. From the findings of this survey, it seems safe to assume that corporations haven't yet initiated, or if so fully completed, the transition from traditional structural forms to new organizational schemes in order to adapt to the new challenges. Although the literature is compelling and content management is expected to be major marketing trend for 2016 (SmartInsights.com, 2016), the shift in management mindset is not yet attempted, creating a gap between what needs to be done and what can really be done. The digital world is not a marketing hype or a technical achievement. It is a new era that influences all management aspects to the core and calls for immediate and drastic change in every level, including the perception of the customer roles as active co-creators rather than passive consumers. In the times of "me-formation", where users overflow the internet with personal stories, brands need to be altruistic, extrovert and beyond their self-referential messages, they have to stop talking to customers and start talking with people. For this step to be made, marketing practitioners also have to move beyond "me", to a more collaborative, participative mindset of creating value for everyone, together.

INTERVIEW WITH PERSADO'S DIRECTOR OF PRODUCT, MR. ALEXIOS BALLAS (WWW.PERSADO.COM)

1. You have launched a very innovative solution, like the cognitive content platform. What is the research behind your service - why and how did you decide to focus on cognitive content creation?

Persado's cognitive content platform is a smart system that combines natural language processing and machine learning technologies to generate the precise words, phrases, and images that can inspire any given audience to act, every time. It is widely known that the most ancient and influential parts of our thinking deals with basic survival. Drawing from the world's largest database of emotional and motivational language, Persado generates & identifies cognitive triggers that inspire action.

Persado is a technology that spans out of a mobile marketing company called Upstream. Upstream run highly impactful SMS marketing campaigns, and it soon becomes evident that the right words could make a huge difference in the success of a campaign, sometimes with even bigger impact than the marketing offer itself. While Upstream developed a technology that created better messages, it soon became clear that this was something bigger and that it could be applied to all forms of communication. Thus, Persado was born.

2.   Can you describe for us in detail how your service works, to which companies it is mainly addressed and what is the value added to them?

Persado's cognitive content platform generates language that inspires action. Powered by cognitive computing technologies, the platform eliminates the random process behind traditional message creation. Persado arms organizations and individuals with "smart content" that maximizes the efficacy of communication with any audience at scale, while delivering unique insight into the specific triggers that drive action. Using Persado, leading brands such as American Express, Citi, MetLife, Microsoft, Neiman Marcus, Staples and Verizon Wireless have realized one billion dollars in incremental revenue and an average uplift of 49.5% in conversions across marketing campaigns.

3.   From your point of view and your experience, what are the major digital marketing trends for the years to come? Research findings place content management at the top of the trends, do you agree with this?

The consolidation of the marketing platforms in one login do-all solutions seems to be the major trend in the movement. The biggest players in the field are trying to unify all the single point marketing solutions to fully integrated marketing clouds. Content management is an important part of this trend as

Figure 11.

[PERSADO]

it touches all the ever increasing number of marketing channels that have increased dramatically as the consumer's digital life keeps growing. More digital touch points mean more work in coordinating and producing effective content for every moment, consumer and place.

Answers

1. The online environment is very cluttered with every kind of information and users, usually, do not intent to spend much time sorting out what it's interesting and what is not; they engage only in whatever is really relevant to them. Engagement is a result of exposure, of course; the more people see a post, for example, the higher the possibilities for some of them to like it, but mostly it is the response to the quality of the shared information. Brands, even smaller ones, that excel in creating high quality content can stand up against their strong competition and even win the battle for engagement.

2. Building a loyal audience, one that trusts you as an authoritative source of information on a specific subject, one that engages and co-creates, is a very promising start for successful sales. For example, if you are a food retailer you can benefit from an online strategy based on recipes and a cooking community exchanging tips and variations. Naturally, you will get the chance to promote your products also, but, in this context, the cooking website is the heart of your marketing campaign, the core of your audience building and, ultimately a product itself.

3. Using the traditional 4Ps analogy, the e-product is the overall online experience, from the website to the content and the participatory benefits of communities and sharing. Online pricing is a complex process of giving away, offering multiple alternatives to pricing co-creation through auctions. E-placement, in fact, refers to the domain name and the links that lead to the website; it is a completely new concept, very much related to the SEO efforts. Finally, for the promotion aspect, marketers have a wide toolbox of alternatives to identify and target specific personas and niche markets in an unprecedented cost effective manner.

4. Digital marketing doesn't happen in a vacuum neither it is a self-purpose. Rather it is a part of a holistic, integrated marketing strategy that combined online with traditional tactics to provide customers with a consistent seamless experience. Yet, surveys reveal that companies today fail to integrate due to lack of communication and collaboration

among the different marketing functions. Obviously, this is a matter of strategic decision making and leadership initiatives, to overcome the barriers and bring together the different facets of the same effort and infuse an integrated marketing perceptive throughout the company.

REFERENCES

B2CEurope.eu. (2015). *High delivery costs are the no.1 reason for abandoning online purchases*. Retrieved from http://www.b2ceurope.eu/de/news/high-delivery-costs-are-the-no-1-reason-for-abandoning-online-purchases/

Ashley, C., & Tuten, T. (2015). Creative strategies in social media marketing: An exploratory study of branded social content and consumer engagement. *Psychology and Marketing, 32*(1), 15–27. doi:10.1002/mar.20761

Boyd, P. (2016). *Top 10 Tips for an Effective Pay-Per-Click Campaign*. Retrieved from https://www.paperstreet.com/blog/top-10-tips-for-an-effective-pay-per-click-campaign/

Contentmarketinginstitute.com. (2015). *Use Data to Help Your Engagement Conundrum*. Retrieved from http://contentmarketinginstitute.com/2015/04/data-engagement-conundrum/

Deichman, A. (2010). *Wait, what? On Social Network Use and Attention*. Retrieved from steinhardt.nyu.edu/appsych/opus/issues/2010/fall/On_Social_Network_Use_and_Attention

Emarketer. (2014). *Social commerce roundup*. Retrieved from http://www.emarketer.com/public_media/docs/emarketer_social_commerce_roundup.pdf

Google.com. (2014). *Brand Engagement in the participation age*. Retrieved from https://think.storage.googleapis.com/docs/brand-engagement-in-participation-age_research-studies.pdf

Holden, K. (2010). *8 Steps to Successful PPC Campaigns*. Retrieved from https://www.sitepoint.com/seo-ppc-strategy/

Hootsuite.com. (2014). *The social media rule of thirds*. Retrieved from https://blog.hootsuite.com/social-media-rule-of-thirds/

Hubspot.com. (2016). *11 of the best Microsite examples we've ever seen.* Retrieved from http://blog.hubspot.com/marketing/ingenious-microsite-exa mples#sm.0001vvjicfps4euxqfo1m56b35zbm

Kaufmann, H. R., & Manarioti, A. (2016). The Content Challenge: Engaging Consumers in a World of Me-Formation. In The Impact of the digital world on management and marketing (p. 271-285). Academic Press.

Kissmetrics.com. (2015). *5 Ecommerce Stats That Will Make You Change Your Entire Marketing Approach.* Retrieved from https://blog.kissmetrics. com/5-ecommerce-stats/

Laudon, K. C., & Traver, C. G. (2011). *E-commerce 2011. Business, Technology, Society* (7th ed.). UK: Pearson.

Meshi, D., Morawetz, C., & Heekeren, H. R. (2013). Nucleus accumbens response to gains in reputation for the self relative to gains for others predicts social media use. *Frontiers in Human Neuroscience*, 7, 439. doi:10.3389/ fnhum.2013.00439 PMID:24009567

Mullan, E. (2011). *What is content curation?* Retrieved from http://www. econtentmag.com/Articles/Resources/Defining-EContent/What-is-Content-Curation-79167.htm

Naaman, M., Boase, J., & Lai, C. H. (2010, February). Is it really about me? message content in social awareness streams. *Proceedings of the 2010 ACM conference on Computer supported cooperative work* (pp. 189-192). ACM. doi:10.1145/1718918.1718953

Patel, N. (2016). *4 Tips For Mastering Pay-Per-Click Marketing Right Now*. Retrieved from http://www.forbes.com/sites/neilpatel/2016/06/30/4-tips-for-mastering-pay-per-click-marketing-right-now/#3d1815b317e6

Pulizzi, J. (2010). *The 80/20 Rule of corporate content*. Retrieved from http:// contentmarketinginstitute.com/2010/10/the-80-20-rule-of-corporate-content/

Pulizzi, J. (2016). *Content Inc: How entrepreneurs use content to build massive audiences and create radically successful businesses*. McGraw Hill Education.

Relevance.com. (2014). *Using the rule of thirds to build a robust online community*. Retrieved from http://relevance.com/using-rule-thirds-build-robust-online-community-tutorial/

Schaefer, M. (2015). *The Content Code: Six essential strategies to ignite your content, your marketing and your business.* Library of Congress Cataloging-in-Publication Data.

Shopify.com. (2013). *Why Online Retailers Are Losing 67.45% of Sales and What to Do About It.* Retrieved from https://www.shopify.com/blog/8484093-why-online-retailers-are-losing-67-45-of-sales-and-what-to-do-about-it

SmartInsights.com. (2016). *Marketing Trends for 2016- will we be in a post-digital era?* Retrieved from http://www.smartinsights.com/managing-digital-marketing/marketing-innovation/marketing-trends-2016/

Smartinsights.com. (2016). *How to use the power of the 70:20:10 model work to prioritise your digital marketing.* Retrieved from http://www.smartinsights.com/marketing-planning/marketing-models/using-the-702010-rule-in-marketing/

Straker, K., Wrigley, C., & Rosemann, M. (2015). The role of design in the future of digital channels: Conceptual insights and future research directions. *Journal of Retailing and Consumer Services, Col., 26,* 133–140. doi:10.1016/j.jretconser.2015.06.004

Wainwright, M. (2012). *How Even YOU Can Master PPC Campaign Management.* Retrieved from http://blog.hubspot.com/blog/tabid/6307/bid/33882/How-Even-YOU-Can-Master-PPC-Campaign-Management-TEMPLATE.aspx#sm.0000d6pt5u2lpdm5vad1i7rtpl1j0

Watson, L. (2015). *Humans have shorter attention span than goldfish, thanks to smartphones.* Retrieved from http://www.telegraph.co.uk/science/2016/03/12/humans-have-shorter-attention-span-than-goldfish-thanks-to-smart/

Zhu, Y., & Chen, H. (2015). Social media and human need satisfaction: Implications for social media marketing. *Business Horizons, 58*(3), 335–345. doi:10.1016/j.bushor.2015.01.006

Chapter 6
Towards an Integrated Online-Offline Marketing Design:
Integrating Knowledge Management, Multi-Channel Marketing, Big Data, and Customer Analytics

ABSTRACT

Based on a variety of industries, this final chapter aims to provide a coherent helicopter view on interrelated topics in the field of digital marketing integrated with traditional marketing approaches. It combines a body of academic research on the field with practical knowledge. To achieve this aim, mainstream research articles are summarized, illustrating YouTube videos and practical cases, recommendations are presented, interesting future research propositions and questions suggested and conceptualized frameworks provided. The thematic potpourri spans from knowledge management, increased consumer power, multi-channel marketing, integration and channel choice factors, a discussion on business models for multi-channel marketing and online marketing, virtual reality, web and customer analytics and Big Data in relation to corporate performance and corporate competencies. The chapter concludes with a hypothesized summarizing conceptualization on effectively designing online and offline channels, suggestions for future research and strategic foci. The chapter concludes that the path of adopting and anchoring digital marketing is not a mechanical but rather an organic change requiring a holistic change management embracing a cross-functional perspective with strong leadership involvement.

DOI: 10.4018/978-1-68318-012-8.ch006

Questions

1. Performance- wise: what is the gain if we manage to integrate digital with traditional marketing?
2. Can online businesses stand alone or will the brick and mortar option always be the king?
3. What is the strategic aspect of digital marketing?
4. Beyond Google Analytics: what does academia say about web metrics?
5. Is ignorance a bliss for companies?

GENERAL OVERVIEW ON CUSTOMER KNOWLEDGE ARCHITECTURE

Earlier in our book, we have already mentioned some key concepts on customer knowledge management, there with the scope to utilize our insights in order to form realistic and purposeful personas. In this chapter, we take the analysis a step further, focusing the following paragraphs to a general and basic overview of the importance of managing customer knowledge for enhancing marketing performance.

A comprehensive conceptual chapter on Customer Knowledge Management (CKM) aiming to establish the influence of its dimensions on the organizational marketing performance is provided by Panni (2015). The customer relationship profitability as an exemplary and important indicator of marketing performance achieved by Customer Knowledge Management and expressed by the term Customer Life Time Value, has been researched, for example, by Shimp (1997) (Figure 6.1). While adopting an integrated marketing strategy, effective multichannel integration, which facilitates multichannel shopping, is regarded to have a significant bearing on the increase of the Customer Life Time Value.

The model shows that, in case of an increasing rate of retaining the customers, the cumulative Net Present Value Profit and, hence, the live time value per customer increases.

Based on thoroughly researched secondary data, Panni (2015) suggests a framework for customer knowledge management integrating the so far incoherent frameworks as proposed by previous authors. Emanating from this eclectic and chronological literature review, the chapter also suggests further missing links that need to be included in the proposed integrated framework which has led to develop a hypothesized index. The framework and the index

Figure 1. Customer LTV
Source: Shimp (1997, p. 394)

Customer Life Time Value

	Year 1	Year 2	Year 3	Year 4	Year 5
Revenue					
A Customers	1,000	400	180	90	50
B Retention Rate	40%	45%	50%	55%	60%
C Average yearly sales	$ 150	$ 150	$1 50	$ 150	$ 150
D Total Revenue	$ 150,000	$ 60,000	$ 27,000	$ 13,500	$ 7,500
Costs					
E Cost %	50%	50%	50%	50%	50%
F Total Costs	$ 75,000	$ 30,000	$ 13,500	$ 6,750	$ 3,750
Profits					
G Gross Profit	$ 75,000	$ 30,000	$ 13,500	$ 6,750	$ 3,750
H Discount Rate	1	1.2	1.44	1.73	2.07
I NPV Profit	$ 75,000	$ 25,000	$ 9,375	$ 3,902	$ 1,812
J Cumulative NPV Profit	$ 75,000	$ 100,000	$ 109,375	$ 113, 2777	$ 115,088
K Life Time Value (NPV) per Customer	$ 75.00	$ 100	$ 109.38	$ 113.28	$ 115.09

developed from this chapter attempted to provide a clear direction to the future researchers and may be tested empirically in a later study to testify its impact on the organizational marketing performance. The findings of Panni's secondary research can be summarized by the following hypotheses that are useful to structure our thoughts and our research as well:

- **H1:** Knowledge for customer has positive impact on the marketing performance of the organizations.
- **H2:** Knowledge from customers has a positive influence on the marketing performance of the organizations.
- **H3:** Knowledge about customers has a positive effect on the marketing performance of the organizations.
- **H4:** Customer knowledge identification and gathering has a positive influence on the marketing performance of the organizations.
- **H5:** Customer knowledge organization and storage has a positive relationship with the marketing performance of the organizations.
- **H6:** Customer knowledge distribution and sharing has a positive influence on the marketing performance of the organizations.

Figure 2. Underlying factors to integrate traditional and digital marketing

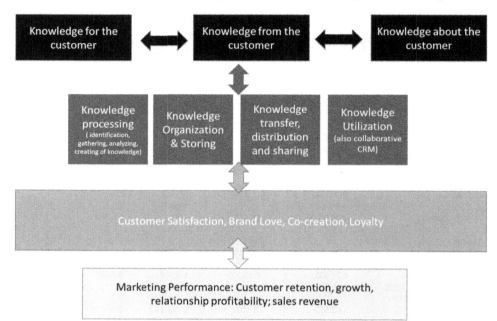

- **H7:** Customer knowledge utilization has a positive association with the marketing performance of the organizations.
- **H8:** The interaction of different CRM elements will be positively related to the marketing performance of the organizations.
- **H9:** The interaction of different KM elements will be positively related to the marketing performance of the organizations.
- **H10:** The interaction of different CRM and KM elements (overall model) will be positively related to the marketing performance of the organizations.

The extensive research of the hypotheses ended up to insightful conclusions that backup one of the fundamental premises of our book, supporting the integration of traditional and digital marketing, as seen on the figure below:

Simply put, at the first stage marketers are using any available source in order to collect information that will assist understanding better what the customers want or need. Having collected this volume of information, then (with their skills are researchers) they reach to conclusions, which are in turn translated into actions, tactics, campaigns and policies. Note that there is no separation between the online and traditional marketing field: data can be used from online sources that lead to conclusions useful for offline practices; or objectives are reached through the collaboration of both available approaches. What is important it's the outcome: when insights are used in a proper manner, then the practices selected reflect the target audiences' needs and wants. That leads to self-expression, and identification –the brands speak a languages that touches and expresses the customers- and this emotional attachment is demonstrated as co-creation and ultimately loyalty. In other words, if we see the marketing function as a knowledge based one, and it is correct to see it like this, channels are working together seamlessly in order to reach the marketing objectives- regardless the nature of the medium.

Attempting to propose a collaborative approach of integrating online and offline business models Kollman and Hasel (2006) held that the rapid growth of Internet technologies induced a structural change in both, social and economic spheres and put a considerable emphasis on digital channels. Digital channels have become an integral part of daily life, and their influence on the transfer of information has become ubiquitous. In line with Dickley and Lewis (2009), the authors see new possibilities emerging with respect to how enterprises create value on an electronic level.

As already indicated by Hansen's (2006, in Dickley and Lewis, 2009) research, Kollman and Hasel (2006) stressed the importance of a combination of physical and electronic trade channels for ensuring higher levels of organizational performance. In their paper, they argue that collaborative concepts represent a promising way of meeting the challenges ahead. Technological advance and changes in customer behavior imply that cross-channel concepts will become a driving force in many industries. Both concepts can complement each other and can ultimately provide some collaborated offerings to the consumers.

Cross channel co-operation enables firms to integrate online and offline business models without extending themselves beyond their own means or competencies. Building, in terms of strategic management or business model aspects, upon market- and resource-based considerations, they argue why and how cross-channel co-operation contributes to competitive advantage and propose a classification of the resulting forms of collaboration. In many industries, online and offline integrated business concepts become a prerequisite for successfully utilizing customer touch points and achieving customer loyalty. To achieve this end, strategic business concepts must be combined with the technology perspective (Hippner, 2005, in Kollman and Hasel, 2006)).

Evolution of Customer Power

Another proposition that is constant throughout the book refers to the urgent need for a mindset shift, as a result of the "revenge of the customer", the evolution of the consumer power in the digital age (Labrecque et al., 2013). In the wave of dizzily swift changes of internet technology, digitalization and social media, this paper is dedicated to the noticeable power shift in consumer – marketer relationship swinging the pendulum clearly to the consumer. Facing a more empowered customer, marketers face, so far unknown challenges to create new brand consumer relationships as well as manage their demand. Although the phenomenon of consumer empowerment is still in a fledgling phase, it will become the more influential the more the digitalized marketing will be even more widespread and, hence, calls for more research.

Labrecque et al. (2013) provide a framework that depicting four distinct consumer power sources:

- Demand power (individual based)
- Information power (individual based)
- Network power (network based)
- Crowd-based power (network based)

Resorting to previous literature (Bakos, 1991; Deighton and Kornfeld, 2009; Kozinets, 1999; Levine et al., 2000; Shipman, 2001; Cattaneo and Chapman, 2010; Clegg, 1989; Sadan, 1997; Kozinets et al., 2010 in Labrecque et al., 2013) this article highlights technology's instrumental role for this trend to consumer empowerment triggered mainly by increasingly available information.

The four sources of Consumer Power discussed in the paper are summarized as follows (Day, 2011, Anderson, 2004; Brynjolfsson, Hu, and Smith, 2003; Hennig-Thurau et al., 2004; Brynjolfsson, Hu, and Simester, 2011; Grégoire, Laufer, and Tripp, 2010; Ward and Ostrom, 2006; Schau and Gilly, 2003; Liu-Thompkins and Rogerson, 2012; Goldenberg, Oestreicher-Singer and Reichman, 2012, in Labrecque et al., 2013):

1. Demand-Based Power: Facilitated transaction processes and ubiquitous access to retail service options. Consumers today has immediate access to multiple offering not limited by geographical boundaries. Comparative advantages based on claims are now put on dispute, since consumers can validate whether a seller really offers "the best price one can find".

Remember that millennials have the tendency to check and compare prices online, while being in the store, so that pushes a lot of extra pressure on the companies.

2. Information-Based Power:
   a. Through content consumption, as consumers now have easier access to more information, to an extent that private issues of the company are becoming public and transparency has become a must. The main sources of the information based power result from:
      i. Reducing information asymmetry by a multitude of channels
      ii. Better informed and educated consumers
      iii. Electronic word of mouth increases objectivity (independent journalists, rating agencies or private product reviews)
      iv. Better market diffusion of information
      v. Contributing to shorten product life cycles and higher levels of innovation
   b. Through content production. As we said earlier, we are living in the world of meformation, everyone can be a content producer. This is a threat and an opportunity at the same time, for the brands: a threat because the vast volumes of content produce exhaust consumers that become more eclectic, while algorithms of popular media (like Facebook and Instagram) prioritize personal over branded content; thus, extra effort is needed in the content creation field to manage to stand out. At the same time, it's an opportunity for brands that broadcast clear, coherent messages that are self-expressive to a specific audience and therefore upgrade their relationship through daily engagement. By the same token, the power to review is a pressing call for quality but also a great leverage to trigger streams of positive online reputation. In a nutshell, information based power comes from:
      i. Higher levels of self-expression by producing user-generated content
      ii. Extending opportunities for individual reach and to influence markets (i.e. by praising, liking, sharing experiences, complaining, supporting social causes, initiating change)

3. **Network-Based Power:** The power of working together, even with no physical presences and to collaborate and share to everyone's benefit, like in the case of content curation. Apart from this, some other facets of network based power are:

    a.   Content dissemination (e.g., sharing and organizing content through networks)

    b.   Content completion (e.g., commenting on and contributing to blog posts; tagging)

    c.   Content modifications or repurposing (i.e. videos, images)

    d.   Social Media instrumental for higher levels of consumers' proactivity in sharing information (i.e. user-generated links)

4.   **Crowd-Based Power:** There are two aspects of crowd-based power: in the first case, the crowd is structured to a community, where common goals and objectives are pursued. It can be a community for strays' rescue or a group of knowledge sharing about Branding, but in this context, people that don't know each other work together to everyone's benefit. The other version of this crowd- based power can be found in the different crowdfunding or crowdsourcing websites, where the scope is to serve a personal goal or find support for a project.

    a.   **Structured (i.e. Brand Community)**: Motivating community members to create a resource pool (knowledge, economic/financial, social), hence, supporting the communities objectives/initiatives fosters the social identity of the community members

    b.   **Unstructured (i.e. Individual):** Customers reap personal benefits; Generating, albeit, pooled resources of individuals for co-creation, i.e. new product development.

Case Studies on Marketing Responses to Network-based and Crowd-based Power exemplified by Online Music Communities (Salo, 2012). Salo's (2012) interesting case studies on the online communities in the music industry are summarized below:

Case Study Indie

The Indie Company uses artist marketing featuring their pop/rock/metal music artists through the online system. They exert their marketing activities on YouTube and other social platforms. Most of the company's artists maintain personal profiles where users can listen to the band's songs and can get additional band related information. To generate further attention, other features like ringtones and wallpapers are offered for fans and those who have just accidentally accessed their profile. Artists' music videos and concert performances are also shown on YouTube.

Case Study Affiliate

As Affiliate normally focuses on relatively older customer segment they are quite reluctant to use internet or digital platforms in making their music programs and artists known to this segment. Consequently, social web and internet are not yet considered as a massive marketing channel. However, exciting news is that, via a customer survey, it was found that their customers have started to feel the importance of the internet and online based marketing. As a result, a number of communities were identified for marketing their artists.

Case Study: Sony

Sony, a world reputed multi-national company, represents world famous artists like Beyoncé, Britney Spears, Kelly Clarkson, Bruce Springsteen and the Foo Fighters. The company relies both on traditional marketing channels (like radio, television and print) as well as online channels. To be en vogue, Sony currently emphasizes online and internet marketing. It appreciates the benefits of online and internet based marketing such as the ability for speeding communication and quickly updating material and interactively communicating with customers. Other advantages as identified by the Sony team are cost efficiency and a sense of communality. Sony's digital team usually decides on a case to case basis on the mediums on marketing each artist for different occasions differentiating the content as to target groups to enhance interest. Through digital marketing Sony aims to give an added value to consumers, thus, making the necessary interactive communication tools available to the customers. Sony's marketing on the digital platforms is remarkable. For example, it provides the consumers with the opportunity to listen an album free of charge before the official release date for the purpose of promotion or intends to let consumers stream music free of charge. The underlying business model is to sell music files in MP3 format, compatible with the majority of music players, whose downloads can be bought by consumers from music stores. Rather than relying on expensive marketing campaigns to the online communities, the company focuses on electronic word-of-mouth marketing taking place between consumers.

Additionally, Sony engages in viral marketing using their personal online networks such as Facebook in order to disseminate and share messages about interesting artists to friends and business partners.

Multi-Channel Marketing

Customer Knowledge Management is instrumentally utilized by multi-channel marketing with its key objective to harmonizing corporate, marketing as well as customer motives and objectives. Apparently, since the early days of this concept the channels and circumstances have changed, however, key meaning and the strategic purpose remain valid and valuable, as you will realize yourself.

Regarding corporate objectives in this context, profitability can be increased through increasing sales and customer loyalty as well as decreasing costs (Gronover, 2003)- a concept that remains very much applicable even if the contexts have changed in some ways.

Consistently, the marketing objectives relate to exciting, attracting and moving customers to buy and engage for co-creation via integrated traditional and online channels (Customer Centric Marketing Strategies) (Kaufmann and Panny, 2015; Staeger, 1999)

Figure 3. Consequences of multi-channel management
(Gronover, 2003, p. 18)

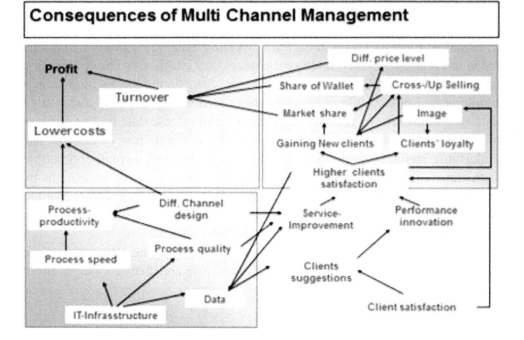

Figure 4. Customer orientation by multi-channel marketing
(Staeger, 1999, p. 12)

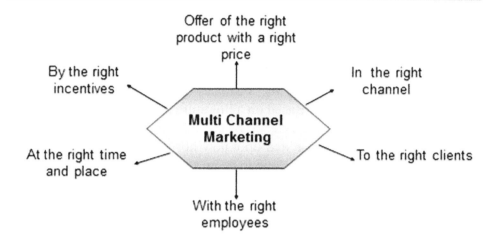

Clients should perceive and feel attracted to the Corporate Identity consistently across all channels. For this to engineer, the Corporate/Brand Identity should match with Client Identity in all direct, indirect, online and offline channels. Latter reflects the new identity paradigm and era in Marketing leading to Brand Love) (Kaufmann et al., 2012; Loureiro & Kaufmann, 2012; Kaufmann & Manarioti, 2015).

The following SAP YouTube video (https://www.youtube.com/watch?v=cFC9Xb07Ye8) emphasizes the need to design meaningful, value based and customized messages and experiences consistent across all channels to the customers at a moment where they are ready to engage. An exemplary application of the concept of identity as a tailored communication platform is shown by the consumer motives of the Generation Y (Straker, Wrigley and Rosemann, 2015) culminating in becoming a Co-Creator. Perceiving themselves as sitting in the 'driving seat', being empowered and in control, they are attracted from online and detached from traditional channels. They are more critical and ready to voice concerns and use different channels for different parts of purchase process. They are regarded as being more active, interactive and engaged with and contributing to companies expecting, however, 24/7 contact. Customers want to be asked for permission. Aiming to be highly self-expressive, they would like to create their own content. Mirroring the key features of social media, they would like to socialize, experience and share. This is a major reason why we so intensively preach for the mindset shift and the urgent call for integration. Brands that continue to rely on traditional practices will, eventually, find themselves being ignored by the new generations that are more and more absorbed by the digital sirens. Simultaneously, traditional practices that are based on decades of research and answer very profound psychological needs cannot be thrown away; they have to be updated by the marketing forces of researchers and practitioners.

Let's take the example of the business models for online groceries (Dickley and Lewis, 2009). Based on a literature review, Dickley and Lewis (2009) stressed the high importance of the internet for marketing arguing that internet marketing has added up a new horizon in modern marketing. The attractiveness of the web is due to be an effective medium and efficient channel for advertising, marketing communication, selling and the distribution of goods.

Dickley and Lewis (2009) examined various business models that could be used by online grocers and the nature of customer value these are designed to deliver compared to traditional channels. The components of a Business Model (Rappa, 2004, in Dickley and Lewis, 2009) are:

- Conductor to business success focusing on efficiency, the customer and profit
- Explaining the relationships between revenue generation, costs and profitability
- Basis for assessing business viability
- Visualization of business activities
- Infrastructure for daily activities

Furthermore, they investigated the impact that the development of new, possibly more effective business models (which include e-business) could have on future trends in online grocery shopping.

In their study they examined the nature and key determinants of the value which can be delivered to consumers with an online business model in the grocery industry to be instrumental for the development of recommendations for business model advancement for grocers. According to the paper, value relates to the business model design itself, and, finally, the business model must be able to deliver these values. This emphasis on value delivery is confirmed by Groenroos (2006) perceiving marketing in a crisis, mainly due to a lack of understanding of customer value and strategic focus. Groenroos points to the paramount research task to assess those factors consumers regard as valuable. In assessing and meeting these values Marketing should be regarded as a value based corporate wide philosophy spanning also non-marketing business functions (i.e. delivery, logistics, maintenance, warehousing, repair) as long the latter represent a customer touch point.

Coming back to the example of groceries, depending on this value delivery, the question should be answered whether an online channel should be included as an ancillary business avenue of traditional grocers or whether online grocery businesses can succeed on their own as stand-alone businesses.

According to Bevan and Murphy (2001, in Dickley and Lewis, 2009), the Internet to be a successful medium for consumer spending, its technologies will need to match or exceed the value or utility provided by traditional (bricks-and-mortar) retail formats. The key to online grocery shopping is to devise a business model that offers the benefits sought by the online shopper that outweighs the costs of online shopping. In this context, a differentiation focus (based on Porter's (2001) generic strategies- cost leadership, differentiation, focus on one market niche (cost or differentiation) would seem to be the most appropriate strategy for Internet marketers. This would require the online grocer to focus on one type of end buyer, such as the consumer who wanted delivery of a particular type of grocery product of the highest quality at the lowest price. It would be accurate to consider this to be the "value" proposition.

Hansen's (2006, in Dickley and Lewis, 2009) research results suggest some significant indicators of online shopping where they argued that consumer's attitudes towards online grocery buying is positively affected by perceived offline physical effort and negatively affected by offline shopping enjoyment. Their study results also indicated that consumers may hesitate from repeat online buying if they are faced with high online complexity. Successfully establishing trust will be crucial to the overall success of online grocery shopping, and once again, add value. In summary, web is an opportunity to achieve a competitive advantage by further meeting the needs of consumers. Finally, Superior Value Delivery in Online Channels referred to:

- Convenience (most important online customer value)
- Excellence
- High Quality Food
- Time Saved
- Trust

Figure 5. E-business models derived from Smith and Chaffey (2005) and Laudon and Trevor (2011)

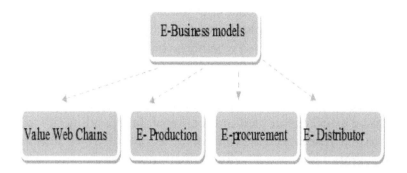

New E-Business Models
Business Models for e-marketing

- Satisfaction
- Cost Efficiencies
- Customization of Offerings,
- Opportunity to Build Stronger Relationships with Customers

A very general suggestion for e-marketing business models is derived from Smith and Chaffey (2005) and Laudon and Trevor (2011)

Different Views on Digital Marketing

Market-Based View: It Is Not All Gold What Glitters

The market-based view is based on the assumption that the uniqueness and the success of firms are determined by their position in the market. In that sense, understanding the market is a prerequisite for the formulation of a successful competitive strategy. According to Porter's 'Five Forces' model, the competitive forces driving competition within a market include rivalry among existing competitors, bargaining power of suppliers, bargaining power of buyers, threat of substitute products, and barriers to entry (Porter, 1980). Although the deployment of internet technologies brings many new benefits, it is often found to have some negative effects as well:

- Online offerings are difficult to keep proprietary, reduce differences between competitors and, thus, increase rivalry among them.
- Online channels within an industry reduce switching costs and, thus, shift bargaining power to end users.
- Online channels represent a new substitution threat for nearly all kinds of offline channels

Resource-Based View (RBV)

RBV postulates that companies displaying internal resources that are

- Valuable
- Rare
- Inimitable
- Non substitutable

are able to achieve competitive advantage by strategies that cannot be easily duplicated by their competitors (Prahalad and Hamel, 1990; Barney, 1991; Wernerfeld, 1995, in Kollman and Hasel, 2006).

First of all, engaged audiences and co-creating brand communities can be very sustainable sources of advantage, as they are idiosyncratic, valuable, rare and very difficult to imitate (even if one copies the practice, they cannot guarantee the result!) But, when talking about integration, a balance must be obtained, one that is actually very beneficial for companies as, though core competencies of e-ventures and traditional firms are very different from each other and, thus, have different advantages and require different competencies; from this point of view, both the traditional firm and e-ventures can complement their advantages and competencies. These resource combinations may be referred to as cross-channel complementarities (Kollmann and Häsel, 2006).

Reasons for complementing offline and online assets, hence, acquiring dynamic capabilities (Ernst et al., 2001; Amit and Zott, 2001; Jones and Spiegel, 2003; Wiedman et al., 2002, in Kollmann and Häsel, 2006; Kollmann and Häsel, 2006) are:

- Aftersales services provided by offline outlets
- Internet based resources require support in terms of technical knowledge and know how

- Traditional firms still contribute most of the assets (brands, products, distribution and supplier networks, customer relationships, and physical sites)
- Optimization of advertising efforts and cross-media co-operation:
  - Online Channels: Fast and comprehensive for interactive relationships
  - Print Media: Attracting attention and quickening interests
  - Combined information and knowledge resources (i.e. to provide high quality
  - Customer profiles) facilitate customer centric strategies and sustainable customer relationships

Distribution structure can provide a fruitful field of application for the discussed synergistic concept. First of all, an overview of a structural design of a distribution System is provided by Meffert et al. (2008)

Figure 6.
Source: Channel Structure. Translated by the authors from Meffert et al. (2008, p. 560)

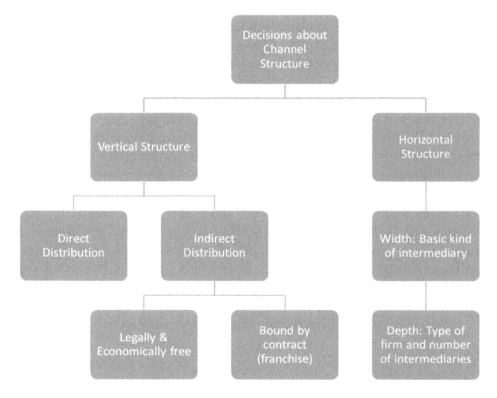

This model is exemplified by the multichannel distribution system of Nike, as the company applies both direct and indirect distribution. Direct Distribution is done virtually via nike.com and by own subsidiaries, so called flagship stores in big cities as well as selling surplus stock in Nike Factory stores. Indirect distribution is conducted via online traders such as Amazon or traditional offline retailers such as Karstadt or via surplus stock traders on virtual markets such as ebay (based on Mohammed et al. 2004, in Meffert et al., 2008, p. 579).

Trenz (2015) has portrayed the offline, online and multichannel trade and business practices and perceptions particularly from the consumer perspective. Most importantly, this chapter highlights the issues and factors concerning the multichannel integration.

Channel configuration determinants or drivers (Golsbee, 2001; Montoya-Weiss et al., 2003; Chiang et al., 2006; Frambach et al., 2007; Pavlou and Fygenson, 2006; Verhagen and van Dolen, 2009; Bendoly et al., 2005; Konus, et al. 2008; Chintagunta et al., 2012; Forman et al., 2009; Janakiraman and Niraj, 2011; Frambach et al., 2007; Keen et al., 2004; Dholakia et al., 2005, in Trenz, 2015)

- Prices
- Experience
- Perceived Service Qualities
- Online Channel characteristics: ease of use, purchase effort, convenience
- Inhibitors of Online Channel usage: risk, privacy, security
- Online and/or offline channel product assortments
- Demographic influences: still ambivalent research findings
  -males and younger people with online preference
  -demographics seemingly irrelevant for channel choice
- Geographic proximity to store: Offline channel preference
- Internet and IT skills
- Channel of entry into the relationship
- Psychographic characteristics of shoppers: innovativeness, shopping enjoyment and

Price consciousness (multichannel preference)

As repeatedly mentioned, multichannel integration services such as "purchase online with service in store" can loosen this tie to one channel. A distribution system integrating a variety of channels is, for example, applied by Nike. Via nike.com products are directly distributed to the customers through the internet.

Multichannel Shoppers: The Jewels in the Crown?

Keen et al. (2004, in Trenz, 2015) find differentiated group behavior in that one group of purchasers that have a very strong preference for a specific channel, while other types of would move between channels. Dholakia et al. (2005, in Trenz, 2015) study a multichannel retailer and find that the channel of entry influences multichannel shopping behavior since most multichannel shoppers were leads resulting from the online channel. Konus et al. (2008) identify that customers who are enthusiastic multichannel shoppers are characterized by innovativeness, shopping enjoyment, and price consciousness. With regards to the value of multichannel shoppers, early empirical studies suggest that multichannel shoppers are generally more valuable than consumers that stick to one channel in terms of revenue (Kumar and Venkatesan, 2005, Venkatesan et al., 2007, in Trenz, 2015) and retention (Venkatesan et al., 2007, in Trenz, 2015).

Relating to a wide ranging literature review, Trenz (2015) provides three types of Multichannel Integration which is summarized as follows. His study has shown an overall perspective/aspect of the different types of integration in the multiple channel integration in reputed outlets like Walmart, BestBuy, Macy's, Target, Sears, Otto, Notebooksbilliger, Conrad, Cyberport, Weltbild, Bonprix, C&A and Mediamarkt. This categorization on multichannel integration, however, is still research in progress. Especially, the behavioral consequences of individual integration services are suggested by Oh and Teo (2010, in Trenz, 2015) to be subject of further investigation.

1. **Co-Ordination:** Exploiting synergies between channels and increasing efficiency: managing complexity within organization and supply chain
   a. Centralized administration and inventory
2. **Information:** Co-ordinating the information flow between channels, consumers and firm (see Customer Knowledge Management) (controllable or uncontrollable by the firm)
   a. More effective communication with the customer
   b. Sharing of promotion, product, price and transaction information between channels
3. **Services:** Managing the Experience of the customer by matching respective online and offline benefits and utilizing spillover effects

a. Inventory systems, warehousing, marketing and pricing 1 (with still existing challenges to valuate these services; a further still existing challenge is the expansion of the marketing function to these often non-marketing functions as highlighted by Groenroos (2006).

Getting comfortable with disruptive innovation and cultivating customer knowledge, experiences, ecosystems and implicit competencies for business modeling (Weill and Woerner, 2015)

The following summary of Weill's and Woerner's (2015) paper reflects how the knowledge on digital business modeling has advanced. Beyond the aforementioned generic strategies of Porter, market, resource based view and customer value, customer experience in the context of life events is emphasized as paramount for designing the business model. The paper culminates in calling for cultivating customer knowledge and provides suggestions for digital managerial competencies to put the respectively chosen business model into reality. The paper illustrates some crucial and burning issues relating to the digital marketing operating model perspective and some guidelines and contexts.

Weill and Woerner (2015) prepared a paper on digitalization in marketing focusing on digital interruption. According to this paper, the business world is rapidly digitizing which leads to the breakdown of many traditional practices. From a disruptive perspective, this is creating both, barriers as well as opportunities whilst at the same time destroying long-successful business models. This process is known as digital disruption. Technology-enabled change and history shows that the impact of such mind-blowing change can be greater than we ever could have imagined. If we remember the past success stories of steam engines, cars, airplanes, TVs, telephones and, most recently, mobile phones and e-books, we can taste the flavor of such change. With e-books, the market has been slow to develop and traditionalists doubt the possibility to replace the experience with a paper book. Recently, however, e-books are gaining momentum as they are cheaper than paper books, faster to acquire and easier searchable.

Due to the ambivalent nature of disruptive innovation, companies should be very careful in assessing their possible opportunities and threats. A significant amount of top managers believe that their company's revenue will be under threat from digital disruption in the next five years. On the other hand, it is argued in the article that companies can benefit from digitalization by leveraging strong customer relationships and increase cross and up selling opportunities. Weill and Woerner (2015) present a framework supported by examples and financial performance impacts, for helping managers to contemplate about their competitive environments in the digital era. In fact, the authors provide an important insight in that businesses will experience problems if they too narrowly focused on value chains rather than on ecosystems in the digital era.

The authors studied where companies intended to move in the next five to seven years. Based on this view, the authors observed leading companies that were operating on one or more new digital initiatives to see what works reflecting a less than wholehearted commitment. Companies perceived high levels of threats from competitors with competing products due to high disruption potential and potentially attacking their core business.

It has been found that companies were seeking to transform in two dimensions: to know more about their end customers by collecting, consolidating and using deeper customer insights. In addition, companies increasingly operate in a digital ecosystem and shift their emphasis from individual direct customer relationships to a web of ecosystem relationships to provide for customer centered products/services. Against this background, based on Weill and Woerner (2015), the following four future business model alternatives are presented:

1. Suppliers' Potential Loss of Power Compared to Independent Agents
   a. Easier search opportunities might exert pressure on prices and induce industry consolidation
   b. Possible examples: Chubb Group (insurances), Sony (electronic goods), Vanguard (Mutual Funds), Procter & Gamble
2. Omni Channel/Multi Channel businesses
   a. Greater customer choice and seamless experience
   b. Ever increasing customer knowledge and avoiding customer churn
   c. Emphasis is on controlling integrated value chain and 'owning' the customer relationship
   d. Possible examples: Carrefour, Nordstrom, Walmart (retailing), CIBC and BBVA (banks)
3. Ecosystem drivers
   a. Establishing relations with other providers to create platforms for complementary or even competing services
   b. Various degrees of platform openness
   c. Utilizing high brand equity, great customer experience and one-stop shopping
   d. Often concentrating on one business domain
   e. Excel in customer knowledge

  f. Building reputation and revenues from customer ratings and reviews.

  g. Possible examples: Google, Apple, Fidelity Vanguard

4. Modular Producers

  a. Hypercompetitive environment

  b. Plug and Play Products adaptable to a variety of Ecosystems

  c. Continuous and well-priced product and service innovation avoiding commodity business

  d. Often limited to customers' transaction data (compared to ecosystem drivers)

  e. Possible Examples: PayPal, Apple Play, Square

The implicit and conditional corporate competencies to fully exploit the relevant business model are the following:

- Timely synthesizing information on customers' goals and life events: centralizing customer data often scattered in different departments, systems or geographical settings
- Cultivating a Customer centered corporate culture: champion the customer by the use of Customer satisfaction metrics; in addition to Weill's and Woerner's (2015) suggestions, Behavioral Branding is suggested as a promising to route to follow; Behavioral Branding refers to create high identification and emotional association levels of employees with brand values, hence acting as brand ambassadors. Transformational leadership is instrumental to achieve this objective (i.e. Kaufmann et al., 2012)
  - Accessing and reacting to customers' honest perceptions via social media
  - Using big-data analytics to continuously learn
  - Creating an evidence based culture and make decisions based on evidence due to vastly improved data analytics
  - Putting customer values and their life events center stage: providing multi products and multi channels simultaneously
  - Be top of mind positioned and become first choice: achieving customers' identification with the brand, receiving great customer recommendations and not compromising on world-class performance
  - Becoming excellent in networking with ecosystem partners (and even competitors) to provide for more holistic fulfillment of customer needs

- ○ Provide service-enabled interfaces for others to make business rules and activities available.
- ○ Making business transactions, knowledge and services available also for outsiders to drive innovation and reduce time to market.
- ○ Be the pupil in the master class in terms of efficiency and Compliance: knowing efficiencies, reasons for potential service disruption, responsibilities, cyber threats and opportunities; thrive on legitimacy in terms of privacy issues and compliance to regulations from government and other global regulators.

A New Consumer Trend: Shopping in Virtual Reality

A virtual community is considered as a sort of society that gathers consumers with similar interests. Hence, researchers investigate the consumers' human interactions within the social structure of virtual communities. Based on important general issues concerning human interaction in virtual communities, Lau, Kan and Lau (2013) shed light on consumer shopping behavior in virtual environments. The authors, furthermore, explained the difference between Bricks- and –Mortar and virtual shopping.

Figure 7.

Human Interactions in Virtual Communities

Virtual technology provides consumers with a unique time and space in the shopping ambience which is different from 2D web-based and real world shopping. In virtual environments, consumers can interact and communicate in virtual communities representing social groups organized largely on the basis of individuals' habits, tastes and interests. As virtual communities differ in terms of styles of living, mode of interaction and communication, their product and service demands differ as well. Prior literature argued that the consumers in virtual communities usually gain product and service knowledge by means of social and functional interactions among the members within that particular community. In this regard, social media like Facebook, Twitter, Youtube and Wikipedia (Chen et al., 2013; Molesworth, 2006; Gabisch and Gwebu, 2011; Hsiao and Chiou, 2012; in Lau, Kan and Lau, 2013) are of vital importance.

Trustfulness in Virtual Communities

Lau, Kan and Lau (2013) posited the importance of trustfulness in online and virtual environments. This trustfulness relates to online information, privacy, company policy and the confidence with retailers and marketers. Wu et al. (2010, in Lau, Kan and Lau, 2013) attempted to elicit the impact of the trust factor on virtual community members. According to these authors trust in virtual environments entails relationship commitment and member adhesion. Latter authors also claim that the provided privacy policies of virtual communities could increase the consumers' level of trust having a positive effect on the member's adhesion and commitment.

Social trust, according to Mathwick et al. (2008, in Lau, Kan and Lau, 2013) is besides reciprocity and voluntarism an ingredient of social capital and, therefore, a glue for the social structure in a virtual community.

Consumers' Social Presence in Virtual Communities

Lau, Kan and Lau (2013) refer to generally two types of communication in virtual communities: the human interaction between consumer to marketer and that between consumer to consumer. As per the various prior literatures, social presence is a factor that generates interaction within a social community. Shin and Shin (2011, in Lau, Kan and Lau, 2013) noted that consumers'

Figure 8. Trust in the virtual communities
based on Lau, Kan, and Lau (2013)

Figure 9. Social presence in virtual communities
based on Shin and Shin (2011; as cited in Lau, Kan, & Lau, 2013)

behavioral attitude and perception of security is influenced by social presence in virtual environment.

Virtual Communities: Achieving Co-Creation via Virtual Interaction Tools

The authors have pointed out the types of marketing tools for targeting and reaching consumers in virtual communities. Füller and Matzler (2007, in Lau, Kan and Lau, 2013) argued that virtual interaction tools are useful for providing virtual experiences, enhance relationships and help consumers to share their explicit and implicit innovative ideas with the company's R&D team. Gabisch and Gwebu (2011, in Lau, Kan and Lau, 2013) regarded both, functional and social interaction between consumers as effective communication tools in virtual communities and could contribute in enhancing consumer brand knowledge and relationships.

Complementary: Bricks-and-Mortar Shopping – Virtual Shopping

A significant amount of research explains the difference between the traditional bricks-and-mortar shopping and virtual shopping by differentiating the respective factors of these types of shopping. Gabisch and Gwebu (2011, in Lau, Kan and Lau, 2013) attempted to find out the multiple effects of virtual reality shopping and its difference with the traditional shopping trend. Gabisch (2011, in Lau, Kan and Lau, 2013) also found that virtual shopping brand experiences usually have a positive effect on the consumers' real world purchasing intention.

Regarding exclusively virtual shopping behavior, the virtual store layout design is regarded a key determinant to attract the consumers involved in virtual shopping. Apparently, both bricks-and-mortal shopping and virtual shopping still complement each other.

Figure 10.

The paper concludes that the human aspects are most important to diffuse and establish virtual shopping practice among different communities.

The trend to embrace virtual worlds and virtual realities might also have an impact on education (i.e. online learning). On the one hand, online learning might provide more pupils and students with access to cheaper, more flexible and more global educational products (i.e. Moocs online courses by Harvard and MIT). In addition, this teaching methodology might take the specific characteristics of the young generations into account, being highly computer and Social Network Services affine, being very proactive in information and knowledge search, question the status quo and interested in self- creating content. Supported by modern communication and information technology, teaching of the future could be provided 'on demand'. Teaching might be even skipped with the teacher/professor becoming more a coach on suggested solutions to case study problems.

On the other hand, parents working in the Silicon Valley for Google, Yahoo or Apple prefer to send their children to Waldorf schools dedicated to "a holistic approach that integrates the intellectual, practical and creative development of pupils" (Jenkin, 2015). This Guardian report refers to an OECD study refuting a beneficial effect of computer technology on International Student Assessment tests (Pisa). Vice versa, social media, so the reference to other reports, result in disruptive behavior of pupils when using IPhones or tablets. Representatives of Waldorf schools refer to teaching and learning methodologies which stood the test of time, such as imaginative thinking, movement, human interaction and attention and concentration spans, play or artistic activities. They restrict the exposure to television, computers, internet or smartphones to pupils over the age of 12. It will be interesting to see if electronic books will be swapped again for tangible ones or if technology wins the upper hand in the classroom.

Framework for Investigating the Use of Performance Metrics Systems

In their study Järvinen and Karjaluoto (2015) applied web analytics to measure the digital marketing performance. For this purpose, the authors reviewed performance measurement literature and applied it to the use of Web analytics. Latter offers companies a metrics system to measure their digital marketing performance. The study shows that an organization's efforts to use marketing metrics systems and its resulting outcomes must be underpinned by

- The reasoning behind the chosen metrics' content
- The processing of metrics data
- The organizational context surrounding the use of the system.

Given the continuously growing importance of digital marketing in the industrial sector, this study illustrates how industrial companies characterized by complex selling processes can harness Web analytics, however, concludes on diverse practices in the chosen industrial sectors.

Pettigrew's et al.'s (1989) widely used framework (Bourne et al., 1999, 2002, 2005, Martinez et al., 2010, in Järvinen and Karjaluoto (2015) was used as a guiding model because it provides a sound structure for organizing disparate findings from the performance measurement literature to develop a holistic understanding of the elements that affect the firm's ability to design and exploit a marketing metrics system.

In this paper, the authors chose the case study approach as their research method. The study was conducted as part of a two-year Digital Marketing (DM) research project that was supported by seven large industrial firms and seven service providers, such as DM agencies. During exploratory discussions with the participating companies, the authors found, that DM performance measurement emerged as being a top-priority research theme and that multiple companies had already used web analytics (WA) for this purpose. Three of seven industrial companies that participated in the research project reported that they are actively using WA for DM performance measurement. These three companies were largely similar in terms of digital marketing activities and channels in use and, thus, have been considered in this study. The three companies' product categories are steel, paper and machinery. Among them steel has been found to better use the web analytics performance system in comparison to paper and machinery.

Performance Measurement Content

As per the study the exact design of an effective metrics system is likely to depend on the particular organization in question. Thus, there are no clear standards for building a metrics system that would fit the needs of all organizations. However, research indicates that to develop a successful metrics system, organizations should focus on

- Aligning metrics and strategy and
- Aligning definitions, dimensions, and structure of the metrics.

Referring to a number of prior studies (Phippen et al., 2004; Weischedel & Huizingh, 2006; Welling & White, 2006, in Järvinen and Karjaluoto, 2015), the authors state that little is known regarding the underlying reasons why organizations select certain WA metrics and ignore others, especially on how companies resolve the challenge of compiling a comprehensive yet manageable set of WA metrics. Moreover, whether quantitative WA metrics can substitute for subjective qualitative marketing measures remains unclear.

In case of web analytics measurement content, in comparison to steel, machinery and paper encountered more difficulties in designing a holistic WA metrics system. Likewise, machinery and paper measure the generation of sales leads; however, they do not follow how many of these leads result in transactions. Thus, they are unable to link their DM activities with financial outcomes.

Performance Measurement Process

From reviewing previous studies (e.g., Bourne, Mills, Wilcox et al., 2000; Bourne et al., 2005, in Järvinen and Karjaluoto, 2015) on the implementation and processing of measurement systems, key phases of the performance measurement process have been identified:

- Data gathering
- Data analysis and interpretation
- Result reporting
- Taking action
- Updating the metrics system.

Especially, the reporting phase is regarded to contribute to transmitting favorable managerial attitudes and behavior to marketers (Curren et al., 1992; Pauwels et al., 2009; Järvinen and Karjaluoto (2015).

However, the authors pointed to a lack of answers on the following questions:

1. How should reporting be organized?
2. How detailed should the information be that management is willing to receive from DM results?
3. How should responsibility regarding WA data be shared and co-ordination be performed (Eccles, 1991; Simons, 1991, in Järvinen and Karjaluoto, 2015)?

With regards to the web analytics measurement process, Steel had outlined a clear process and clear responsibilities for their use of WA data. Steel's customer data are properly stored by the data expert and campaign manager whose main responsibilities are to analyze and interpret the data and to draw insights from the data.

Performance Measurement Context

Research on the internal performance measurement context has identified various factors that influence the use of performance measurement systems. These findings complement and, partially, confirm the earlier competencies suggestions derived from Weill's and Woerner's (2015) article.

These factors include referring to previous studies (Chaffey & Patron, 2012; Court et al., 2012; Germann et al., 2013; Lenskold, 2002; O'Sullivan &Abela, 2007; Patterson, 2007, in Järvinen and Karjaluoto, 2015)

- Analytics skills and resources
- Information technology infrastructure
- Senior management commitment (i.e. investment in recruiting an expanding team of specialists and the allocation of substantial monetary resources to DM activities)
- Leadership and organizational culture (i.e. allocation of responsibilities and reporting of findings)

In this study it is stated that the use of analytics is more effective when the organizational culture applies effective change management (Davenport, 2013; McAfee & Brynjolfsson, 2012, in Järvinen and Karjaluoto, 2015), favors data-driven decision making, co-operation, and information sharing.

Regarding the information technology infrastructure, Järvinen and Karjaluoto (2015) pointed to primary advantages of WA tools in that they can be synchronized with other enterprise software, such as customer relationship management (CRM) and social analytics software (Digital Marketing Depot, 2014, in Järvinen and Karjaluoto, 2015). The authors, furthermore, notified that the integration of WA tools with other information technology platforms has not yet been fully explored in the academic literature.

The following SAS YouTube on Big Data visualizes the enormous data growth, especially also in emerging markets with only 0.5% being already analyzed and half of the data stored being unprotected: https://www.youtube.com/watch?v=-Gj93L2Qa6c

Consumer analytics is a major application field of th Big Data revolution. Technology, hereby, is the main enabler to capture rich and a large quantity data on consumer phenomena in real time. Thus, unprecedented volume, velocity, and variety of primary data, Big Data, are available from individual consumers. In this paper Erevelles, Fukawa and Swayne (2016) have proposed a conceptual framework on consumer analytics and big data analysis and have derived different propositions from it.

Defining Consumer Big Data

Big Data has a very significant influence on both, consumers and companies. Whilst consumers have become increasingly vigilant and informed buyers, the marketers have more traditional, structured, transactional data as well as more contemporary, unstructured, behavioral data at their disposal. However, the sheer magnitude of data challenges the marketers when requested to transforming them into efficient marketing decision making.

The following three dimensions help define Big Data, commonly referred to as the 3 Vs: volume, velocity, and variety (IBM, 2012; Lycett, 2013; Oracle, 2012; Lycett, 2013; Integreon Insight, 2012, in (Erevelles, Fukawa and Swayne, 2016).

The 3 Vs of Big Data

Figure 11.

The 3 Vs of Big Data

- Volume (the primary distinguishing characteristic)
  - Measured in petabytes, exabytes,or zettabytes with one petabyte being the equivalent to 20 million traditional filing cabinets of text

- Velocity
  - Relentless speed of continuous new rich, insightful and current data creation; Enhances evidence marketing decision making based on data created at real time

- Variety
  - Shift from transactional data to unstructured behavioral data retrieved from diverse sources

- Volume (the primary distinguishing characteristic)
- Measured in petabytes, exabytes,or zettabytes with one petabyte being the equivalent to 20 million traditional filing cabinets of text
- Velocity
- Relentless speed of continuous new rich, insightful and current data creation;
  Enhances evidence marketing decision making based on data created at real time
- Variety
- Shift from transactional data to unstructured behavioral data retrieved from diverse sources

Theoretical Framework

Resource-based theory has been often applied to digital data regarding them as precious resources to positively influence marketing performance and competitive advantage (RBT) (Barney, 2014, Day, 2014, Kozlenkova, Samaha, and Palmatier, 2014, Wu, 2010, Barney, 1991, Bharadwaj, El Sawy, Pavlou, and Venkatraman, 2013, Barth, & Bean, 2012, in Erevelles, Fukawa and Swayne, 2016).

Types of Resources

As Big Data relates to physical capital, human capital, and organizational capital resources they are most important from an organizational perspective. In this context, physical capital resources comprise software or platforms to collect, store, or analyze Big Data. Regarding human capital resources, the companies need to recruit data scientists and strategists to transform scattered insights into intelligent marketing action.

The Reason Why Ignorance Is Beneficial for Companies

Big Data on consumers' transactional and behavioral data provide the company with enhanced dynamic and adaptive capabilities necessary for innovative value creation in various marketing activities (Ambrosini & Bowman, 2009, Day, 2011, Bharadwaj et al., 2013 in Erevelles, Fukawa and Swayne, 2016). One of the limitations of RBT relates to the origin of these resources and capabilities (Barney, 2014, in Erevelles, Fukawa and

Swayne, 2016). Interestingly, to address this issue, the concept of ignorance has been suggested as a unique resource requirement or precondition for firms to achieve sustainable competitive advantage using Big Data. Rather than traditionally focusing on what they know, marketers and researchers should understand what they do not know, referred to as ignorance (Proctor & Schiebinger, 2008, Sammut & Sartawi, 2012, in Erevelles, Fukawa and Swayne, 2016). In other words, following the Socrates phrase of 'scio me nihil scire', the pursuit of knowledge sometimes requires researchers to recognize ignorance which exceeds often the amount of our knowledge (Smithson, 1985; Ungar, 2008; Firestein, 2012; Vitek & Jackson, 2008 in Erevelles, Fukawa and Swayne, 2016). Thus, as the source of competitive advantage moves from the knowledge itself to the speed of generating creative ideas (Erevelles, Horton, & Fukawa, 2007), ignorance is likely to become a more crucial cultural orientation for facilitating creativity within an organization (Erevelles, Horton, & Fukawa, 2007). In such a context, an ignorance-based view, rather than a knowledge-based view, enables researchers to be more effective as it allows them to observe phenomena using inductive reasoning and grounded theory based on new data without being possibly biased by existing knowledge.

Development of Propositions

Expanding What Marketers Don't Know

Drawing on a discussion on the benefits of more quantitative, deductive, linear research methodologies and more qualitative and inductive ones, also related to innovation and creativity levels, the authors provide the following propositions to guide future research in this important research stream (Erevelles, Horton, & Fukawa, 2007):

Proposition 1a. As the richness (volume, velocity and variety) of data increases, both linear and non-linear advances in understanding marketing phenomena will increase.

Proposition 1b. Non-linear advances in understanding marketing phenomena will occur more often with inductive techniques using Big Data than with deductive techniques using traditional data.

Proposition 2a. Firms that embrace inductive techniques in analyzing Big Data will be able to identify information needs arising from partial ignorance with greater success than firms that embrace deductive techniques.

Proposition 2b. Firms with greater awareness of information needs arising from partial ignorance will uncover more hidden consumer insights from Big Data that facilitate adaptive capabilities than firms with little awareness of information needs. (p. 900).

Proposition 3. A firm creates greater value with Big Data through radical innovation than with incremental innovation.

Proposition 4. Firms that embrace an ignorance-based view (embedded in human and organizational capital resources) will be able to create the valuable, rare, and imperfectly imitable resource from Big Data to facilitate sustainable competitive advantage with greater success than firms with a knowledge-based view.

Proposition 5. Firms with greater creative intensity in human and organizational capital resources will extract more hidden insights from Big Data than firms with little creative intensity. (pp. 900-901)

Based on and further developed from the paper the following managerial implications for companies are derived. Companies should be able to:

- Transform Big Data on consumer transactions and behavior into intelligent adaptive and innovative marketing strategies and tactics.
- Assess those capital resources (physical, human, organizational) which, both inhibit and enhance consumer analytics.
- Create a corporate culture embracing the ignorance based view to thrive on adaptive and innovative capabilities leading to competitive advantage.

Key Insights From McKinsey's DataMatics 2013 Survey: Customer Intelligence Correlated With Return on Assets

The paper emphasizes the use of customer intelligence to materialize corporate customer centric perspectives. As, so far, the high expectations of big data were not met, a key research question for McKinsey's global quantitative survey on big data with 400 top managers of large international companies addresses a possible correlation between the use of customer analytics and corporate performance.

Initially self-assessed corporate capabilities were later, with a sub-sample, correlated with objective performance criteria, resulting in a significant correlation of customer intelligence with the companies' return on assets.

The key findings of the survey in a nutshell:

- It is less a sophisticated IT customer analytics tool which matters in the first place, albeit instrumental, but more an integrated use of IT systems, strategy orientated analytics skills to underpin effective customer centric corporate decision making.
- It is key that customer analytics are integrated across functions and channels.
  - Generally, it is important to integrate real time data across all channels and giving frontline personnel access to it. This is preferred to exploiting new sources of data.
  - In particular: "enabling integrated multi-channel marketing, expanding customer analytics across the value chain, embedding analytics on the front line and processing real-time data" (McKinsey, 2013)
- "High Performers hire C-level executives with the 'data gene' in their DNA" (McKinsey, 2013) and involve senior management in customer analytics.

Regarding managerial implications the survey provides very useful wide ranging recommendations:

- Pursuing a cross functional approach
- Creating an internal Turntable or Center of Competence for customer centric analytics
- Providing standard reports to all relevant business functions
- Affirmatively and harmoniously anchor the transformation in the corporate culture and organizational processes regarding: mindsets, behavior, skills; organization; tools and process integration; data; IT; analytic methods
- Leaders' and senior management's commitment is crucial
- "Target group programs"
- "Guided selling devices for branch staff"

- "Shopping apps for customers"
- "Web shops with personalized content"

Whether termed "strategic analytics," "business intelligence" or "customer analytics," effective interpretation of consumer data has already become an absolutely necessary and integral part of any business process. These consumer data analytic system interfaces are crucial to prescribe models that match segments to campaigns, offers, and content using every conceivable channel. Hence, consumer data analytics is key to maintaining a competitive edge. In view of these developments, it is necessary that every company will be performing customer analytics as a condition in the near future. But champion organizations always need to remain active to be the major player in any industry. Since all the players will be in the game and improving by the minute, champions need to prepare themselves for a pure-play strategy that elevates them to strategic and operational excellence, with the lowest costs coupled with the greatest possible benefits.

Ethical Aspects of Digitalization

Brahmbhatt (2015) based on wide ranging literature review portrays various ethical perspectives on marketing communication particularly in the context of digitalization.

Ethics in marketing communication consists of the following factors or standards:

- Perception of right or wrong deed implying morality (De George, 1999 in Brahmbhatt, 2015)
- Representation and expression should not be "misleading, deceitful, exploitative, demeaning, irritating, wasteful, arrogant and servile" (Varey, 2002, p.325, in Brahmbhatt, 2015)
- Customers are the focus for ethical marketing practice (Laczniak and Murphy,2006, in Brahmbhatt, 2015)
- Following ethical principles in the conduct of business (Brahmbhatt, 2015).
- Ethical Marketing is context specific (Robin and Reidenbach, 1993, in Brahmbhatt, 2015)
- Such as truth telling through advertisements, treatment of vulnerable groups, representation of groups, infringement of personal privacy through direct marketing, images of women and men in advertising and

stereotyping people, culture and region (Attas, 1999; Borgerson and Schroeder, 2002; Carrigan and Szmigin, 2003;, Christy & Mitchell, 1999; Packard, 1960; Strachan & Pavie-Latour, 2008, in Brahmbhatt, 2015; p.38).

Kuldeep Brahmbhatt (2015) notified the following factors influencing ethical marketing perspective which are as follows:

1. Personal, Organizational and Institutional Factors (Sparks and Hunt, 1998; Hunt & Vittel, 1992; Hawkins and Cocanougher, 1972, in Brahmbhatt, 2015)
   a. Judging organizational practices
   b. Supervisory actions
   c. Machiavellianism
   d. Cognitive moral development
   e. Deontological norms
   f. Importance and moral intensity of ethical issues
   g. Religion
   h. Individual value system
   i. Strength and moral character
   j. Ethical sensitivity
   k. Educational institutions environment
2. Contextual Factors (Clampitt, 1991, in Brahmbhatt, 2015)
   a. On behalf of the communicator: feelings attached, information to be sent and motives
   b. On behalf of the message receiver: moral stance when interpreting the message;
3. Competitive Environment (Johnson and Busbin, 2000)
   a. Digitalization creates new paradigm speeding competition and information
   b. Dissemination resulting in new marketing concepts (i.e. buzz and viral marketing or electronic word of mouth)

Based on research, the Institute of Business Ethics (IBE) (2011) highlights the key ethical concerns for companies in relation to social media and refers to best practices to overcome them.

Integrity Risk

Ninety five per cent of employees, so a DLA Piper Survey (in IBE, 2011), use social media both, for personal as well as work reasons. This elevates, according to 6 of 7 surveyed large companies, Integrity Risk to the top ethical corporate concern as, in case of potentially irresponsible social media use by employees on behalf of the company, the ethical code and reputation of a company might be affected. Exemplarily, offensive responses of content managers to fan's comments (i.e. Nestle) might jeopardize corporate reputation. The same effect might occur when employees spread negative comments about their employer through their personal social media profiles.

How to remedy the dilemma? "To ensure that work-related discussion amongst employees is internal to the organization, Serco Group, a large UK-listed international services company, has developed an „internal Facebook". This is for staff to use to discuss work topics with colleagues rather than using public forums, as a way of dealing with integrity risk" (IBE, 2011, p.2).

Responsible Marketing

Interactive engagement with consumers and ever closer brand consumer relationships raises the bar for socially responsible marketing. Exemplarily, "to avoid misleading consumers, employees can declare that they are representing/have an interest in the company e.g. if writing product reviews" (IBE, 2011, p. 2).

Recruitment Practices

The assessment of the professional qualification of an applicant, based on primarily private information on Social Media profiles, as done by the majority of researched recruiters or using the social media screening service of specialized organisations (IBE, 2011) is questionable ethical practice. A transparent and outspoken corporate policy in the case of using Social Media for recruitment purposes is recommended.

The Duty of Care

The employees' simultaneous use of social media for private and work activities, might prevent the employer fulfilling its duty of care for employees, for example, in case of cyber bullying, harassment and discrimination. "The challenge for companies is identifying acceptable levels of monitoring employees" personal use of social media, without being seen to limit their freedom of expression" (IBE, 2011, p.3). As a company opts for monitoring employees' private social media communication, again, a transparent communication of the practices and reasons for doing so is recommended. As in the other critical points mentioned before, the solution is seen in having a continuously updated Social Media Policy in place which is consistent with the ethical code of the company (IBE, 2011) and empathetically and constantly reminding the employee on her/his responsibility for the company when using Social Media. Exemplarily, KPMG's practice of using on screen alerts is mentioned in this context. The Social Media Policy is suggested to be co-created by different functions, the employees, customers/fans/members of the brand community and other stakeholder of the company and reflected by the terms of use.

Online Price Discrimination

Relating to the Wall Street Journal which published websites that differentiated prices due to certain factors of consumer statistics, Shpania in his blog (2013) questions these practices to be appropriate for a reliable and fair electronic market place. He refers to practices where websites differentiated prices due to browsers' location, browsing history or operating system and suggests: "However, the federal trade commission can interfere in cases where online information has been used to manipulate the prices. Well, this is just an idea for those who have been victims of this pricing strategy" (Shpania, 2013). Besides the ethical issues involved, it is questionable if loyal consumers agree with websites using cookies to track user behavior and changing the price according to increased page visits.

Interesting Philosophical Discussion with Practical Implications

A comprehensive and interesting discussion on ethical issues in the context of Social Networking Services is provided by the Stanford Encyclopedia of

Philosophy (2015). Exemplarily, the following two ethical topics referring to Privacy and Virtual identities are summarized. Whilst a more comprehensive philosophical discussion is regarded to go beyond the scope of this book, the reader is strongly recommended to read the full original article and to engage in the discussion.

Privacy

In addition to the ethical pragmatic factors mentioned before, the Stanford Encyclopedia of Philosophy (2015) points to the sense of urgency, i.e. in the light of privacy practices of some Social Network Services (SNS), in debating the following concerns:

- "The potential availability of users' data to third parties for the purposes of commercial marketing, data mining, research, surveillance or law enforcement;
- The capacity of facial-recognition software to automatically identify persons in uploaded photos;
- The ability of third-party applications to collect and publish user data without their permission or awareness;
- The frequent use by SNS of automatic 'opt-in' privacy controls;
- The use of 'cookies' to track online user activities after they have left a SNS;
- The potential use of location-based social networking for stalking or other illicit monitoring of users' physical movements;
- The sharing of user information or patterns of activity with government entities; and, last but not least,
- The potential of SNS to encourage users to adopt voluntary but imprudent, ill-informed or unethical information sharing practices, either with respect to sharing their own personal data or sharing data related to other persons and entities".

Ethics and Virtual Identities

In addition, the Stanford Encyclopedia of Philosophy (2015, http://plato. stanford.edu/entries/ethics-social-networking/) also raises interesting ethical questions relating to the creation of virtual identities and communities. A potential problem might arise when, previously anonymously in SNS constructed, virtual alter-egos are nowadays linked with real-world networks and a number of questions are triggered to be debated and researched: "Yet SNS still enable users to manage their self-presentation and their social networks in ways that offline social spaces at home, school or work often do not permit. The result, then, is an identity grounded in the person's material reality and embodiment but more explicitly "reflective and aspirational" (Stokes 2012, p. 365) in its presentation. This raises a number of ethical questions: first, from what source of normative guidance or value does the aspirational content of an SNS user's identity primarily derive? Do identity performances on SNS generally represent the same aspirations and reflect the same value profiles as users' offline identity performances? Do they display any notable differences from the aspirational identities of non-SNS users? Are the values and aspirations made explicit in SNS contexts more or less heteronomous in origin than those expressed in non-SNS contexts? Do the more explicitly aspirational identity performances on SNS encourage users to take steps to actually embody those aspirations offline, or do they tend to weaken the motivation to do so?"

Bridging an Apparent Gap: Integrated Online and Offline Channel Design

This chapter, and this book, concludes with a proposed summarizing framework depicting an integrated online-offline channel strategy, suggestions for future research and future strategic foci.

1. Suggestions for further research based on the following general research questions in addition to the propositions developed by reviewed papers:
    a. Which customer segments are valuable in which channels?
    b. Which channels are valuable for which segments?
    c. How to match digital customer identity with corporate identity?
    d. How are channels linked to corporate objectives, customer needs, industries, and Marketing strategies?
    e. Can brand love be increased by digital channels?
    f. How can companies excite and engage customer in online and offline channels (addressing all 5 Senses)?

Figure 12. Integrated online and offline channel design

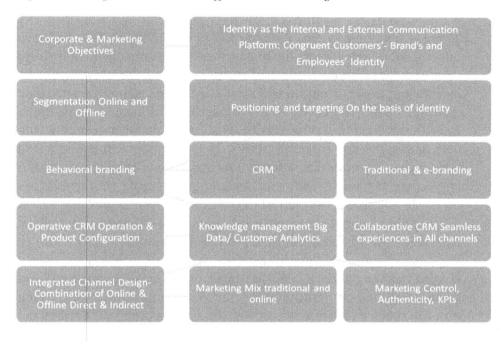

g. How does channel preference affect product category (i.e. hedonic and utilitarian)?

h. How do the various sources of consumer power influence corporate performance and profitability?

2. Selected Strategic Aspects

a. Better understanding and appreciation of customer value and satisfying them via Integrated multi-channel marketing

b. Better appreciation of social, community, ecosystem touch points

c. Affirmative coping with still existing challenges ('shitstorming', privacy, security, ethics)

d. Designing and configurating channels according to key performance indicators

e. Corporate objectives should focus more on achieving customer co-creating, co-designing, co producing

Answers

1. There is a premise in customer knowledge marketing that the better we understand our customers the higher their retention rates (aka loyalty), therefore, the profitability-related ratios. First of all, the internet provides us with ample opportunities to collect and utilize customer related data, therefore betters our customer knowledge and ultimately- as the model goes- the profitability ratios. Obviously, there are steps between collecting data and improving the profitability. But, simply put, imagine a state where you can combine information about your customers' in-store and online behaviour and start designing marketing strategies based on these: you must possibilities to craft the right strategies that will be self-expressive for your targeted customers, who will in turn reward you with their loyalty and impact the profitability ratios.

2. For centuries the customer behaviour is formed in brick-and-mortar contexts, characterized by interpersonal communication, touch and feel, problem solving etc. Truth be told, the younger consumers seem quite prone to replace - in some sectors- traditional shopping with online but, in the larger scale, we support that there is a two way evolution happening right now: online retailers struggle to simulate the "real" experience, even with the use of virtual reality and advanced features. At the same time, however, the traditional shops are evolving as well, incorporating advanced technology. The example of the recent Amazon Go brick and mortar shop is a loud call for integration in this field.

3. From a market-based view, where the position in the market determines the leader, the better understanding of our customers through the utilization of the big data, in fact allows us to better define the market and then lead it. From a resource based view, loyal communities and engaged audiences that are gained via digital marketing practices are amongst the most sustainable versions of competitive advantage. From a channel structure point of view, finally, integrating traditional and online stores can, like many leading retailers, in a synergistic rather that competitive mentality, can result to a very efficient business model and a source of competitive advantage, as well.

4. It is true that Google Analytics is a fairly easy to use tool that allow marketers to mine data about their consumers' behaviour. But, this is not a process that takes place in vacuum and this is something modern businesses have to consider: There is a what, a how and a who that

need to be answered in advance. First of all, our metrics need to be meaningful, bonded to some conversion goals, otherwise we face the risk of paralysis by analysis. Then, it's the process we measure performance, the reports we issue and the time we do it, the use of the conclusions etc. And last but not least, it's the who: are the people responsible to handle the analysis of data properly equipped with knowledge, skills and experience both from marketing and analysis fields? As you might already see, answering these questions is much more difficult that signing up to Google Analytics, yet, it's not a step that can be skipped.

5. There is a stream of thought suggesting that too much information might make companies too confident about themselves and the antidote to this is the concept of ignorance. The supporters of ignorance- based view (as an opposite to knowledge-based view) propose that as the source of competitive advantage moves from the knowledge itself to the speed of generating creative ideas, constantly pursuing what we don't know is a better source of innovation than utilizing what we know.

REFERENCES

Ali Khan Panni, M. F. (2015). Basic model of CKM in terms of Marketing Performance and some important antecedents and dimensions. In H.R. Kaufmann (Ed.), Handbook of Research on Managing and Influencing Consumer Behavior. Hershey, PA: IGI Global.

Brahmbhatt, K. (2015). Ethical marketing communication in the era of digitalization. *Indore Management Journal*, 7(2), 26–44.

Dickley, I. J., & Lewis, W. F. (2009). Furthering the integration of online marketing in the grocery industry through business model and value assessment. *Proceedings of ASBS Annual Conference.*

Erevelles, S., Fukawa, N., & Swayne, L. (2016). Big Data consumer analytics and the transformation of marketing. *Journal of Business Research*, 69(2), 897–904. doi:10.1016/j.jbusres.2015.07.001

Gronover, S. (2003). *Multi-Channel-Management - Konzepte, Techniken und Fallbeispiele aus dem Retailbereich der Finanzdienstleistungsbranche* (Doctoral thesis). UniSG.

Grönroos, C. (2006). On defining marketing: Finding a new roadmap for marketing. *Marketing Theory, 6*(4), 395–417. doi:10.1177/1470593106069930

Institute of Business Ethics. (2011, December). The Ethical Challenges of Social Media. *Business Ethics Briefing, 22.*

Järvinen, J., & Karjaluoto, H. (2015). The use of web analytics for digital marketing performance measurement. *Industrial Marketing Management, 50,* 117–127. doi:10.1016/j.indmarman.2015.04.009

Jenkin, M. (2015). Tablets out, imagination in: the school that shun technology. *The Guardian.* Retrieved from https://www.theguardian.com/teacher-network/2015/dec/02/schools-that-ban-tablets-traditional-education-silicon-valley-london

Kaufmann, H. R., & Ali Khan Panni, M. F. (2014). *Handbook of Research on Consumerism in Business and Marketing: Concept and Practices.* Hershey, PA: IGI Global. doi:10.4018/978-1-4666-5880-6

Kaufmann, H. R., Loureiro, S., & Manarioti, A. (2016). Exploring Consumer-Brand Relationships: A synthesized model exploring the relationship among behavioral branding, brand love and brand co- creation. *Journal of Product and Brand Management, 25*(6), 516–526. doi:10.1108/JPBM-06-2015-0919

Kaufmann, H. R., Vrontis, D., Czinkota, M., & Hadiono, A. (2012). Corporate branding and transformational leadership in turbulent times. *Journal of Product and Brand Management, 21*(3), 192–204. doi:10.1108/10610421211228810

Kollman, T., & Hasel, M. (2006). Cross channel cooperation: a collaborative approach of integrating online and offline business models. *Lecture Notes in Informatics.* Retrieved from http://subs.emis.de/LNI/Proceedings/Proceedings92/gi-proc-092-004.pdf

Labrecque, L. I., vor dem Esche, J., Mathwick, C., Novak, T. P., & Hofacker, C. F. (2013). Consumer power: Evolution in the digital age. *Journal of Interactive Marketing, 27*(4), 257–269. doi:10.1016/j.intmar.2013.09.002

Lau, H.-f., Kan, C.-w., & Lau, K.-w. (2013). How consumers shop in virtual reality? How it works? *Advances in Economics and Business, 1*(1), 28–38.

Laudon, K. C., & Trevor, C. G. (2011). *Ecommerce 2011* (7th ed.). Pearson Higher Education.

Loureiro, S., Kaufmann, H. R., & Vrontis, D. (2012). Brand Emotional Connection and Loyalty. *Journal of Brand Management, 20*(1), 13–27. doi:10.1057/bm.2012.3

McKinsey. (2014). *Using customer analytics to boost corporate performance: Key insights from McKinsey's DataMatics 2013 survey.* Retrieved from https://www.mckinseyonmarketingandsales.com/sites/default/files/pdf/Datamatics.pdf

Meffert, H., Burmann, C., & Kirchgeorg, M. (2008). *Marketing- Grundlagen Marktorientierter Unternehmensfuehrung.* Berlin: Springer Verlag.

Salo, J. (2012). Customer experience management in the music industry online communities. *International Journal of Music Business Research, 1*(2), 7–29.

Shimp, T.A. (1997). *Advertising, Promotion, and Supplemental Aspects of Integrated Marketing Communications.* Dryden Press.

Shpania, A. (2013). Online price discrimination: A surprising reality in ecommerce. *Econsultancy.* Retrieved from https://econsultancy.com/blog/62699-online-price-discrimination-a-surprising-reality-in-ecommerce/

Smith, P. R., & Chaffey, D. (2005). EMarketing excellence: The heart of Ebusiness. Elsevier Butterworth-Heinemann.

Staeger, C. (1999). *Multi Channel Management: Mehrdimensionale Optimierung der Kundenbeziehung zur nachhaltigen Steigerung der Profitabilität im Retail Banking.* Bern: Paul Haupt Verlag.

Stanford Encyclopedia of Philosophy. (2015). *Social networking and ethics.* Retrieved from http://plato.stanford.edu/entries/ethics-social-networking/

Straker, K., Wrigley, C., & Rosemann, M. (2015). Typologies and touchpoints: Designing multi-channel digital strategies. *Journal of Research in Interactive Marketing, 9*(2), 110–128. doi:10.1108/JRIM-06-2014-0039

Trenz, M. (2015). *Offline, Online and Multichannel Commerce. Multichannel Commerce, Consumer Perspective on the Integration of Physical and Electronic Channel.* Springer International Publishing.

Weill, P., & Woerner, S. L. (2015). Thriving in an increasingly digital ecosystem. *MIT Sloan Review, 56*(4), 27–34.

Related Readings

To continue IGI Global's long-standing tradition of advancing innovation through emerging research, please find below a compiled list of recommended IGI Global book chapters and journal articles in the areas of economic development, business productivity, and business technology. These related readings will provide additional information and guidance to further enrich your knowledge and assist you with your own research.

Abidi, N., Bandyopadhayay, A., & Gupta, V. (2017). Sustainable Supply Chain Management: A Three Dimensional Framework and Performance Metric for Indian IT Product Companies. *International Journal of Information Systems and Supply Chain Management*, *10*(1), 29–52. doi:10.4018/IJISSCM.2017010103

Akçay, D. (2017). The Role of Social Media in Shaping Marketing Strategies in the Airline Industry. In V. Benson, R. Tuninga, & G. Saridakis (Eds.), *Analyzing the Strategic Role of Social Networking in Firm Growth and Productivity* (pp. 214–233). Hershey, PA: IGI Global. doi:10.4018/978-1-5225-0559-4.ch012

Alizadeh, T., & Sipe, N. (2016). Vancouvers Digital Strategy: Disruption, New Direction, or Business as Usual? *International Journal of E-Planning Research*, *5*(4), 1–15. doi:10.4018/IJEPR.2016100101

Ambani, P. (2017). Crowdsourcing New Tools to Start Lean and Succeed in Entrepreneurship: Entrepreneurship in the Crowd Economy. In W. Vassallo (Ed.), *Crowdfunding for Sustainable Entrepreneurship and Innovation* (pp. 37–53). Hershey, PA: IGI Global. doi:10.4018/978-1-5225-0568-6.ch003

Antonova, A. (2015). Emerging Technologies and Organizational Transformation. In M. Wadhwa & A. Harper (Eds.), *Technology, Innovation, and Enterprise Transformation* (pp. 20–34). Hershey, PA: IGI Global. doi:10.4018/978-1-4666-6473-9.ch002

Azevedo, P. S., Azevedo, C., & Romão, M. (2017). Benefits and Value of Investments in Information Systems: The Case of Enterprise Resource Planning (ERP) Systems in the Hospitality Industry. In P. Vasant, & K. M. (Eds.), Handbook of Research on Holistic Optimization Techniques in the Hospitality, Tourism, and Travel Industry (pp. 251-262). Hershey, PA: IGI Global. doi:10.4018/978-1-5225-1054-3.ch011

Baig, V. A., & Akhtar, J. (2016). Supply Chain Process Efficiency (SCPE) and Firm's Financial Efficiency (FFE): A Study of Establishing Linkages. In A. Dwivedi (Ed.), *Innovative Solutions for Implementing Global Supply Chains in Emerging Markets* (pp. 49–70). Hershey, PA: IGI Global. doi:10.4018/978-1-4666-9795-9.ch003

Baporikar, N. (2017). Business Excellence Strategies for SME Sustainability in India. In P. Ordóñez de Pablos (Ed.), *Managerial Strategies and Solutions for Business Success in Asia* (pp. 61–78). Hershey, PA: IGI Global. doi:10.4018/978-1-5225-1886-0.ch004

Bartens, Y., Chunpir, H. I., Schulte, F., & Voß, S. (2017). Business/IT Alignment in Two-Sided Markets: A COBIT 5 Analysis for Media Streaming Business Models. In S. De Haes & W. Van Grembergen (Eds.), *Strategic IT Governance and Alignment in Business Settings* (pp. 82–111). Hershey, PA: IGI Global. doi:10.4018/978-1-5225-0861-8.ch004

Berberich, R. (2017). Creating Shared Value and Increasing Project Success by Stakeholder Collaboration: A Case in European Manufacturing. In M. Camilleri (Ed.), *CSR 2.0 and the New Era of Corporate Citizenship* (pp. 101–122). Hershey, PA: IGI Global. doi:10.4018/978-1-5225-1842-6.ch006

Blazeska-Tabakovska, N., & Manevska, V. (2015). The Impact of Knowledge Management Information System on Businesses. In M. Wadhwa & A. Harper (Eds.), *Technology, Innovation, and Enterprise Transformation* (pp. 92–117). Hershey, PA: IGI Global. doi:10.4018/978-1-4666-6473-9.ch005

Boachie, C. (2017). Public Financial Management and Systems of Accountability in Sub-National Governance in Developing Economies. In E. Schoburgh & R. Ryan (Eds.), *Handbook of Research on Sub-National Governance and Development* (pp. 193–217). Hershey, PA: IGI Global. doi:10.4018/978-1-5225-1645-3.ch009

Boitan, I. A. (2017). Nonparametric Estimation of National Promotional Banks' Efficiency and Productivity. In *Examining the Role of National Promotional Banks in the European Economy: Emerging Research and Opportunities* (pp. 77–107). Hershey, PA: IGI Global. doi:10.4018/978-1-5225-1845-7.ch004

Bookhamer, P., & (Justin) Zhang, Z. (. (2016). Knowledge Management in a Global Context: A Case Study. *Information Resources Management Journal*, 29(1), 57–74. doi:10.4018/IRMJ.2016010104

Caffrey, E., & McDonagh, J. (2015). Aligning Strategy and Information Technology. In M. Wadhwa & A. Harper (Eds.), *Technology, Innovation, and Enterprise Transformation* (pp. 233–261). Hershey, PA: IGI Global. doi:10.4018/978-1-4666-6473-9.ch011

Camilleri, M. A. (2017). The Corporate Sustainability and Responsibility Proposition: A Review and Appraisal. In M. Camilleri (Ed.), *CSR 2.0 and the New Era of Corporate Citizenship* (pp. 1–16). Hershey, PA: IGI Global. doi:10.4018/978-1-5225-1842-6.ch001

Can, M., & Doğan, B. (2017). The Effects of Economic Structural Transformation on Employment: An Evaluation in the Context of Economic Complexity and Product Space Theory. In F. Yenilmez & E. Kılıç (Eds.), *Handbook of Research on Unemployment and Labor Market Sustainability in the Era of Globalization* (pp. 275–306). Hershey, PA: IGI Global. doi:10.4018/978-1-5225-2008-5.ch016

Cano, I. M., Ozuna, M. G., Hernández, M. D., Contreras, J. A., & Láinez, J. J. (2016). Influence of ICT in the Industrial Sector MSMEs. In G. Alor-Hernández, C. Sánchez-Ramírez, & J. García-Alcaraz (Eds.), *Handbook of Research on Managerial Strategies for Achieving Optimal Performance in Industrial Processes* (pp. 197–217). Hershey, PA: IGI Global. doi:10.4018/978-1-5225-0130-5.ch010

Carillo, K. D. (2016). How to Engrain a Big Data Mindset into Our Managers' DNA: Insights from a Big Data Initiative in a French Business School. In A. Aggarwal (Ed.), *Managing Big Data Integration in the Public Sector* (pp. 71–91). Hershey, PA: IGI Global. doi:10.4018/978-1-4666-9649-5.ch005

Castellano, E., Zubizarreta, P. X., Pagalday, G., Uribetxebarria, J., & Crespo Márquez, A. (2017). Service 4.0: The Reasons and Purposes of Industry 4.0 within the Ambit of After-Sales Maintenance. In M. Carnero & V. González-Prida (Eds.), *Optimum Decision Making in Asset Management* (pp. 139–162). Hershey, PA: IGI Global. doi:10.4018/978-1-5225-0651-5.ch007

Castro, O. A., Arias, C. L., Ibañez, J. E., & Bulla, F. J. (2017). Universities Fostering Business Development: The Role of Education in Entrepreneurship. In I. Hosu & I. Iancu (Eds.), *Digital Entrepreneurship and Global Innovation* (pp. 193–224). Hershey, PA: IGI Global. doi:10.4018/978-1-5225-0953-0.ch010

Chen, E. T. (2016). Examining the Influence of Information Technology on Modern Health Care. In P. Manolitzas, E. Grigoroudis, N. Matsatsinis, & D. Yannacopoulos (Eds.), *Effective Methods for Modern Healthcare Service Quality and Evaluation* (pp. 110–136). Hershey, PA: IGI Global. doi:10.4018/978-1-4666-9961-8.ch006

Chkiwa, M., Jedidi, A., & Gargouri, F. (2017). Semantic / Fuzzy Information Retrieval System. *International Journal of Information Technology and Web Engineering*, *12*(1), 37–56. doi:10.4018/IJITWE.2017010103

Cole, M. T., Swartz, L. B., & Shelley, D. J. (2015). Enhancing Business Education with Technology Using Social Media to Aid Learning. In M. Khosrow-Pour (Ed.), *Encyclopedia of Information Science and Technology* (3rd ed.; pp. 699–708). Hershey, PA: IGI Global. doi:10.4018/978-1-4666-5888-2.ch067

Dau, L. A., Moore, E. M., Soto, M. A., & LeBlanc, C. R. (2017). How Globalization Sparked Entrepreneurship in the Developing World: The Impact of Formal Economic and Political Linkages. In B. Christiansen & F. Kasarcı (Eds.), *Corporate Espionage, Geopolitics, and Diplomacy Issues in International Business* (pp. 72–91). Hershey, PA: IGI Global. doi:10.4018/978-1-5225-1031-4.ch005

David-West, O. (2016). E-Commerce Management in Emerging Markets. In I. Lee (Ed.), *Encyclopedia of E-Commerce Development, Implementation, and Management* (pp. 200–222). Hershey, PA: IGI Global. doi:10.4018/978-1-4666-9787-4.ch016

Dawson, M., Leonard, B., & Rahim, E. (2015). Advances in Technology Project Management: Review of Open Source Software Integration. In M. Wadhwa & A. Harper (Eds.), *Technology, Innovation, and Enterprise Transformation* (pp. 313–324). Hershey, PA: IGI Global. doi:10.4018/978-1-4666-6473-9.ch016

De Coster, R., & McEwen, C. (2015). The Commercialisation and Adoption of Emerging Technologies: The Role of Professional Service Firms. In A. Szopa, W. Karwowski, & D. Barbe (Eds.), *Competitive Strategies for Academic Entrepreneurship: Commercialization of Research-Based Products* (pp. 227–255). Hershey, PA: IGI Global. doi:10.4018/978-1-4666-8487-4.ch011

de Vrieze, P., & Xu, L. (2016). Internet Enterprise Service Design Based on Existing Architectural Knowledge. In I. Lee (Ed.), *Encyclopedia of E-Commerce Development, Implementation, and Management* (pp. 818–826). Hershey, PA: IGI Global. doi:10.4018/978-1-4666-9787-4.ch057

Delgado, J. (2015). Structural Services: A New Approach to Enterprise Integration. In M. Wadhwa & A. Harper (Eds.), *Technology, Innovation, and Enterprise Transformation* (pp. 50–91). Hershey, PA: IGI Global. doi:10.4018/978-1-4666-6473-9.ch004

Deshpande, M. (2017). Best Practices in Management Institutions for Global Leadership: Policy Aspects. In N. Baporikar (Ed.), *Management Education for Global Leadership* (pp. 1–27). Hershey, PA: IGI Global. doi:10.4018/978-1-5225-1013-0.ch001

Di Caprio, D., Santos-Arteaga, F. J., & Tavana, M. (2015). Technology Development through Knowledge Assimilation and Innovation: A European Perspective. *Journal of Global Information Management*, *23*(2), 48–93. doi:10.4018/JGIM.2015040103

Ditizio, A. A., & Smith, A. D. (2017). Transformation of CRM and Supply Chain Management Techniques in a New Venture. In M. Tavana, K. Szabat, & K. Puranam (Eds.), *Organizational Productivity and Performance Measurements Using Predictive Modeling and Analytics* (pp. 96–114). Hershey, PA: IGI Global. doi:10.4018/978-1-5225-0654-6.ch006

Duffy, A. (2017). How Social Media Offers Opportunities for Growth in the Traditional Media Industry: The Case of Travel Journalism. In V. Benson, R. Tuninga, & G. Saridakis (Eds.), *Analyzing the Strategic Role of Social Networking in Firm Growth and Productivity* (pp. 172–187). Hershey, PA: IGI Global. doi:10.4018/978-1-5225-0559-4.ch010

Easton, J., & Parmar, R. (2017). Navigating Your Way to the Hybrid Cloud. In J. Chen, Y. Zhang, & R. Gottschalk (Eds.), *Handbook of Research on End-to-End Cloud Computing Architecture Design* (pp. 15–38). Hershey, PA: IGI Global. doi:10.4018/978-1-5225-0759-8.ch002

El-Gohary, H., & El-Gohary, Z. (2016). An Attempt to Explore Electronic Marketing Adoption and Implementation Aspects in Developing Countries: The Case of Egypt. *International Journal of Customer Relationship Marketing and Management*, 7(4), 1–26. doi:10.4018/IJCRMM.2016100101

Escribano, A. J. (2017). Transitions toward Sustainability in the Livestock Business: Developing Countries and Disfavored Areas. In N. Ray (Ed.), *Business Infrastructure for Sustainability in Developing Economies* (pp. 192–214). Hershey, PA: IGI Global. doi:10.4018/978-1-5225-2041-2.ch010

Esen, S. K., & El Barky, S. S. (2017). Drivers and Barriers to Green Supply Chain Management Practices: The Views of Turkish and Egyptian Companies Operating in Egypt. In U. Akkucuk (Ed.), *Ethics and Sustainability in Global Supply Chain Management* (pp. 232–260). Hershey, PA: IGI Global. doi:10.4018/978-1-5225-2036-8.ch013

Eze, U. C. (2016). A TOE Perspective of E-Business Deployment in Financial Firms. In I. Lee (Ed.), *Encyclopedia of E-Commerce Development, Implementation, and Management* (pp. 653–673). Hershey, PA: IGI Global. doi:10.4018/978-1-4666-9787-4.ch048

Fernandes da Anunciação, P., Lobo, M., Pereira, O., & Mateus, G. (2017). The Importance of Perception and Appreciation of the Information Management for Effective Logistics and Supply Chain in Transport Sector. In G. Jamil, A. Soares, & C. Pessoa (Eds.), *Handbook of Research on Information Management for Effective Logistics and Supply Chains* (pp. 453–468). Hershey, PA: IGI Global. doi:10.4018/978-1-5225-0973-8.ch024

Fernando, Y., Mathath, A., & Murshid, M. A. (2016). Improving Productivity: A Review of Robotic Applications in Food Industry. *International Journal of Robotics Applications and Technologies*, *4*(1), 43–62. doi:10.4018/IJRAT.2016010103

Fields, Z., & Atiku, S. O. (2017). Collective Green Creativity and Eco-Innovation as Key Drivers of Sustainable Business Solutions in Organizations. In Z. Fields (Ed.), *Collective Creativity for Responsible and Sustainable Business Practice* (pp. 1–25). Hershey, PA: IGI Global. doi:10.4018/978-1-5225-1823-5.ch001

Gleghorn, G. (2015). Business Competence and Acumen of Information Technology Professionals. In M. Wadhwa & A. Harper (Eds.), *Technology, Innovation, and Enterprise Transformation* (pp. 302–312). Hershey, PA: IGI Global. doi:10.4018/978-1-4666-6473-9.ch015

Gleghorn, G. D., & Harper, A. (2015). Logistics and Supply Chain Management and the Impact of Information Systems and Information Technology. In M. Wadhwa & A. Harper (Eds.), *Technology, Innovation, and Enterprise Transformation* (pp. 295–301). Hershey, PA: IGI Global. doi:10.4018/978-1-4666-6473-9.ch014

Gokhale, A. A., & Machina, K. F. (2017). Development of a Scale to Measure Attitudes toward Information Technology. In L. Tomei (Ed.), *Exploring the New Era of Technology-Infused Education* (pp. 49–64). Hershey, PA: IGI Global. doi:10.4018/978-1-5225-1709-2.ch004

Gomes, J., & Romão, M. (2017). Aligning Information Systems and Technology with Benefit Management and Balanced Scorecard. In S. De Haes & W. Van Grembergen (Eds.), *Strategic IT Governance and Alignment in Business Settings* (pp. 112–131). Hershey, PA: IGI Global. doi:10.4018/978-1-5225-0861-8.ch005

Heni, N., & Hamam, H. (2016). Databases and Information Systems. In P. Papajorgji, F. Pinet, A. Guimarães, & J. Papathanasiou (Eds.), *Automated Enterprise Systems for Maximizing Business Performance* (pp. 123–149). Hershey, PA: IGI Global. doi:10.4018/978-1-4666-8841-4.ch008

Hernandez, A. A., & Ona, S. E. (2016). Green IT Adoption: Lessons from the Philippines Business Process Outsourcing Industry. *International Journal of Social Ecology and Sustainable Development*, *7*(1), 1–34. doi:10.4018/IJSESD.2016010101

Hunter, M. G. (2015). Adoption. In *Strategic Utilization of Information Systems in Small Business* (pp. 136–169). Hershey, PA: IGI Global. doi:10.4018/978-1-4666-8708-0.ch005

Hunter, M. G. (2015). Information Systems. In *Strategic Utilization of Information Systems in Small Business* (pp. 78–108). Hershey, PA: IGI Global. doi:10.4018/978-1-4666-8708-0.ch003

Hunter, M. G. (2015). Strategy. In *Strategic Utilization of Information Systems in Small Business* (pp. 184–194). Hershey, PA: IGI Global. doi:10.4018/978-1-4666-8708-0.ch007

Hunter, M. G. (2015). Theories for Investigations. In *Strategic Utilization of Information Systems in Small Business* (pp. 109–135). Hershey, PA: IGI Global. doi:10.4018/978-1-4666-8708-0.ch004

Hurst, R. R., Lloyd, J. T., & Miller, J. C. (2017). Raising the Bar: Moving Evaluation of Training From the Classroom Into the Business. In S. Frasard & F. Prasuhn (Eds.), *Training Initiatives and Strategies for the Modern Workforce* (pp. 41–60). Hershey, PA: IGI Global. doi:10.4018/978-1-5225-1808-2.ch003

Islam, D., Ashraf, M., Rahman, A., & Hasan, R. (2015). Quantitative Analysis of Amartya Sens Theory: An ICT4D Perspective. *International Journal of Information Communication Technologies and Human Development*, 7(3), 13–26. doi:10.4018/IJICTHD.2015070102

Jean-Vasile, A., & Alecu, A. (2017). Theoretical and Practical Approaches in Understanding the Influences of Cost-Productivity-Profit Trinomial in Contemporary Enterprises. In A. Jean Vasile & D. Nicolò (Eds.), *Sustainable Entrepreneurship and Investments in the Green Economy* (pp. 28–62). Hershey, PA: IGI Global. doi:10.4018/978-1-5225-2075-7.ch002

Jha, A. K., & Bose, I. (2015). Innovation Styles, Processes, and their Drivers: An Organizational Perspective. In M. Wadhwa & A. Harper (Eds.), *Technology, Innovation, and Enterprise Transformation* (pp. 143–163). Hershey, PA: IGI Global. doi:10.4018/978-1-4666-6473-9.ch007

Joseph, E., & O'Dea, E. (2017). Integrating Spatial Technologies in Urban Environments for Food Security: A Vision for Economic, Environmental, and Social Responsibility in South Bend, Indiana. In W. Ganpat, R. Dyer, & W. Isaac (Eds.), *Agricultural Development and Food Security in Developing Nations* (pp. 263–299). Hershey, PA: IGI Global. doi:10.4018/978-1-5225-0942-4.ch012

Joshua-Gojer, A. E., Allen, J. M., & Gavrilova-Aguilar, M. (2015). Technology Integration in Work Settings. In M. Wadhwa & A. Harper (Eds.), *Technology, Innovation, and Enterprise Transformation* (pp. 1–19). Hershey, PA: IGI Global. doi:10.4018/978-1-4666-6473-9.ch001

Jovanovic, M., Rakicevic, J., Jaksic, M. L., Petkovic, J., & Marinkovic, S. (2017). Composite Indices in Technology Management: A Critical Approach. In V. Jeremic, Z. Radojicic, & M. Dobrota (Eds.), *Emerging Trends in the Development and Application of Composite Indicators* (pp. 38–71). Hershey, PA: IGI Global. doi:10.4018/978-1-5225-0714-7.ch003

Jridi, K., Jaziri-Bouagina, D., & Triki, A. (2017). The SCM, CRM Information System, and KM – An Integrating Theoretical View: The Case of Sales Force Automation. In G. Jamil, A. Soares, & C. Pessoa (Eds.), *Handbook of Research on Information Management for Effective Logistics and Supply Chains* (pp. 239–254). Hershey, PA: IGI Global. doi:10.4018/978-1-5225-0973-8.ch013

Kalaian, S. A., Kasim, R. M., & Kasim, N. R. (2017). A Conceptual and Pragmatic Review of Regression Analysis for Predictive Analytics. In M. Tavana, K. Szabat, & K. Puranam (Eds.), *Organizational Productivity and Performance Measurements Using Predictive Modeling and Analytics* (pp. 277–292). Hershey, PA: IGI Global. doi:10.4018/978-1-5225-0654-6.ch014

Kalhori, M., & Kargar, M. J. (2017). An Analytical Employee Performance Evaluation Approach in Office Automation and Information Systems. In M. Tavana, K. Szabat, & K. Puranam (Eds.), *Organizational Productivity and Performance Measurements Using Predictive Modeling and Analytics* (pp. 324–343). Hershey, PA: IGI Global. doi:10.4018/978-1-5225-0654-6.ch016

Kasemsap, K. (2015). The Role of E-Business Adoption in the Business World. In N. Ray, D. Das, S. Chaudhuri, & A. Ghosh (Eds.), *Strategic Infrastructure Development for Economic Growth and Social Change* (pp. 51–63). Hershey, PA: IGI Global. doi:10.4018/978-1-4666-7470-7.ch005

Kasemsap, K. (2015). The Role of Information System within Enterprise Architecture and their Impact on Business Performance. In M. Wadhwa & A. Harper (Eds.), *Technology, Innovation, and Enterprise Transformation* (pp. 262–284). Hershey, PA: IGI Global. doi:10.4018/978-1-4666-6473-9.ch012

Kasemsap, K. (2016). The Roles of Information Technology and Knowledge Management in Global Tourism. In A. Nedelea, M. Korstanje, & B. George (Eds.), *Strategic Tools and Methods for Promoting Hospitality and Tourism Services* (pp. 109–138). Hershey, PA: IGI Global. doi:10.4018/978-1-4666-9761-4.ch006

Kasemsap, K. (2016). Utilizing Communities of Practice to Facilitate Knowledge Sharing in the Digital Age. In S. Buckley, G. Majewski, & A. Giannakopoulos (Eds.), *Organizational Knowledge Facilitation through Communities of Practice in Emerging Markets* (pp. 198–224). Hershey, PA: IGI Global. doi:10.4018/978-1-5225-0013-1.ch011

Kasemsap, K. (2016). Utilizing Complexity Theory and Complex Adaptive Systems in Global Business. In Ş. Erçetin & H. Bağcı (Eds.), *Handbook of Research on Chaos and Complexity Theory in the Social Sciences* (pp. 235–260). Hershey, PA: IGI Global. doi:10.4018/978-1-5225-0148-0.ch018

Kasemsap, K. (2017). Management Education and Leadership Styles: Current Issues and Approaches. In N. Baporikar (Ed.), *Innovation and Shifting Perspectives in Management Education* (pp. 166–193). Hershey, PA: IGI Global. doi:10.4018/978-1-5225-1019-2.ch008

Kasemsap, K. (2017). Mastering Business Process Management and Business Intelligence in Global Business. In M. Tavana, K. Szabat, & K. Puranam (Eds.), *Organizational Productivity and Performance Measurements Using Predictive Modeling and Analytics* (pp. 192–212). Hershey, PA: IGI Global. doi:10.4018/978-1-5225-0654-6.ch010

Kasemsap, K. (2017). Mastering Intelligent Decision Support Systems in Enterprise Information Management. In G. Sreedhar (Ed.), *Web Data Mining and the Development of Knowledge-Based Decision Support Systems* (pp. 35–56). Hershey, PA: IGI Global. doi:10.4018/978-1-5225-1877-8.ch004

Kasemsap, K. (2017). Mastering Web Mining and Information Retrieval in the Digital Age. In A. Kumar (Ed.), *Web Usage Mining Techniques and Applications Across Industries* (pp. 1–28). Hershey, PA: IGI Global. doi:10.4018/978-1-5225-0613-3.ch001

Kasemsap, K. (2017). Text Mining: Current Trends and Applications. In G. Sreedhar (Ed.), *Web Data Mining and the Development of Knowledge-Based Decision Support Systems* (pp. 338–358). Hershey, PA: IGI Global. doi:10.4018/978-1-5225-1877-8.ch017

Kasemsap, K. (2017). The Importance of Entrepreneurship in Global Business. In B. Christiansen & F. Kasarcı (Eds.), *Corporate Espionage, Geopolitics, and Diplomacy Issues in International Business* (pp. 92–115). Hershey, PA: IGI Global. doi:10.4018/978-1-5225-1031-4.ch006

Kaur, R., & Malhotra, H. (2016). SWOT Analysis of M-Commerce. In S. Madan & J. Arora (Eds.), *Securing Transactions and Payment Systems for M-Commerce* (pp. 48–67). Hershey, PA: IGI Global. doi:10.4018/978-1-5225-0236-4.ch003

Kekwaletswe, R. M. (2015). Towards A Contingency Model for Assessing Strategic Information Systems Planning Success in Medium Enterprises. In T. Iyamu (Ed.), *Strategic Information Technology Governance and Organizational Politics in Modern Business* (pp. 1–30). Hershey, PA: IGI Global. doi:10.4018/978-1-4666-8524-6.ch001

Khan, I. U., Hameed, Z., & Khan, S. U. (2017). Understanding Online Banking Adoption in a Developing Country: UTAUT2 with Cultural Moderators. *Journal of Global Information Management*, 25(1), 43–65. doi:10.4018/JGIM.2017010103

Khan, N., & Al-Yasiri, A. (2016). Cloud Security Threats and Techniques to Strengthen Cloud Computing Adoption Framework. *International Journal of Information Technology and Web Engineering*, 11(3), 50–64. doi:10.4018/IJITWE.2016070104

Kiberiti, B. S., Sanga, C. A., Mussa, M., Tumbo, S. D., Mlozi, M. R., & Haug, R. (2016). Farmers Access and Use of Mobile Phones for Improving the Coverage of Agricultural Extension Service: A Case of Kilosa District, Tanzania. *International Journal of ICT Research in Africa and the Middle East*, 5(1), 35–57. doi:10.4018/IJICTRAME.2016010103

Kohle, F. H. (2017). Social Media in Micro SME Documentary Production. In V. Benson, R. Tuninga, & G. Saridakis (Eds.), *Analyzing the Strategic Role of Social Networking in Firm Growth and Productivity* (pp. 188–213). Hershey, PA: IGI Global. doi:10.4018/978-1-5225-0559-4.ch011

Kumar, M., Singh, J., & Singh, P. (2017). A Causal Analytic Model for Labour Productivity Assessment. In M. Tavana, K. Szabat, & K. Puranam (Eds.), *Organizational Productivity and Performance Measurements Using Predictive Modeling and Analytics* (pp. 235–260). Hershey, PA: IGI Global. doi:10.4018/978-1-5225-0654-6.ch012

Kumar, S., & Sharma, D. (2015). Factors Influencing ICT Development in BRICS Countries. *International Journal of Social and Organizational Dynamics in IT*, *4*(2), 30–40. doi:10.4018/IJSODIT.2015070103

Kumar, V., & Pradhan, P. (2016). Reputation Management Through Online Feedbacks in e-Business Environment. *International Journal of Enterprise Information Systems*, *12*(1), 21–37. doi:10.4018/IJEIS.2016010102

Lazzareschi, V. H., & Brito, M. S. (2017). Strategic Information Management: Proposal of Business Project Model. In G. Jamil, A. Soares, & C. Pessoa (Eds.), *Handbook of Research on Information Management for Effective Logistics and Supply Chains* (pp. 59–88). Hershey, PA: IGI Global. doi:10.4018/978-1-5225-0973-8.ch004

Lederer, M., Kurz, M., & Lazarov, P. (2017). Usage and Suitability of Methods for Strategic Business Process Initiatives: A Multi Case Study Research. *International Journal of Productivity Management and Assessment Technologies*, *5*(1), 40–51. doi:10.4018/IJPMAT.2017010103

Lee, L. J., & Leu, J. (2016). Exploring the Effectiveness of IT Application and Value Method in the Innovation Performance of Enterprise. *International Journal of Enterprise Information Systems*, *12*(2), 47–65. doi:10.4018/IJEIS.2016040104

Leminen, S., Rajahonka, M., & Westerlund, M. (2017). Actors in the Emerging Internet of Things Ecosystems. *International Journal of E-Services and Mobile Applications*, *9*(1), 57–75. doi:10.4018/IJESMA.2017010104

Loya, V. M., Alcaraz, J. L., Reza, J. R., & Gayosso, D. G. (2017). The Impact of ICT on Supply Chain Agility and Human Performance. In G. Jamil, A. Soares, & C. Pessoa (Eds.), *Handbook of Research on Information Management for Effective Logistics and Supply Chains* (pp. 180–198). Hershey, PA: IGI Global. doi:10.4018/978-1-5225-0973-8.ch010

Lu, W. (2015). Literature Review. In *Information Acquisitions and Sharing through Inter-Organizational Collaboration: Impacts of Business Performance in China* (pp. 76–139). Hershey, PA: IGI Global. doi:10.4018/978-1-4666-8527-7.ch004

Lu, Y. (2016). Public Financial Information Management for Benefits Maximization: Insights from Organization Theories. *International Journal of Organizational and Collective Intelligence*, *6*(3), 50–74. doi:10.4018/IJOCI.2016070104

Lyakurwa, F. S., & Sungau, J. (2017). Information and Communication Technologies (ICTs) for Industrial Development: Challenges and Opportunities. In T. Tossy (Ed.), *Information Technology Integration for Socio-Economic Development* (pp. 306–319). Hershey, PA: IGI Global. doi:10.4018/978-1-5225-0539-6.ch012

Mabe, L. K., & Oladele, O. I. (2017). Application of Information Communication Technologies for Agricultural Development through Extension Services: A Review. In T. Tossy (Ed.), *Information Technology Integration for Socio-Economic Development* (pp. 52–101). Hershey, PA: IGI Global. doi:10.4018/978-1-5225-0539-6.ch003

Maes, K., De Haes, S., & Van Grembergen, W. (2017). A Business Case Process for IT-Enabled Investments: Its Perceived Effectiveness from a Practitioner Perspective. In S. De Haes & W. Van Grembergen (Eds.), *Strategic IT Governance and Alignment in Business Settings* (pp. 1–23). Hershey, PA: IGI Global. doi:10.4018/978-1-5225-0861-8.ch001

Makoza, F., & Chigona, W. (2016). Ex-Post Stakeholder Analysis of National ICT Policy Subsystem: Case of Malawi. *International Journal of ICT Research in Africa and the Middle East, 5*(1), 15–34. doi:10.4018/IJICTRAME.2016010102

Mazini, S. R. (2015). New Technologies and the Impact on the Business Environment. In M. Wadhwa & A. Harper (Eds.), *Technology, Innovation, and Enterprise Transformation* (pp. 35–49). Hershey, PA: IGI Global. doi:10.4018/978-1-4666-6473-9.ch003

Mazini, S. R. (2015). Strategic Role of Information and Information Technology in Shop Floor Control in Footwear Industry Sector. In Z. Luo (Ed.), *Robotics, Automation, and Control in Industrial and Service Settings* (pp. 225–242). Hershey, PA: IGI Global. doi:10.4018/978-1-4666-8693-9.ch008

Mezgár, I., & Grabner-Kräuter, S. (2015). Privacy, Trust, and Business Ethics for Mobile Business Social Networks. In D. Palmer (Ed.), *Handbook of Research on Business Ethics and Corporate Responsibilities* (pp. 390–419). Hershey, PA: IGI Global. doi:10.4018/978-1-4666-7476-9.ch019

Mphahlele, L., & Iyamu, T. (2015). Enterprise Architecture for Business Objectives: Understanding the Influencing Factors. In T. Iyamu (Ed.), *Strategic Information Technology Governance and Organizational Politics in Modern Business* (pp. 171–187). Hershey, PA: IGI Global. doi:10.4018/978-1-4666-8524-6.ch009

Mushi, R., Jafari, S., & Ennis, A. (2017). Measuring Mobile Phone Technology Adoption in SMEs: Analysis of Metrics. *International Journal of ICT Research in Africa and the Middle East*, 6(1), 17–30. doi:10.4018/IJICTRAME.2017010102

Najmaei, A., & Sadeghinejad, Z. (2016). Designing Business Models for Creating and Capturing Shared Value: An Activity-System Perspective. In Z. Fields (Ed.), *Incorporating Business Models and Strategies into Social Entrepreneurship* (pp. 40–65). Hershey, PA: IGI Global. doi:10.4018/978-1-4666-8748-6.ch003

Ncibi, F., Hamam, H., & Ben Braiek, E. (2016). Android for Enterprise Automated Systems. In P. Papajorgji, F. Pinet, A. Guimarães, & J. Papathanasiou (Eds.), *Automated Enterprise Systems for Maximizing Business Performance* (pp. 19–42). Hershey, PA: IGI Global. doi:10.4018/978-1-4666-8841-4.ch002

Nekaj, E. L. (2017). The Crowd Economy: From the Crowd to Businesses to Public Administrations and Multinational Companies. In W. Vassallo (Ed.), *Crowdfunding for Sustainable Entrepreneurship and Innovation* (pp. 1–19). Hershey, PA: IGI Global. doi:10.4018/978-1-5225-0568-6.ch001

Ogunsanya, O. (2017). Connecting the Dots: Bisociation, Collective Creativity, and Sustainable Business. In Z. Fields (Ed.), *Collective Creativity for Responsible and Sustainable Business Practice* (pp. 26–41). Hershey, PA: IGI Global. doi:10.4018/978-1-5225-1823-5.ch002

Patro, C. (2017). Impulsion of Information Technology on Human Resource Practices. In P. Ordóñez de Pablos (Ed.), *Managerial Strategies and Solutions for Business Success in Asia* (pp. 231–254). Hershey, PA: IGI Global. doi:10.4018/978-1-5225-1886-0.ch013

Pegoraro, A., Scott, O., & Burch, L. M. (2017). Strategic Use of Facebook to Build Brand Awareness: A Case Study of Two National Sport Organizations. *International Journal of Public Administration in the Digital Age*, 4(1), 69–87. doi:10.4018/IJPADA.2017010105

Pekkarinen, S., & Melkas, H. (2017). Digitalisation in Health Care and Elderly Care Services: From Potholes to Innovation Opportunities. *International Journal of Information Systems and Social Change, 8*(1), 24–45. doi:10.4018/IJISSC.2017010102

Pereira, G. V., Macadar, M. A., & Testa, M. G. (2016). A Sociotechnical Approach of eGovernment in Developing Countries: An Analysis of Human Development Outcomes. *International Journal of Systems and Society, 3*(1), 67–79. doi:10.4018/IJSS.2016010105

Pinho, C. S., & Ferreira, J. J. (2017). Impact of Information Technologies, Corporate Entrepreneurship and Innovation on the Organizational Performance: A Literature Review. *International Journal of Social Ecology and Sustainable Development, 8*(1), 32–48. doi:10.4018/IJSESD.2017010103

Poças Rascão, J. (2017). Information System for Logistics and Distribution Management. In G. Jamil, A. Soares, & C. Pessoa (Eds.), *Handbook of Research on Information Management for Effective Logistics and Supply Chains* (pp. 374–414). Hershey, PA: IGI Global. doi:10.4018/978-1-5225-0973-8.ch021

Rahdari, A. H. (2017). Fostering Responsible Business: Evidence from Leading Corporate Social Responsibility and Sustainability Networks. In M. Camilleri (Ed.), *CSR 2.0 and the New Era of Corporate Citizenship* (pp. 309–330). Hershey, PA: IGI Global. doi:10.4018/978-1-5225-1842-6.ch016

Rajabi, M., & Bolhari, A. (2015). Business Transformations: Inevitable Changes of the Era. In E. Sabri (Ed.), *Optimization of Supply Chain Management in Contemporary Organizations* (pp. 61–86). Hershey, PA: IGI Global. doi:10.4018/978-1-4666-8228-3.ch003

Rajagopal. (2017). Competing on Performance on the Global Marketplace: Applying Business Analytics as a Robust Decision Tool. In Rajagopal, & R. Behl (Eds.), *Business Analytics and Cyber Security Management in Organizations* (pp. 1-13). Hershey, PA: IGI Global. doi:10.4018/978-1-5225-0902-8.ch001

Ramirez, J. (2016). The Use of Technology in Organizations. In M. Khan (Ed.), *Multinational Enterprise Management Strategies in Developing Countries* (pp. 108–128). Hershey, PA: IGI Global. doi:10.4018/978-1-5225-0276-0.ch006

Ramos, S., Armuña, C., Arenal, A., & Ferrandis, J. (2016). Mobile Communications and the Entrepreneurial Revolution. In J. Aguado, C. Feijóo, & I. Martínez (Eds.), *Emerging Perspectives on the Mobile Content Evolution* (pp. 32–43). Hershey, PA: IGI Global. doi:10.4018/978-1-4666-8838-4.ch002

Rathnayake, C. (2015). Social Construction of Colombo Lotus Tower: Intertwined Narratives of Religion, Economic Development, and Telecommunication. *International Journal of Information Systems and Social Change*, 6(3), 1–14. doi:10.4018/IJISSC.2015070101

Ristimäki, P. (2015). Explorative Actions in Search for a New Logic of Business Activity. In T. Hansson (Ed.), *Contemporary Approaches to Activity Theory: Interdisciplinary Perspectives on Human Behavior* (pp. 181–197). Hershey, PA: IGI Global. doi:10.4018/978-1-4666-6603-0.ch011

Romero, J. A. (2015). Effects of Information Technology on Business Performance and the Use of Accounting Measures. In M. Wadhwa & A. Harper (Eds.), *Technology, Innovation, and Enterprise Transformation* (pp. 285–294). Hershey, PA: IGI Global. doi:10.4018/978-1-4666-6473-9.ch013

Rossetti di Valdalbero, D., & Birnbaum, B. (2017). Towards a New Economy: Co-Creation and Open Innovation in a Trustworthy Europe. In W. Vassallo (Ed.), *Crowdfunding for Sustainable Entrepreneurship and Innovation* (pp. 20–36). Hershey, PA: IGI Global. doi:10.4018/978-1-5225-0568-6.ch002

Roy, S., Ponnam, A., & Mandal, S. (2017). Comprehending Technology Attachment In The Case Of Smart Phone-Applications: An Empirical Study. *Journal of Electronic Commerce in Organizations*, 15(1), 23–43. doi:10.4018/JECO.2017010102

Rutigliano, N. K., Samson, R. M., & Frye, A. S. (2017). Mindfulness: Spiriting Effective Strategic Leadership and Management. In V. Wang (Ed.), *Encyclopedia of Strategic Leadership and Management* (pp. 460–469). Hershey, PA: IGI Global. doi:10.4018/978-1-5225-1049-9.ch033

Saiz-Alvarez, J. M., & Leal, G. C. (2017). Cybersecurity Best Practices and Cultural Change in Global Business: Some Perspectives from the European Union. In G. Afolayan & A. Akinwale (Eds.), *Global Perspectives on Development Administration and Cultural Change* (pp. 48–73). Hershey, PA: IGI Global. doi:10.4018/978-1-5225-0629-4.ch003

Saiz-Alvarez, J. M., & Olalla-Caballero, B. (2017). EFQM in Management Education: A Tool for Excellence. In N. Baporikar (Ed.), *Management Education for Global Leadership* (pp. 221–240). Hershey, PA: IGI Global. doi:10.4018/978-1-5225-1013-0.ch011

Seidenstricker, S., & Ardilio, A. (2015). Increase the Diffusion Rate of Emergent Technologies. In M. Khosrow-Pour (Ed.), *Encyclopedia of Information Science and Technology* (3rd ed.; pp. 5381–5391). Hershey, PA: IGI Global. doi:10.4018/978-1-4666-5888-2.ch531

Selmoune, N., & Alimazighi, Z. (2017). A New Multidimensional Design Method Based on Meta Model Assistance. *International Journal of Knowledge-Based Organizations*, 7(1), 1–18. doi:10.4018/IJKBO.2017010101

Serkani, E. S., Najafi, S. E., & Nejadi, A. (2017). Application of Malmquist Productivity Index in Integrated Units of Power Plant. In F. Lotfi, S. Najafi, & H. Nozari (Eds.), *Data Envelopment Analysis and Effective Performance Assessment* (pp. 83–137). Hershey, PA: IGI Global. doi:10.4018/978-1-5225-0596-9.ch003

Shalan, M. A. (2017). Considering Middle Circles in Mobile Cloud Computing: Ethics and Risk Governance. In K. Munir (Ed.), *Security Management in Mobile Cloud Computing* (pp. 43–72). Hershey, PA: IGI Global. doi:10.4018/978-1-5225-0602-7.ch003

Shalan, M. A. (2017). Risk and Governance Considerations in Cloud Era. In J. Chen, Y. Zhang, & R. Gottschalk (Eds.), *Handbook of Research on End-to-End Cloud Computing Architecture Design* (pp. 376–409). Hershey, PA: IGI Global. doi:10.4018/978-1-5225-0759-8.ch016

Shirima, C., & Sanga, C. A. (2017). Assessment of Contribution of ICT for Sustainable Livelihoods in Kilosa District. In T. Tossy (Ed.), *Information Technology Integration for Socio-Economic Development* (pp. 260–283). Hershey, PA: IGI Global. doi:10.4018/978-1-5225-0539-6.ch010

Silatchom, F., Rutigliano, N. K., & Fiorino, J. (2017). Employee Development for Organizational Success: The Pressures, the Economics, the Rewards. In V. Wang (Ed.), *Encyclopedia of Strategic Leadership and Management* (pp. 845–860). Hershey, PA: IGI Global. doi:10.4018/978-1-5225-1049-9.ch059

Smith, A. D. (2017). New Product Development and Manufacturability Techniques and Analytics. In M. Tavana, K. Szabat, & K. Puranam (Eds.), *Organizational Productivity and Performance Measurements Using Predictive Modeling and Analytics* (pp. 80–95). Hershey, PA: IGI Global. doi:10.4018/978-1-5225-0654-6.ch005

Sodhi, I. S. (2015). Application of Information Technology to Global Financial Crisis: Policy Response and Reforms in India. *International Journal of Public Administration in the Digital Age, 2*(1), 56–74. doi:10.4018/ijpada.2015010104

Srihi, S., Fnaiech, F., Balti, A., & Hamam, H. (2016). Information Security: Application in Business to Maximize the Security and Protect Confidential and Private Data. In P. Papajorgji, F. Pinet, A. Guimarães, & J. Papathanasiou (Eds.), *Automated Enterprise Systems for Maximizing Business Performance* (pp. 244–266). Hershey, PA: IGI Global. doi:10.4018/978-1-4666-8841-4.ch013

Stancu, S., Bodea, C., Naghi, L. E., Popescu, O. M., & Neamtu, A. (2017). Use of New Innovative Technologies in Business by All Age Groups. In I. Hosu & I. Iancu (Eds.), *Digital Entrepreneurship and Global Innovation* (pp. 79–103). Hershey, PA: IGI Global. doi:10.4018/978-1-5225-0953-0.ch005

Szopa, A., & Kopeć, K. D. (2016). Strategic Crowdsourcing as an Emerging Form of Global Entrepreneurship. In N. Baporikar (Ed.), *Handbook of Research on Entrepreneurship in the Contemporary Knowledge-Based Global Economy* (pp. 244–259). Hershey, PA: IGI Global. doi:10.4018/978-1-4666-8798-1.ch011

Talamantes-Padilla, C. A., García-Alcaráz, J. L., Maldonado-Macías, A. A., Alor-Hernández, G., Sánchéz-Ramírez, C., & Hernández-Arellano, J. L. (2017). Information and Communication Technology Impact on Supply Chain Integration, Flexibility, and Performance. In M. Tavana, K. Szabat, & K. Puranam (Eds.), *Organizational Productivity and Performance Measurements Using Predictive Modeling and Analytics* (pp. 213–234). Hershey, PA: IGI Global. doi:10.4018/978-1-5225-0654-6.ch011

Tambunan, T. T. (2017). Economic Growth, Labor Market Segmentation, and Labor Productivity: A Story from Indonesia. In F. Yenilmez & E. Kılıç (Eds.), *Handbook of Research on Unemployment and Labor Market Sustainability in the Era of Globalization* (pp. 345–370). Hershey, PA: IGI Global. doi:10.4018/978-1-5225-2008-5.ch019

Terzi, N. (2016). The Impact of E-Commerce on International Trade and Employment. In I. Lee (Ed.), *Encyclopedia of E-Commerce Development, Implementation, and Management* (pp. 2271–2287). Hershey, PA: IGI Global. doi:10.4018/978-1-4666-9787-4.ch163

Trad, A., & Kalpić, D. (2016). The E-Business Transformation Framework for E-Commerce Architecture-Modeling Projects. In I. Lee (Ed.), *Encyclopedia of E-Commerce Development, Implementation, and Management* (pp. 733–753). Hershey, PA: IGI Global. doi:10.4018/978-1-4666-9787-4.ch052

Triandini, E., Djunaidy, A., & Siahaan, D. (2017). A Maturity Model for E-Commerce Adoption By Small And Medium Enterprises In Indonesia. *Journal of Electronic Commerce in Organizations, 15*(1), 44–58. doi:10.4018/JECO.2017010103

Umair, S., Muneer, U., Zahoor, M. N., & Malik, A. W. (2016). Mobile Cloud Computing Future Trends and Opportunities. In R. Kannan, R. Rasool, H. Jin, & S. Balasundaram (Eds.), *Managing and Processing Big Data in Cloud Computing* (pp. 105–120). Hershey, PA: IGI Global. doi:10.4018/978-1-4666-9767-6.ch007

Vaez-Ghasemi, M., & Moghaddas, Z. (2017). Productivity Assessment in Data Envelopment Analysis. In F. Lotfi, S. Najafi, & H. Nozari (Eds.), *Data Envelopment Analysis and Effective Performance Assessment* (pp. 217–264). Hershey, PA: IGI Global. doi:10.4018/978-1-5225-0596-9.ch006

Van der Westhuizen, T. (2017). A Systemic Approach towards Responsible and Sustainable Economic Development: Entrepreneurship, Systems Theory, and Socio-Economic Momentum. In Z. Fields (Ed.), *Collective Creativity for Responsible and Sustainable Business Practice* (pp. 208–227). Hershey, PA: IGI Global. doi:10.4018/978-1-5225-1823-5.ch011

van Wessel, R. M., de Vries, H. J., & Ribbers, P. M. (2016). Business Benefits through Company IT Standardization. In K. Jakobs (Ed.), *Effective Standardization Management in Corporate Settings* (pp. 34–53). Hershey, PA: IGI Global. doi:10.4018/978-1-4666-9737-9.ch003

Venkateswaran, S. (2017). Industrial Patterns on Cloud. In J. Chen, Y. Zhang, & R. Gottschalk (Eds.), *Handbook of Research on End-to-End Cloud Computing Architecture Design* (pp. 73–103). Hershey, PA: IGI Global. doi:10.4018/978-1-5225-0759-8.ch005

Vidal, M., & Vidal-García, J. (2017). Online Banking and Finance. In S. Aljawarneh (Ed.), *Online Banking Security Measures and Data Protection* (pp. 1–26). Hershey, PA: IGI Global. doi:10.4018/978-1-5225-0864-9.ch001

Wolf, R., & Thiel, M. (2017). CSR in China: The Road to New Sustainable Business Models. In D. Jamali (Ed.), *Comparative Perspectives on Global Corporate Social Responsibility* (pp. 258–275). Hershey, PA: IGI Global. doi:10.4018/978-1-5225-0720-8.ch013

Wu, K., Cui, L., Tseng, M., Hu, J., & Huy, P. M. (2017). Applying Big Data with Fuzzy DEMATEL to Discover the Critical Factors for Employee Engagement in Developing Sustainability for the Hospitality Industry under Uncertainty. In H. Chan, N. Subramanian, & M. Abdulrahman (Eds.), *Supply Chain Management in the Big Data Era* (pp. 218–253). Hershey, PA: IGI Global. doi:10.4018/978-1-5225-0956-1.ch012

Wu, S. J., & Raghupathi, W. (2015). The Strategic Association between Information and Communication Technologies and Sustainability: A Country-Level Study. *Journal of Global Information Management*, *23*(3), 92–115. doi:10.4018/JGIM.2015070105

Yadav, V. (2016). Technology-Enabled Inclusive Innovation: A Case from India. *International Journal of Innovation in the Digital Economy*, *7*(1), 1–11. doi:10.4018/IJIDE.2016010101

Zahidy, A. H., Azizan, N. A., & Sorooshian, S. (2017). An Analytical Algorithm for Delphi Method for Consensus Building and Organizational Productivity. In M. Tavana, K. Szabat, & K. Puranam (Eds.), *Organizational Productivity and Performance Measurements Using Predictive Modeling and Analytics* (pp. 62–79). Hershey, PA: IGI Global. doi:10.4018/978-1-5225-0654-6.ch004

Zezzatti, C. A. (2017). Improving Decision-Making in a Business Simulator Using TOPSIS Methodology for the Establishment of Reactive Stratagem. In G. Sreedhar (Ed.), *Web Data Mining and the Development of Knowledge-Based Decision Support Systems* (pp. 12–21). Hershey, PA: IGI Global. doi:10.4018/978-1-5225-1877-8.ch002

About the Author

Hans Ruediger Kaufmann, after appointments as manager, consultant, and academic in five European countries, is currently Full Professor in Marketing in the School of Business of the University of Nicosia. He was President of CIRCLE (2007-2009) and is currently Vice-President of EMBRI and was a founding member in both institutions. He is a board member of the American Marketing Association Global Marketing SIG. He is member of the editorial board of a variety of journals and an Associate Editor of the World Review of Entrepreneurship, Management and Sustainable Development. He published a large number of journal articles and is author/editor of 8 books (mainly in the field of Consumer Behaviour and Marketing) and 4 Electronic Books (Thompson Reuters accredited conference proceedings). He is Visiting Professor to the International Business School of Vilnius University and an Adjunct Professor of the University of Vitez.

Index

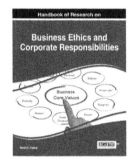

Stay Current on the Latest Emerging Research Developments

Become an IGI Global Reviewer for Authored Book Projects

Premier Reference Source

Solutions for High-Touch Communications in a High-Tech World

Premier Reference Source

Advanced Research on Biologically Inspired Cognitive Architectures

Premier Reference Source

Workforce Development Theory and Practice in the Mental Health Sector

Premier Reference Source

Resource Management and Efficiency in Cloud Computing Environments

The overall success of an authored book project is dependent on quality and timely reviews.

In this competitive age of scholarly publishing, constructive and timely feedback significantly decreases the turnaround time of manuscripts from submission to acceptance, allowing the publication and discovery of progressive research at a much more expeditious rate. Several IGI Global authored book projects are currently seeking highly qualified experts in the field to fill vacancies on their respective editorial review boards:

Applications may be sent to:
development@igi-global.com

Applicants must have a doctorate (or an equivalent degree) as well as publishing and reviewing experience. Reviewers are asked to write reviews in a timely, collegial, and constructive manner. All reviewers will begin their role on an ad-hoc basis for a period of one year, and upon successful completion of this term can be considered for full editorial review board status, with the potential for a subsequent promotion to Associate Editor.

If you have a colleague that may be interested in this opportunity, we encourage you to share this information with them.

IGI Global
Proudly Partners with

eContent Pro

eContent Pro specializes in the following areas:

Academic Copy Editing

Our expert copy editors will conduct a full copy editing procedure on your manuscript and will also address your preferred reference style to make sure your paper meets the standards of the style of your choice.

Expert Translation

Our expert translators will work to ensure a clear cut and accurate translation of your document, ensuring that your research is flawlessly communicated to your audience.

Professional Proofreading

Our editors will conduct a comprehensive assessment of your content and address all shortcomings of the paper in terms of grammar, language structures, spelling, and formatting.

Become an IRMA Member

Members of the **Information Resources Management Association (IRMA)** understand the importance of community within their field of study. The Information Resources Management Association is an ideal venue through which professionals, students, and academicians can convene and share the latest industry innovations and scholarly research that is changing the field of information science and technology. Become a member today and enjoy the benefits of membership as well as the opportunity to collaborate and network with fellow experts in the field.

IRMA Membership Benefits:

- **One FREE Journal Subscription**
- **30% Off Additional Journal Subscriptions**
- **20% Off Book Purchases**
- Updates on the latest events and research on Information Resources Management through the IRMA-L listserv.
- Updates on new open access and downloadable content added to Research IRM.
- A copy of the Information Technology Management Newsletter twice a year.
- A certificate of membership.

InfoSci®-OnDemand

Continuously updated with new material on a weekly basis, InfoSci®-OnDemand offers the ability to search through thousands of quality full-text research papers. Users can narrow each search by identifying key topic areas of interest, then display a complete listing of relevant papers, and purchase materials specific to their research needs.

Comprehensive Service

- Over 81,600+ journal articles, book chapters, and case studies.
- All content is downloadable in PDF format and can be stored locally for future use.

No Subscription Fees

- One time fee of $37.50 per PDF download.

Instant Access

- Receive a download link immediately after order completion!

Database Platform Features:

- Comprehensive Pay-Per-View Service
- Written by Prominent International Experts/Scholars
- Precise Search and Retrieval
- Updated With New Material on a Weekly Basis
- Immediate Access to Full-Text PDFs
- No Subscription Needed
- Purchased Research Can Be Stored Locally for Future Use

"It really provides an excellent entry into the research literature of the field. It presents a manageable number of highly relevant sources on topics of interest to a wide range of researchers. The sources are scholarly, but also accessible to 'practitioners'."

- Lisa Stimatz, MLS, University of North Carolina at Chapel Hill, USA

"It is an excellent and well designed database which will facilitate research, publication and teaching. It is a very very useful tool to have."

- George Ditsa, PhD, University of Wollongong, Australia

"I have accessed the database and find it to be a valuable tool to the IT/IS community. I found valuable articles meeting my search criteria 95% of the time."

- Lynda Louis, Xavier University of Louisiana, USA

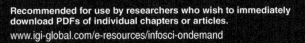

Recommended for use by researchers who wish to immediately download PDFs of individual chapters or articles.
www.igi-global.com/e-resources/infosci-ondemand

Lightning Source UK Ltd.
Milton Keynes UK
UKOW07n0838120917
309006UK00011B/83/P